Tourist Organizations

Tourist Organizations

Douglas Pearce *Senior Lecturer in Geography*
University of Canterbury, New Zealand

Copublished in the United States with
John Wiley & Sons, Inc., New York

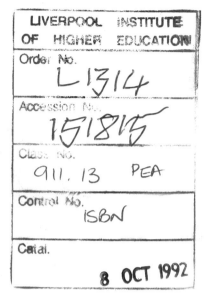
Longman Group UK Ltd,
Longman House, Burnt Mill, Harlow, Essex CM20 2JE, England
and Associated Companies throughout the world.

Copublished in the United States with
John Wiley & Sons, Inc., 605 Third Avenue, New York, NY 1015

First published 1992
ISBN 0-582-07010-4
British Library Cataloguing in Publication Data
A catalogue record for this book is available from the British Library

Library of Congress Cataloging-in-Publication Data
A catalogue record for this book is available from the Library of Congress

Set by 8 in Ehrhardt 9½/12pt

Printed in Hong Kong
WP/01

Contents

List of Figures

List of Tables

List of Plates

Acknowledgements

Most of the research on which this book is based was undertaken during a year's study leave overseas from the University of Canterbury, New Zealand, in 1989. I am grateful to the University Council for granting this leave and providing travel assistance. Research in Germany at this time was also supported by a study grant from the Deutscher Akademischer Austauschdienst. Later, fieldwork within New Zealand benefited from a grant from the Department of Geography at the University of Canterbury. During the course of this research many individuals from a large number of tourist organizations and associated government departments and tourism companies gave generously of their time and provided valuable information, insights and assistance; I am particularly grateful to James Williams, Brian Hay and David Burt. The hospitality and assistance of friends and colleagues overseas not only made fieldwork in distant places enjoyable but also enabled a lot to be achieved in a comparatively short time. Many thanks to Professors Russell King and Des Gillmor at Trinity College, Dublin; to Myriam Jansen-Verbeke, Theo de Haan, Jan Bergsma, Victor Bareno, Greg Ashworth in the Netherlands and to the Nationale Hogenschool voor Toerisme en Verkeer in Breda which provided a base for my work on Dutch organizations; to Professors Erdmann Gormsen, Peter Weber, Jorg Maier and Klaus Wolf and also Peter Schnell in Germany; to Guy and Susan

Robinson and Gordon and Aileen Dickinson in Scotland; to Dean Chuck
Gee, Pauline Sheldon, Juanita Liu, Jack Foote, Peter Stafford and other
colleagues at the School of Travel Industry Management, University of
Hawaii. Special mention must be made here of Madame Biart for her
hospitality and welcome base in Brussels. Pauline Sheldon, Juanita Liu, Des
Gillmor, Stephen Page and Theo de Haan read and reviewed drafts of
individual chapters while Bob Mings cheerfully reviewed the first draft of the
entire manuscript. My thanks also go to Doug Johnston for assistance with
computing, to Alastair Dyer and Tony Shatford who drafted the maps and
figures, to Chris Pennington for photographic assistance and to Linda
Harrison and Anna Moloney for typing the manuscript. I am also grateful to
Longman Group UK Ltd for editorial advice and assistance. Chantal and
Rémi's company increased the pleasure of carrying out fieldwork in 1989
and their subsequent patience and support have enabled the successful
completion of the manuscript.

Doug Pearce
Christchurch
September 1991

We are indebted to the following for permission to reproduce copyright
figures and tables.

Bord Fáilte for Table 7.2 (1989); Canterbury Tourism Council for Plate 8.3;
Deutsche Zentrale für Tourismus e.V. for Plate 4.1 (DZT); Hawaii Visitors
Bureau for Plate 3.1; Keauhou Visitors Association for Plate 3.2; *The Journal
of Tourism Studies* for Figs 8.1, 8.3 & Tables 8.1, 8.2, 8.3 (Pearce, 1990b);
Munich City Tourist Office for Plate 4.2; New Zealand Tourism
Department for Plates 1.1, 8.1, 8.2; Poipu Beach Resort Association for
Plates 3.1 & 3.2; Scottish Tourist Board for Tables 5.4 & 5.6 (STB, 1989a),
5.5 (STB, 1989b), 5.9 (STB, 1986b); Tourism Taranaki for Fig. 8.5 (1991);
U.S. Travel Data Center for Table 2.6 (1989a).

Whilst every effort has been made to trace the owners of copyright material,
in a few cases this has proved impossible and we take this opportunity to
offer our apologies to any copyright holders whose rights we may have
unwittingly infringed.

We are indebted to the following for permission to reproduce copyright
material:

Butterworth–Heinemann for extracts from the article 'Tourism in Ireland'
by Douglas Pearce in *Tourism Management* 11 (2), 133–57; Highlands &
Islands Enterprise for material in Chapter 5.

Acronyms and Abbreviations

ANVV	Algemene Nederlandse Vereniging van VVVs (General Netherlands Association of Tourist Information Offices)
ARC	Auckland Regional Council
ATB	Area Tourist Board (Scotland)
BTA	British Tourist Authority
COTCI	Central Otago Tourism Council Incorporated
CTC	Canterbury Tourism Council
CVB	Convention and Visitors Bureau
DBED	Department of Business and Economic Development (Hawaii)
DBEDT	Department of Business, Economic Development and Tourism (Hawaii)
DBV	Deutschen Bäderverbändes
DFV	Deutsche Fremdenverkehrsverband
DEHOGA	Deutscher Hotel- und Gaststättenverband
DLS	Donegal Leitrim and Sligo
DPED	Department of Planning and Economic Development (Hawaii)
DRV	Deutscher Reisebüro-Verband
DTPA	Dunedin Tourist Promotion Association

DZT	Deutsche Zentrale für Tourismus
EC	European Community
ECU	European Currency Unit
ERDF	European Regional Development Fund
ETB	English Tourist Board
FVV	Fremdenverkehrsverband (tourist organization)
FY	Financial Year
GBT	Gelders Bureau voor Toerisme
GTB	Government Tourist Bureau
HIDB	Highlands and Islands Development Board (from 1 April 1991 HIDB was superseded by Highlands and Islands Enterprise)
HISWA	Nederlandse Vereniging van Ondernemingen in de Bedrijfstak Waterrereatie
HVB	Hawaii Visitors Bureau
IHF	Irish Hotels Federation
ITIC	Irish Tourist Industry Confederation
KBOA	Kaanapali Beach Operators Association
KVA	Keahou Visitors Association
LFV	Landfremdenverkehrsverband (state tourist organization)
MCVA	Maui County Visitors Association
NBT	Nederlands Bureau voor Toerisme
NITB	Northern Ireland Tourist Board
NTA	National Tourist Administration
NTO	National Tourist Organization
NZTD	New Zealand Tourism Department
NZTP	New Zealand Tourist and Publicity Department
OECD	Organization for Economic Cooperation and Development
PATA	Pacific Asia Travel Association
PPP	Public Private Partnership
PR	Public Relations
QPB	Queenstown Promotions Bureau
Recron	Vereniging Recreatie Ondernemers Nederland
REDPP	Regional Economic Development Partnership Program
RLO	Regional Liaison Officer (NZ)
RPAS	Regional Promotion Assistance Scheme
RTAC	Regional Tourism Action Campaign
RTO	Regional Tourist Organization
SCOT	Scottish Confederation of Tourism
SFADCo	Shannon Free Airport Development Company
SIPA	South Island Promotion Association
STB	Scottish Tourist Board
STO	State Travel Office (USA)
	State Tourism Office (Hawaii)
THC	Tourist Hotel Corporation (NZ)

TIC	Tourist Information Centre (UK)
TIF	Tourist Industry Federation (NZ)
TIMS	Tourism Impact Management System
TPA	Tourism Promotion Agency
TROP	Toeristisch Recreatieve Ontwikkelings Plan (tourism and recreation development plan)
TSMG	Tourism Strategic Marketing Group
USTS	United States Travel Service
USTTA	United States Travel and Tourism Administration
VFR	Visiting friends and relatives
VVV	Vereniging voor Vreemdelingenverkeer
WBOA	Waikiki Beach Operators Association
WCTC	West Coast Tourism Council
WDA	Wailea Destination Association
WIA	Waikiki Improvement Association
WOVA	Waikiki/Oahu Visitors Association
WTB	Wales Tourist Board
WTO	World Tourism Organization

1

Organizations, Tourism and Tourist Organizations

Today's society is very much 'an organizational society' (Presthus, 1962; Etzioni, 1964). The activities and impacts of organizations of various forms and sizes influence and impinge on virtually all aspects of everyday living and all sectors of society and the economy. Tourism is no exception as the analysis of any holiday demonstrates.

In taking a holiday, tourists, knowingly or unconsciously, are likely to come in contact with organizations and organizational activities at each stage of their trip. The decision to take a holiday and select a particular destination may have been influenced by the marketing activities of some destination organization. The conditions of travel to, from and within the destination are likely to have been determined in some degree by various organizations. International travel by air, for example, is subject to agreements and regulations reached and imposed by intergovernmental and other organizations affecting factors such as routes, schedules, prices and safety. Other travel,

particularly that within destinations, will be facilitated by maps and brochures produced and distributed by tourist organizations. The hotel in which the stay is spent may have been built with financial assistance provided by some organization, it may be operated subject to regulations imposed by others and the booking may have been made through yet another. The hotelier is likely to belong to some trade association and possibly to some broader destination organization. Attractions visited during the course of the holiday may also be promoted, operated or partially financed by some organization. As with the accommodation and transport, the attractions may have been developed within the context of some tourism plan conceived and implemented by an organization. Many of the organizations mentioned thus far are likely to have been public or semi-public. Other goods and services, perhaps the hotel accommodation and the air transport, may have been provided by private sector business firms which are also organizations. Finally, the tourists and their holiday are likely to have been recorded as statistics by the research division of some organization, these statistics in turn being used by researchers in some other organization, for example a university.

The extent and nature of organizational activity will of course vary from place to place and one form of tourism to another. Independent, informal holidays in rural areas close to one's home, for example, may be less exposed to organizational influence than more structured ones taken abroad. Whatever the form, there can be no doubt, however, that tourism too is very much part of today's organizational society.

It is therefore surprising that there has been comparatively little research on tourist organizations, whether in the tourism or the organization literature. In this latter, broader field virtually no attention at all appears to have been given to tourism, Usdiken's (1983) study of tourist-receiving operators in Turkey being a rare exception. Rather, the emphasis among organization scholars has been on industrial, military, educational, medical, judicial and related organizations (Dunkerley, 1972). Tourism would appear to share in a more general neglect of the commercial service sector as a focus for organizational research despite its growing social and economic significance: upwards of half the population in most developed countries now take an annual holiday, with tourism today ranking as a leading economic sector and item in international trade.

Within the now extensive tourism literature tourist organizations have largely been ignored. Certainly a number of textbooks have a chapter on tourist organizations (eg Burkart and Medlik, 1974; Mill and Morrison, 1985; Lavery, 1987) but this is generally descriptive and simply outlines the nature and role of such organizations without much analysis of how they work or what they actually accomplish. Other work on tourism is concerned primarily with techniques or results rather than with who is using these techniques or implementing the findings of this research. The emphasis is on how to undertake market research, how to plan for tourism, how to assess the impacts of tourist development. Very little attention is given to who undertakes this research, who plans and who may attempt to mitigate negative impacts and enhance positive ones. Only rarely is the role of the tourist organization, the 'who' in many of these cases, addressed explicitly, for example by Wahab, Crampon and Rothfield (1976), Doering (1979), Jefferson and Lickorish (1988) and Middleton (1988) with regard to tourism marketing and Cook (1987) and Taylor (1987) in terms of tourism research. If tourist organizations are considered, it is more often as a consequence of some broader interest in governmental policies or intervention (eg Airey, 1983; Elliott, 1987; Hall, 1991) with Heeley's work in Britain being particularly notable (Heeley, 1981, 1985, 1986b, 1989).

The most comprehensive review so far of tourist organizations at a national level is that undertaken by the World Tourism Organization (WTO, 1979). While wide-ranging in coverage, the WTO study is somewhat skeletal in treatment, outlining the role and structure of the different organizations without much analysis of what they actually do and achieve. To know that most National Tourist Organizations (NTOs) engage in marketing and research, for example, is a useful first step but consideration must also be given to why they become involved in marketing, what sort of marketing is carried out and

what results are achieved. Such issues have been addressed to some extent at the regional or state level by the United States report on state tourism organizations (Council of State Governments, 1979) but in general tourist organizations at this or the smaller, local scale have attracted even less attention than the national organizations.

This book aims to overcome these deficiencies in the existing literature by systematically examining how tourism is organized in selected countries, regions and localities and identifying common issues, problems and solutions. The aim is to go beyond a mere description of the organizations involved and to present an analysis of the interrelationships between different organizations, functions and scales (national, regional and local) and the way these have evolved over time. Attempts will also be made to show how the way tourism is organized reflects different forms of tourism and administrative structures. The emphasis here is not on studying tourist organizations for their own sake, worthy though they might be of such attention, but rather to add to our understanding of the broader phenomenon of tourism by focusing on one of its hitherto neglected components or dimensions.

As a hybrid term, tourist organizations might be expected to reflect and display characteristics of organizations in general and of tourism in particular. Useful concepts, insights, perspectives and methodologies might thus be found both in organization theory and in the tourism literature which could be applied more specifically to the study of tourist organizations. The remainder of this introductory chapter thus begins with a review of organizations and the salient characteristics of tourism. These two sections are then drawn together in a discussion of the general features of tourist organizations. The subsequent section deals with methodological issues. The approach to be adopted throughout this book is then discussed together with an outline of the structure of following chapters.

Organizations

Organizations have been studied by scholars from a

Table 1.1   Definitions of organizations

Organizations are social units (or human groupings) deliberately constructed and reconstructed to seek special goals. . . . Organizations are characterized by: (1) divisions of labour, power and communication . . . deliberately planned to enhance the realisation of specific goals; (2) the presence of one or more power centres which control the concerted efforts of the organization and direct them toward its goals . . . (3) substitution of personnel. Etzioni, 1964, p.3	an organization is a coalition of shifting interest groups that develop goals by negotiation; the structure of the coalition, its activities, and its outcomes are strongly influenced by environmental factors [an open system perspective] Scott, 1981, pp.22–3
Organizations are social inventions or tools developed by men to accomplish things otherwise not possible. Litterer, 1973, p.5	where two or more people unite together and coordinate their activities in order to achieve a set of common goals. Bryans and Cronin, 1984, p.125
a concrete, social structure formally established (incorporated, chartered) for the purpose of achieving specific objectives. Heydebrand, 1973, p.4	a special kind of formal group characterized by technical activities, by externalized values and resources, and by the mobilisation of human energy through substitute inducements, usually wages. Warriner, 1984, p.93
An organization is a contrived open system of coordinated activities by two or more participants to achieve a common goal or goals. Wright, 1977, p.7	Organizations are defined as collections of people joining together in some formal organization in order to achieve group or individual objectives. Dawson, 1986, p.xiii
an organization is a collectivity oriented to the pursuit of relatively specific goals and exhibiting a relatively highly formalized social structure [a rational system perspective] Scott, 1981, p.21	Organizations are defined as associations of persons • set up for a well-defined purpose • requiring more than one person's effort • utilizing resources • not using exchange in markets but other methods of coordination. Beckmann, 1988, p.1

number of disciplines, most notably sociology, psychology, business management and political science: geography has not been at the forefront of this research. Each discipline has brought its own perspective and many definitions of organizations are to be found. Table 1.1 represents a chronological selection of these from which the basic dimensions and some of the more specific elements of organizations can be derived.

Two recurring elements are found in the definitions listed in Table 1.1, suggesting general agreement on the basic characteristics of organizations. First, organizations are set up to achieve goals, and second, these goals are best met by united action accomplished through a formal structuring of the participants involved. Those adopting a more explicit open systems approach also emphasize environmental factors; organizations draw on resources (eg money, labour, information, material inputs) from external sources and their values and activities are externalized, that is they have meaning or benefits for people outside the organization (Scott, 1981; Warriner, 1984). The implications of environmental factors and linkages will be dealt with later.

Goals too have been variously defined but Etzioni's (1964, p.6) definition of an organizational goal as 'a desired state of affairs which the organization attempts to realize' is particularly apt. Etzioni (1964), Perrow (1961) and other organization scholars are quick to point out that there are different sorts of goals and that goals may change over time or be displaced by others. Perrow, in particular, distinguishes between official goals which specify 'the general purposes of the organization as put forth in the charter, annual reports, public statements by key executives and other authoritative pronouncements' and operative goals which 'designate the ends sought through the actual operating policies of the organization [which] tell us what the organization actually is trying to do, regardless of what the official goals say are the aims'. These operative goals may reflect the interests of dominant groups within the organization (see Scott's second definition in Table 1.1), with dominance varying from time to time and from one situation to another. Etzioni (1964, p.7) too notes discrepancies between stated and real goals and notes:

> the real goals of the organization [are] those future states toward which a majority of the organization's means and the major organizational commitments of the participants are directed, and which, in cases of conflict with goals which are stated but command few resources, have clear priority.

Dawson (1986, p.36), argues, however, that the official or stated goals should not be dismissed lightly and that

> They usually represent the outcome of particular debates in an organization's history, for example at foundation and at significant points of change. Their significance is not that they provide a realistic description of organized activities, but that as a symbol they provide legitimacy for some actions and a rallying point for some groups. They can be used to justify or prevent proposed developments. Goals play a key role in the establishment and existence of organizations.

According to Litterer (1973), three basic conditions are needed for an organization to come into being:

- willingness to contribute,
- purposeful activity,
- an ability to communicate.

Goals are an expression of purposeful activity, with people's willingness to contribute being determined by their perception of the balance of the benefits and costs of seeking these goals and the effectiveness with which these goals are communicated and this willingness is co-ordinated. Litterer (1973, p.43) observes that 'most people have ambivalent ideas about organizations, wanting some of the benefits and disliking some of the consequences'. Likewise, Wright (1977, p.26) notes:

> Common purpose is not often automatically achieved. It is encouraged through the design of incentives, roles, role relationships, authority and control so that each participant is rewarded for contributing to the attainment of the overall goals. . . . As long as people believe the trade-offs are in their favour, they will accept a part in the pursuit of organizational objectives.

This brief review of organizations raises several fundamental questions about the nature of tourist organizations. What are their goals? Why can these best be achieved by united action? How can such action best be accomplished? The answers to these questions as they apply to tourist organizations lie to a large extent in the nature of tourism.

Tourism

Tourism too has been defined in various ways but may be thought of as the relationships and phenomena arising out of the journeys and temporary stays of people travelling primarily for leisure or recreational purposes, though business, health or educational travel might also be included. Conceptually, tourism might be seen as an origin-linkage-destination system involving the temporary movement of people from an origin to a destination (or destinations) and usually back home again after at least one overnight stay. The linkage between the origin and a destination is provided in the first instance by the actual movement of tourists but might also be conceived of in terms of flows of information, money and so forth. Tourism is a multi-faceted activity and a geographically complex one as different services and goods are sought and supplied at different stages from the origin (or market) to the destination. Moreover, in any country or region there is likely to be a number of origins and destinations, with most places having both generating (origin) and receiving (destination) functions (Pearce, 1987a, 1989).

The travel and stay attributes of tourism are characterized by the demand for and provision of a wide range of goods and services. In terms of the tourist's destination, these can be grouped into five broad sectors: attractions, transport, accommodation, supporting facilities and infrastructure. The attractions help encourage the tourists to visit the area, transport services enable them to do so, the accommodation and supporting facilities (eg shops, banks, restaurants) cater for their well-being while there, and the infrastructure assures the essential functioning of all of these. Many of these services may be combined and provided by tour operators located at the destination, origin or with links to both, who offer the traveller packages involving transport, accommodation and perhaps sightseeing or some other recreational activity. Sales of these packages and/or individual travel items are often made through retail travel agencies in the origins or markets. Other businesses in the market area may also benefit from tourism: banks (currency exchange), insurance companies (travel insurance), shops (cameras and film, sportswear and equipment, travel goods).

There is then no specific tourism product. Tourists when they travel acquire an experience made up of many different parts, some more tangible than others (a night's accommodation or the thrill of white-water rafting). These many parts, however, are extremely interdependent. One cannot experience the thrill of white-water rafting without having travelled to the appropriate site, without having somewhere to stay, eat and so forth.

While tourist services and facilities may be purchased at the origin and souvenirs and other goods may be bought to take home, most of the actual consumption takes place at or en route to and from the destination, that is the services and goods are consumed in situ, in the places where they are offered or produced. The degree to which this occurs distinguishes tourism from many other activities such as manufacturing and agriculture.

The diversity in the demand for services and facilities sought by tourists is reflected on the supply side by an equally wide range of agents of development, those who cater in one way or another to the needs of the tourist. Many of these will be involved directly and primarily with servicing tourists, for others, tourists will be but one segment of their business or clientele. The opportunities which exist in the field of tourism give rise to a mix of large- and small-scale operators. While market dominance and leadership may lie with the former, the tourist industry in general is characterized by a large number of small operators (Heeley, 1986b).

As the demand for tourism has grown dramatically since the 1950s, so the market has become more diverse. Tourism today is a mass phenomenon but tourists by no means constitute a homogeneous mass market. Rather, the results of market research indicate an increasingly segmented demand for tourist travel (though some of this fragmentation may be the result of more and different ways of identifying segments than an actual evolution in demand).

Tourist organizations

Tourism then is characterized by the interdependence of its different sectors, by the generally small scale of its many operators, by the fragmentation of its markets and by the spatial separation of origins and destinations, in many cases by large distances, especially in the case of international tourism. Interdependence, small size, market fragmentation and spatial separation are all factors which may lead to a desire for combined action, a willingness to unite to achieve common goals, a need to form tourist organizations.

These factors influence the formation and operation of tourist organizations in different ways. Interdependence leads to a need to co-ordinate the different sectors to ensure that they function harmoniously, for example by promoting a common image or avoiding bottlenecks in any sector that might constrain the activities of other parties. Interdependence tends to give rise to destination organizations, that is broadly based organizations located in a specific geographic area which draw together different sectors of the tourist industry. Planning, development and marketing are all functions which are characterized by interdependence and which might therefore be reflected in the goals of these organizations.

The small size of many tourist operators may give rise to united action in order to achieve economies of scale, to accomplish goals which individual operators could not achieve but which become possible when they band together. By pooling resources, for instance, they may be able to acquire a higher profile and stronger voice when lobbying for their interests or undertake more effective marketing campaigns. As interests may vary from sector to sector, specific sectoral organizations may emerge to deal with the interests of hoteliers, carriers, or other operators. However, with marketing, small size may reinforce interdependence in the drive to form destination organizations, with the distance from the origin and the fragmentation of the market also leading to co-ordinated activities in this and other fields. Quite simply, the individual small operator usually does not have the means of reaching specific niches in distant markets and therefore has to depend more on local markets, the efforts of others or some form of joint activity.

Not all operators or businesses in tourism of course are small. A number of large tourism enterprises have also emerged which are complex organizations in their own right, for example hotel chains, airlines and tour operators. Often the growth of these companies has come about through horizontal and vertical integration, processes which reflect an organizational response to some of the factors outlined above (Pearce, 1989).

While recognizing that economic and other factors have led to the growth of tourist enterprises into complex organizations, and that these organizations play a significant role, such organizations do not constitute the focus of this book. Rather, the emphasis is on tourist organizations which deal more generally with tourism or draw together a number of tourist operators and enterprises. Specifically, the emphasis is on public and semi-public destination organizations as well as a range of sector organizations or more broadly based tourist industry organizations. Attention is paid to the relationships between the public and private sector organizations and to the links between organizations at different spatial scales – national, regional and local.

The private sector's prime motivation in tourism is profit maximization. Organizational activity from this sector will primarily be designed to enhance this goal. The public sector, on the other hand, becomes involved in tourism for a variety of reasons (Pearce, 1989), the extent of government intervention varying from country to country in large part as a function of broader political philosophies and policies. Economic factors, nevertheless, are usually to the fore. These include increasing foreign exchange earnings, state revenues (taxes) and employment, economic diversification, regional development and the stimulation of non-tourism investment. Social, cultural and environmental responsibilities may also lead to governmental involvement as may a range of political considerations. The state may also play a key role as landowner or resource manager and a variety of other policies, for instance fiscal policies, will also have an impact on tourist development. According to a recent European Community study (O'Hagan, Scott and Waldron, 1986) the rationale for government involvement in tourism is based 'not only on the nature and extent of perceived economic and social benefits of tourism' but also on 'the impracticability or inability of the enterprises, representative organizations or individuals to undertake certain functions'. Some of these functions have been alluded to above and will be dealt with more fully shortly.

Virtually every country has some national body

responsible for tourism, the basic characteristics of which were reported in the WTO's (1979) inventory of national tourist administrations (NTAs) that is 'the authorities in the central state administration, or other official organization, in charge of tourism development at the national level'. The WTO's survey of 100 NTAs showed two-thirds took the form of ministries or constituted part of a government department. The remaining one-third had their own legal personality, for example they were government corporations, but were linked to or were under the supervision of the central administration. The New Zealand Tourism Department claims to be the oldest NTA, having been established in 1901. Other NTAs were established before the Second World War, but the majority appear to have been set up in the 1960s and 1970s.

The WTO uses the term NTA in preference to the more customary NTO (national tourist organization) to reflect (p.ii) 'the new concept of tourism management at national level and to stress that the majority of countries are moving away from the traditional system, where the National Tourist Organization is essentially a central publicity body, to the newer concept of a national tourism administration which sees promotion and marketing as one of many functions'. Other functions reported by the NTAs surveyed were

- research, statistics and planning,
- inventory of tourist resources and measures for their protection,
- development of tourist facilities,
- manpower development,
- regulation of tourist enterprises and travel,
- facilitation of travel,
- international co-operation in tourism.

Marketing and promotion would nevertheless still seem to be dominant functions (Middleton, 1988). If the functions of tourist organizations reflect their goals, at least their operative goals, then it is important to examine these more closely and to see why such functions are carried out by national and other tourist organizations and how such activities

may differ from those of firms or individual operators.

Marketing

Marketing, according to Kotler (1967, pp.11–12), 'is the analysing, organising, planning and controlling of the firm's customer-impinging resources, policies and activities with a view to satisfying the needs and wants of chosen customer groups at a profit'. It is a process of matching markets and products with 'the notion of consumer satisfaction . . . preponderant . . . as it is the gate leading to the profit goal' (Wahab, Crampon and Rothfield, 1976, p.22). For Wahab et al,

> the whole tourist marketing message from a National Tourist Organization's viewpoint is to identify primary, secondary and opportunity markets for the tourist destination's product, build up a communication system with these markets and to maintain and increase the destination's market share. Therefore the interaction between the product and the market in order for the first to comply with the market conditions and exigencies is paramount. The groups of consumers cannot be identified therefore except through marketing activities.

NTOs and other destination associations have come to fill a particular role in tourism marketing and marketing has become one of their dominant functions for several reasons. First, there is a distinct need to promote destinations *per se*, that is places in their own right. Research on holiday decision-making processes (Jenkins, 1978; Hodgson, 1983; van Raaij and Francken, 1983) suggests that the destination decision is an intermediate one, following first order or generic decisions such as the questions of whether to take a holiday and what type, but preceding product-specific choices concerned with the selection of the type of accommodation, mode of transport and so on. Place-specific images have therefore to be communicated to stimulate an awareness of the desirability of particular destinations so that individual products can be sold, for instance hotels

Replenish thyself.

"Stay where you are, New Zealand. I'm coming over."

1.1 Overseas promotion is an important NTO function: here the Australian regional director of the New Zealand Tourism Department supervises the placement of a billboard advertisement promoting New Zealand in Sydney, Australia
(Courtesy of New Zealand Tourism Department)

or motels, different sightseeing excursions or activity packages (Plate 1.1).

However, general destination promotion tends to benefit all sectors of the tourist industry in the place concerned; it becomes a 'public good'. As Bennett (1984, p.31) has noted elsewhere, 'The public good dilemma faced by organizers of collective action is . . . that the benefits of collective action will accrue to all regardless or whether or not individuals participated'. The question of 'freeloaders' thus arises, for they too will benefit along with those who may have contributed directly to the promotional campaign. Why pay if someone else will bear the expense? Freeloading has bedevilled destination marketing in many places, particularly at the smaller scale, as several conflicting forces come into play. Interdependence

and the smallness of many tourist operators are forces leading towards united action, particularly given the costs and difficulties of penetrating distant markets. At the same time freeloading and the common good element of destination marketing, reinforced again by the smallness of operators and their unwillingness to spend on what is not perceived to be necessary, have led to a reluctance to participate freely in joint activity. Both sets of forces may give rise to the formation of destination associations, with the latter in particular providing a rationale for public-supported organizations as Jeffries (1989, p.79) notes with regard to the British Tourist Authority (BTA):

The argument for government underpinning must be based on the recognition on the one hand that the whole economy benefits and on the other that the taxation system represents the only practical way of collecting at least some of the necessary funding without which the whole exercise would almost certainly collapse.

Where such support has not been forthcoming, there may be relatively little destination marketing, incentives to increase participation or perhaps more specific promotion. Jefferson and Lickorish (1988) also claim a focal point role for the NTO:

> In practice the National Tourist Office is the most powerful motivator for the destination. It concentrates on the national base. Other big promoters, such as air carriers, have many destinations to promote, and do not have the credibility in the public mind of the official government backed services.

The destination organization's focus is solely on its own area which it has an ongoing commitment to promote. In contrast, 'a tour operator's allegiance to any destination is tenuous – it holds only so long as it is sufficiently profitable!' (Ashworth and Goodall, 1988, p.231). Given the 'substitutability' of destinations this can be a major concern. Even where the major air carrier is a state-owned airline it will have an interest at the very least in promoting outbound as well as inbound traffic, with success in the outbound market being to some extent at the expense of the domestic tourist industry.

What distinguishes NTOs and other such organizations in their marketing efforts is that they have only limited control over the services and facilities they are marketing. Burfitt (1988, p.321) notes that 'Few large National Tourist Offices sell the product and few actually own the product'. Rather, as Middleton (1988, p.213) observes, in developed tourist destination countries

> a large number of businesses generates a very wide range of tourist products, most of which are beyond the marketing influence of an NTO with regard to volume, design, price, and promotion decisions.

He concludes:

> It is, therefore, helpful to explain the role of NTO marketing from a perspective of *influence* rather than control; a very different perspective from that used to explain commercial practice.

A similar situation exists with local government promotion at the resort scale (Hughes, 1989, p.16):

> The product promoted . . . is one that is owned and influenced only partially by the promoting organization. There is no necessary community of interest between the providers of the holiday product components and no necessary spirit of 'corporate identity'. The various activities need to be melded into a clearly identifiable product with each component clearly recognising its interdependence with others. A remaining problem is that a local government approach to promotion may not be wholly appropriate in a world of sophisticated marketing approaches.

Moreover, in contrast to much other marketing activity, the NTO or destination organization is not itself the primary beneficiary of this activity.

Middleton (1988) sees two main roles for NTOs in terms of how destination marketing is undertaken: destination promotion and market facilitation. The first role involves directly promoting the destination and developing market awareness through activities such as advertising, information dissemination, public relations and so on. This is a two-level strategy in which heightened awareness of the destination can then be built upon by the private sector or individual operators promoting their own products. Marketing facilitation provides a bridge between these two levels and is achieved by co-ordination and co-operation between the NTO, other destination associations and the various sectors of the industry. In summarizing facilitation strategy Middleton cites Jeffries (1973) who noted that an NTO

> can hardly run the whole of tourism, even in countries where it actually owns hotels and

transportation. Its major role everywhere is to provide leadership and guidance: to indicate marketing opportunities and to produce a climate where all concerned will be prepared to exploit them. Having reached this point its role will be to encourage and assist.

For Middleton (1988, p.225) facilitation is 'the unique marketing role for an NTO; unique in the sense that if the NTO does not fulfil it, it is unlikely that obviously important tasks will be undertaken at all'.

He lists twelve of the most important facilitation processes used by NTOs as

- flow of research data
- representation in markets of origin – through a network of tourist offices
- organization of workshops and trade shows
- familiarization trips
- travel trade manuals
- support with literature production and distribution
- participation in joint marketing schemes or ventures
- information and reservation systems
- support for new products
- trade consortia
- consumer assistance and protection – provision of information services and centres
- general advisory services for the industry.

The balance between promotion and facilitation will depend on a variety of factors, especially the stage of market maturity. Greater promotional activity might be expected in new markets, with facilitation of industry effort being more significant in more established areas. The emphasis each NTO gives to these roles might therefore be expected to change over time.

Visitor servicing

Visitor servicing, what Middleton (1988, p.222) refers to as 'consumer assistance and protection' and what Jefferson and Lickorish (1988) call 'after sales service', is a specific part of marketing and one which might be dealt with separately. Visitor servicing is distinctive in that it occurs at the destination rather than in the origin. The concern here is primarily with reception and providing information, usually at a sub-national, often local, level. Having arrived at a destination, the visitor will want more specific information about where to go, what to see, where to stay, how to get there and so forth. The extent of the information required will depend on the visitor's familiarity with the area (whether it is the first visit or not) and the amount of pre-trip material available, the degree to which the trip is independently organized or prepaid and packaged and the type of holiday undertaken (two weeks on the beach will require less information than a hectic programme of sightseeing). As Middleton (1988, p.222) notes:

> By creating and subsidizing a network of information offices in destination areas, an NTO can extend its influence and communicate messages directly to a wide 'audience' of its visitors; in practice this may be a wider audience than many can hope to reach with available budgets through their promotional efforts in countries of origin. . . . Market research indicates that many visitors to tourist destinations, especially foreign and first-time visitors, are open to suggestion and persuasion from all sources of information, but especially those which have the official endorsement of the NTO and its regional bodies.

Other writers, though, suggest the role of information centres may be exaggerated. Ashworth and Goodall (1988, p.225) note for example:

> research in the important tourist-historic city of Norwich on the role of the Tourist Information Centre (TIC) as a means of transmitting information to existing visitors revealed that only 16 percent of all visitors made any use of its services.

However, there has been comparatively little direct research on the role of tourist information centres, perhaps in part because these are almost exclusively run by destination organizations whose neglect by researchers has already been recorded above.

Provision of information may be complemented by booking services and the handling of tourist complaints. As Jefferson and Lickorish (1988) observe, these aspects of visitor servicing may call for standard setting, regulation, endorsement and so forth. This will often be undertaken by the NTO or some other destination organization and take the form of grading and inspecting hotels or endorsing operators as members of the official organization. In other instances regulations will be imposed or enforced by other organizations, for example the Health or Fire Department with regard to hygiene or fire safety. Day-to-day handling of complaints should be complemented by visitor satisfaction surveys which underline the positive as well as the negative aspects of the visitor's experience. Public sector organizations in particular become involved in these issues, not just as an extension of the marketing effort but as a form of consumer protection.

Development

The public sector in general, and NTOs and other destination organizations in particular, have often been less directly involved in the development of tourism products (Pearce, 1989). The extent of direct involvement varies greatly from country to country but public sector intervention has generally been less in Western liberal economies than the centrally planned economies of the former Soviet bloc or many developing countries. Certain common roles and responsibilities can be recognized.

Because of the scale of development and the element of common good, provision of infrastructure is a widely accepted task of public authorities and one which can greatly facilitate tourist development and selectively direct it to particular areas. This is well illustrated by such major projects as the government-led development of the coast of Languedoc-Roussillon and of Mexican resorts such as Cancun (Pearce, 1983). Exceptions occur nevertheless, as in New Zealand where most ski-field access roads have been built

and are maintained by private developers. Preservation, conservation and enhancement of natural and to a lesser extent historical attractions are a major concern of the public sector, expressed most notably in national parks. Although involved in all sectors, private enterprise has been most active in the accommodation, transport and supporting facilities sectors, in providing purpose-built attractions and in tour operations. Government-owned national airlines and hotel chains, such as the Paradores in Spain, also exemplify state participation in these sectors.

As well as direct involvement, the public sector may also facilitate and encourage the development of tourism by the private sector through the provision of a range of investment incentives in the form of grants, loans, accelerated depreciation and so forth. Bodlender and Davies (1985, p.3) note that

> In general terms for both developed and developing countries their introduction often reflected both the scarcity of domestic investment funds and the widespread ambition to undertake economic development programmes.

In developing countries these incentives were designed primarily to attract foreign capital; in developed countries they were generally introduced to channel growth to selected areas as part of a regional development programme.

Where large-scale projects are being undertaken, new special purpose organizations may be set up to take the initiative, provide the co-ordination and, in developing countries, act as a conduit for international aid and investment (Collins, 1979; McTaggart, 1980). Co-ordination of the development of the coast of Languedoc-Roussillon in France was given over to an Interministerial Commission, much of the actual infrastructural development was carried out by appropriate government departments, local and regional authorities participated directly in the development of the new resorts and the private sector built and operated the accommodation (Pearce, 1989). Elsewhere, when development takes the form not of the creation of massive new projects but of ongoing co-ordination and the encouragement of specific forms of development or development in particular areas through the allocation of various incentives, these responsibilities usually fall to a division of the NTO. They may also be undertaken by a broader based ministry of economic affairs or regional development.

Planning

Marketing and development are not of course independent; products are developed to meet market needs and markets are sought for available tourism resources. In both cases the interdependence of tourism and the existence of many operators and agents of developments requires co-ordination and planning if the marketing and development of tourism are to be successful. Moreover, tourist development not only involves tourists and developers but also touches other sectors of society, is directly related to the economy in general and may impact on the environment at large. Problems arise and costs are increased when the different sectors do not develop harmoniously or when the motives and capabilities of the different development agents conflict. Carried to an extreme, uncontrolled growth of tourism can destroy the very resource base on which it was built. Of the different development processes examined by Pearce (1989), those involving some degree of planning were most often, though not always, shown to reduce the externalities of tourist development and to enhance its positive impacts.

Recognition of the importance and value of planning for tourism is reflected in the number of tourism plans which have been prepared since the 1960s. The WTO (1980) established an inventory of over 1 600 assorted tourism plans in 1980. These ranged in scale from international to local; many were concerned solely with tourism while in others tourism was but one element of a broader, economic or physical plan. Tourism plans often emphasize development or marketing but ideally both activities should be included together with a

clear definition of goals and a broader appreciation of tourism's place in the overall process of economic and social development (Gunn, 1988; Pearce, 1989).

Many different definitions of planning can be found but that by Murphy (1985, p.156) is particularly relevant here:

> Planning is concerned with anticipating and regulating change in a system, to promote orderly development so as to increase the social, economic and environmental benefits of the development process. To do this, planning becomes 'an ordered sequence of operations, designed to lead to the achievement of either a single goal or to a balance between several goals' (Hall, 1970, p.4).

NTOs and other destination organizations might thus plan to achieve their goals or the preparation and implementation of a tourism plan may be one of their major goals. Here again, united action is required to draw together the different operators and agents of development within a given destination, a role appropriate for a destination organization. Where tourism is part of a broader plan, this is likely to be prepared by some other organization such as a local authority or a ministry of planning or economic development.

Tourist organizations face a number of constraints in their efforts to plan for tourism. In general their plans are only indicative in nature, outlining desirable goals and appropriate strategies to attain these. However as noted earlier with regard to marketing, tourist organizations generally exercise only limited control over the product. Some aspects of physical development can be enforced by regulation, for example building and zoning controls, but in most cases tourist planning lacks an inadequate legislative base. Other influence can be exerted through selective allocation of incentives, a leadership role in promotion and the facilitation of marketing but in general it is easier to plan to prevent something from happening than to ensure that something does take place. The WTO (1980) study revealed that about one-third of the more than 1 600 plans inventoried were not implemented, that many plans lacked social and environmental considerations and failed to integrate tourism within broader socio-economic objectives. The WTO concluded (p.22):

> *a desire to plan* exists in the tourism sector, but . . . few countries have been in a position to follow a policy of continuity regarding tourism development. Furthermore, the virtual absence of legislation seems to prejudice applying a directive plan.

The challenge to tourist organizations in this situation is not only to prepare an appropriate tourism plan but also to be able to communicate the goals and strategies to its members and others in order to generate a willingness to participate and implement.

Research

Sound marketing, development and planning are based on good, up-to-date, reliable, relevant information and knowledge. This may come in part from experience but experience in most cases will need to be supported by research. To engage in these other activities effectively most NTOs and other destination organizations will therefore also have a research function. Taylor (1987, p.118) argues that research carried out by an NTO must be viewed as applied and that it must be 'planned and managed in relation to the major functions of the organization'. Likewise Cook (1987, p.155) points out at the state and provincial level in North America:

> The typical travel office has a variety of responsibilities, the most important of which is the marketing and promotion of the state or province as a travel destination. Research is not a primary function, and is not an end result. Research is important only to the extent it provides data to help plan more effective marketing strategies.
>
> To be most effective, research must be based on a thorough assessment of the needs of the particular state or province.

Where, for instance, tourism is already well established the emphasis may be on economic impact studies whereas in less developed states research may be designed primarily to evaluate tourism resources and identify appropriate markets.

Research is thus vital for organizations to perform their other functions effectively and for this reason the specific research required can often best be undertaken internally by the organization's own research division. In other cases existing data or information will be accessed or external researchers will be commissioned (Beaman and Meis, 1987). Taylor (1987) suggests four guidelines for determining the research needs in an NTO (these might also apply to other destination organizations):

- establish an information base to be anchored on periodic and consistent surveys that will supply tourism intelligence on a regular basis,
- provide projectable information on tourism needs for marketing and development planning,
- develop the analytical capacity required to interpret research findings for decision-making purposes,
- develop a research capability to deal with specific problems that are not of a recurring nature.

Taylor (p.149) also suggests that 'it is . . . a responsibility of the research group to ensure that the analysed and interpreted data are presented to the users in a clear and understandable manner'. While other sectors of the organization will often be the primary users of this research, the NTO will usually have a responsibility to communicate appropriate findings to the tourist industry in general and to other sectors of the economy and society, bearing in mind the diverse and small-scale nature of the tourist industry with its concomitant lack of research capability and the desirability of not duplicating effort. A major consideration here is the extent to which data can be disaggregated and used at a regional and local scale, particularly in spatial units which correspond to the boundaries of lower order tourist organizations. Useful reviews of a range of different research techniques and questions applicable to tourism are provided by

Ritchie and Goeldner (1987), Pearce (1987a) and Smith (1989).

Co-ordination and lobbying

Most of the functions noted so far will be undertaken by the NTO or some other destination organization at a lower level. However, as the WTO (1980) points out, because tourism is not 'a clear-cut sector of activity' many of the functions and responsibilities of other government departments and ministries will impinge on tourist development. Agencies with responsibilities for foreign trade, external affairs, customs, immigration, civil aviation, regional development, resource management and so on will all affect the path of tourist development. Consequently, one of the NTO's functions may be to co-ordinate these different policies as they affect tourism or at least ensure there is a tourism voice when these policies are being framed. This requires not only liaison with the other agencies concerned but also the establishment of clear, coherent policies on tourism so that appropriate arguments can be put forward and the needs of tourism clearly identified.

While the NTOs will want to make as strong a case as possible in these situations, the role of tourism will have to be kept in perspective and account taken of broader national policies. Those in the tourist industry, or in particular sectors of it, however, will seek to create as favourable a climate for the pursuit of their individual and common interests as possible. A significant function of sector organizations will thus be to create as powerful a political lobby for their interests as they can. This appears to be the most neglected of all aspects of research on tourist organizations yet as later chapters will show, lobbying can be a very significant function. It is therefore instructive at this stage to look at some findings from other industries.

Assael (1968, pp.24, 26) in his review of the political role of trade associations in the distributive industries of the United States concluded:

1) The more intense the conflict the more likely the resort to political action [as opposed to self-resolution].

2) When issues within an industry are common to all members, it is likely that a national trade association will become involved and resort to political action.
3) Associations whose membership represents a significant majority of the trade have been more successful in obtaining governmental support.
4) The most politically active association . . . has been able to form a strong cohesive organization because of similarities among its members in economic status and background. . . . Without homogeneity, . . . associations have difficulty adopting commonly accepted policies on controversial issues.
5) The most politically active trade associations are formed by the weakest segments in the channel structure.
6) A ready forum for the expression of grievances provides an inducement to trade associations to seek political resolution.
7) Most associations have tended to rely on political action as a last resort.
8) [There has been an] overall lack of success in achieving specific legislative gains on the national level since World War II.

While it would be misleading to transfer Assael's findings directly to the tourist industry, several general trends might be interpreted in the light of these points, particularly the different roles of the sector and destination organizations. Sector organizations are essentially trade associations and like them may seek strength not only through developing a large membership but also in some cases through remaining relatively specific and cohesive. That is, they confine themselves to their individual sectors, for example hotel and motel associations, or tour operator councils. More broadly based tourist organizations may see some of their political effectiveness diminished if increased size and heterogeneity result in a failure to speak with a united voice through a conflict of interest of different members. The public funding of destination organizations may also reduce their scope for overt lobbying and result in fence-sitting on controversial issues. These are all issues which clearly warrant further research.

Approaches to the study of organizations

Many different approaches to the study of organizations have been adopted depending on the nature of the problem examined, the disciplinary perspective employed and the period during which the research was undertaken. Dunkerley (1972) distinguished between three major levels of analysis – role, structural and organizational. In the first, the emphasis is upon the individual role and how individuals relate to the organization. Groups rather than individuals constitute the focus of the second level of analysis with the researcher being concerned with 'the properties of organizational groups and of specific structural characteristics of organizations' (as in the Hawthorne Studies). At the third level, the characteristics of organizations themselves are the major focus, with comparative analyses of organizations being a common approach. While contributions have been made by different disciplines at all levels, certain perspectives are associated with particular problems and levels of inquiry (Litterer, 1973). Business and management specialists, for example, have focused on issues of efficiency and co-ordination at the organizational level while many sociologists and psychologists have dealt with individual and group relations.

Early studies, particularly those concerned with the individual and group level of analysis, tended to view organizations as closed systems, complete in themselves. Later, during the late 1960s and early 1970s, organizations came to be viewed more as open systems which interacted with the environment and were influenced by environmental factors (Scott, 1981). A more macro-level approach was thus adopted by those who sought to incorporate the effect of environmental factors on organizational structure and behaviour. From this approach gradually emerged a fourth level of analysis – interorganizational research – as 'it has become immediately apparent that other organizations are a critical part of the environment of any organization' (Hall et al, 1977, p.458).

Interorganizational analysis

In this form of analysis, the unit to be studied is not a single organization but rather a network of organizations consisting of 'a number of distinguishable organizations engaged in a significant amount of interaction with each other' (Benson, 1975, p.230). Two main approaches to the study of this interaction have emerged (Hall et al, 1977; Schmidt and Kochan, 1977), one based on exchange theory as presented in the seminal paper by Levine and White (1961), the second stressing a power-dependency approach as expressed in Benson's (1975) paper which treated the interorganizational network as a political economy.

For Levine and White (1961, p.588):

> Organizational exchange is any voluntary activity between two organizations which has consequences, actual or anticipated, for the realization of their respective goals or objectives.

Their emphasis is thus on voluntary, goal-oriented exchange in a broad sense, not just the transfer of material goods. Organizations perceive the chances of attaining their goals in some domains are greater by acting jointly rather than behaving independently.

Benson (1975, p.232), however, lays greater stress in the analysis of interorganizational interaction on the importance of resource acquisition, particularly the acquisition and defence of money and authority:

> Authority refers to the legitimation of activities, the right and responsibility to carry out programs of a certain kind, dealing with a broad problem area or focus. Legitimated claims of this kind are termed domains. The possession of a domain permits the organization to operate in a certain sphere, claim support for its activities and define proper practices within its realm. . . . Money and authority are interrelated in that there is a generalized expectation of balance or correlation between the two.

Organizations seek an adequate supply of authority and money from the political economy to fulfil their programme requirements, maintain their domain, maintain an orderly and reliable flow of resources and to defend their paradigm or way of doing things. Their ability to do this is likely to vary and depend on two differential power bases, first, characteristics of the internal network structure (eg centrality), and second, the external linkages of network organizations.

Benson (pp.235–6) further postulated the idea of some state of interorganizational equilibrium or balance existing, the four dimensions of this being:

1) Domain consensus: agreement regarding . . . the appropriate role and scope of an agency,
2) Ideological consensus: agreement . . . regarding the nature of the tasks confronted by the organizations and appropriate approaches to those tasks,
3) Positive evaluation: the judgement by workers in one organization of the value of the work of another organization,
4) Work coordination: patterns of collaboration and cooperation between organizations. Work is coordinated to the extent that programs and activities in two or more organizations are geared into each other with a maximum of effectiveness and efficiency.

Balance is said to be reached when 'participant organizations are engaged in highly coordinated, cooperative interactions based on normative consensus and mutual respect'.

Other writers have elaborated on the bases of interorganizational interaction and forms of co-ordination that may be found. The voluntary and power-induced bases are extended by what Hall et al (1977) term 'voluntary but standardized through some form of formal agreement' and by mandated interaction. In this latter case (Raelin, 1982, p.244):

the legal-political mandate . . . assembles units into a network by a mandate, rather than under the inducement of a particular actor or set of actors, in order to accomplish a

designated task(s). It differs from the exchange basis in that although the interacting organizations are expected to be willing participants, the motivation to interact is provided by the mandate rather than by the parties' mutual consent.

Hall et al (1977, p.459) define co-ordination as 'the extent to which organizations attempt to ensure that their activities take into account those of other organizations'. They suggest that not only will the bases of interaction differ but also the form and degree of co-ordination are also likely to vary widely, ranging from the minimal and informal, to comprehensive formalized linkages. Given the multi-faceted nature of tourism and the many different activities that tourist organizations have been shown to engage in, questions of co-ordination and interorganizational interaction are likely to be critical in any analysis of tourist organizations.

Desirable as co-ordination may seem to be, the difficulties of achieving it should not be under-estimated. Writing from a policy implementation perspective, O'Toole (1983, p.130) observed:

Organizational goals, world views and routines may act as constraints against implementing certain policies. Co-ordination of all parties in an interorganizational network may be tough to achieve. And the sheer complexity of inducing cooperation across a number of varied but interdependent units could reduce chances of success.

Other writers go further, stressing the inevitability of conflict when interaction between organizations occurs (Scott, 1964; Dunkerley, 1972). Conflict is especially likely to occur under conditions of resource scarcity with Litwak and Hylton (1962, p.397) noting that its existence is one of the distinguishing features between inter- and intra-organizational analysis:

This conflict between organizations is taken as a given in interorganizational analysis, which starts out with the assumption that there is a situation of partial conflict and investigates the forms of social interaction under such conditions. From this point of view the elimination of conflict is a deviant instance and likely to lead to the disruption of interorganizational relations (ie organizational mergers and the like). By contrast, intraorganizational analysis assumes that conflicting values lead to a breakdown in organizational structure.

Organizations and their environment

As Benson (1975, p.238) and other researchers adopting an open-systems approach have recognized, 'The interorganizational network is affected in important ways by environmental conditions. These conditions provide a social context within which network relationships are negotiated.' This is also the case with individual organizations. The environment has been conceived in various ways from simply 'anything external to it [the organization]' (Hicks and Gullet, 1975) to 'those *events, circumstances and factors* which occur *outside* the boundaries of the organization and which may influence what may happen within it' (Bryans and Cronin, 1984, p.54).

From an organizational perspective, what is important is identifying those features of the environment which influence organizations the most and in analysing environments in those terms. Thus for Benson the environment is important insofar as it affects the supply of money and resources and the distribution of power within a network. The important dimensions of the structure of the environment are then depicted as resource concentration/dispersal, power concentration/dispersion and network autonomy/dependence. Similarly, Bryans and Cronin (1984) employ dimensions of environmental capacity (rich or lean in resources) and homogeneity/heterogeneity. Hage (1978) argues a case for specifying a larger number of environmental variables and lists a number of these for three sorts of contexts: the environment as a resource and performance context, as a network of interorganizational relationships and as a societal context.

Other writers (eg Hicks and Gullett, 1975; Dawson, 1986) emphasize the interactions between organizations and the environment in terms of the exchange or acquisition of inputs and outputs, with the environment being seen as providing both opportunities and constraints in these areas. Dawson also identifies a third source of environmental influence as external regulation; this may take the form of either formally established laws, rules and procedures or the attitudes and values of members of the focal organization and constituents of its environment. Dawson argues (p.90):

> To speak of organization is thus to speak of environment as well. The inevitability of needing to secure inputs, to disburse outputs and of attempts to regulate, inextricably links the members of any focal organization with the members of its environment in a form of 'love–hate' relationship. 'Love' because of the opportunities the environment provides and 'hate' because of the constraints and losses it can impose; 'inextricably linked' because of an inability for anyone to have the opportunities without the possibility of constraints.

Dawson goes on to point out that the environment to some extent is always a source of uncertainty for a focal organization. For this reason much organizational effort will be directed to generating and collecting information about relevant environmental attributes and influencing and controlling aspects of the environment.

Studying tourist organizations

The preceding section has reviewed a variety of approaches and concepts used in the broader field of organizational studies, many of which could be usefully applied to the study of tourist organizations. Concepts of exchange, resource acquisition, domain consensus, co-ordination and partial conflict appear to be potentially valuable tools for examining tourist organizations given the multi-faceted but interdependent nature of tourism

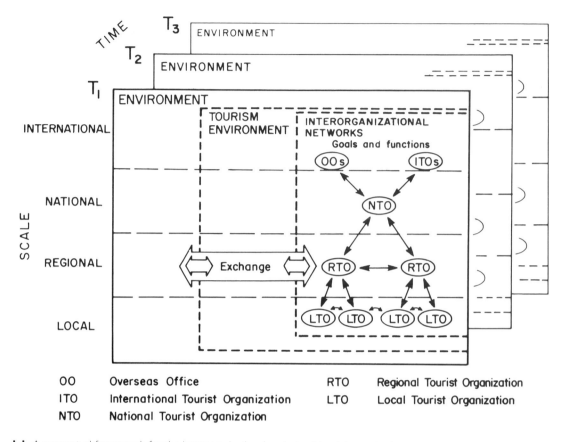

OO   Overseas Office   RTO   Regional Tourist Organization
ITO   International Tourist Organization   LTO   Local Tourist Organization
NTO   National Tourist Organization

1.1 A conceptual framework for the interorganizational analysis of tourist organizations

and the diversity of goals and activities which these organizations have been shown to pursue. In view of the paucity of work on tourist organizations it is not surprising that these concepts have gained little or no currency in the tourism literature. Other ideas have been more widely used in other areas of tourism research. The significance of the environment or context has been stressed elsewhere, notably with regard to the development, impact and spatial structure of tourism (Pearce, 1987a; 1989, pp.52–6, 185–6). What is needed now to launch a more substantial and systematic study of tourist organizations is an integrative framework which not only draws on the existing organizational literature but also takes account of the features and characteristics of the specific field of study, in this case, tourism. Figure 1.1 represents the conceptual model which underpins the substantive chapters

that follow; it may also serve as the first step in developing an integrative framework for subsequent work in this field.

Figure 1.1 depicts an approach to the study of tourist organizations which stresses a number of interrelated components and the relationships between these. It is an open-systems model which emphasizes not only the links within the specific field of study – the interorganizational network of tourist organizations – but the setting of this network in the broader environment, a sub-environment of which is the tourism environment, with which a variety of exchanges occur. Figure 1.1 also gives explicit recognition to the questions of spatial scale and temporal change (T1, T2, T3 . . .), dimensions which add further complexity to the basic organization-environment models of the organizational literature (Scott, 1981;

Bryans and Cronin, 1984). Finally, in the context of this book, Figure 1.1 constitutes a comparative framework for the study of tourist organizations in six different countries.

Interorganizational networks

The primary interest here is in elucidating the role of tourist organizations in the broader field of tourism. The concern is with what tourist organizations actually do, a concern expressed by focusing on their goals and functions. The available evidence and a priori reasoning indicate a variety of goals might be sought and a range of functions undertaken by a spectrum of tourist organizations. A comprehensive interorganizational approach exploring the nature of these goals and activities and the interactions between these organizations thus suggests itself for this new and essentially undeveloped area of study rather than the lower levels of analysis outlined by Dunkerley (1972) – role, structural and organizational.

The range of functions to be examined has been reviewed earlier (marketing, development, planning, research). The aim, however, is not just to identify the function, for example marketing, but to examine what specific aspects are undertaken, by which organizations, how and why. A wide range of tourist organizations may exist in any country and a selection of these may have to be made for practical purposes. The focal organizations examined in subsequent chapters are primarily destination organizations, usually public or semi-public, with consideration being given to sectoral and other related organizations where time and space permit or where particular problems warrant their inclusion. The emphasis on destination organizations enables a range of these to be examined at different spatial scales with national, regional and local tourist organizations being included in the network and attention being given to international links through the operation of overseas offices or membership of international organizations.

The inclusion of the scale element in the interorganizational network is a departure from similar studies in the organizational literature which have commonly been concerned with the interaction of related organizations within a given area or community, for example community-level planning organizations (Warren, 1967), agencies dealing with community chests and social service exchanges (Litwak and Hylton, 1962) and those dealing with problem youth (Hall et al, 1977). As the latter point out (p.458), in these cases 'the domain is [often] subdivided so that the interorganizational network becomes a situation of "sequential interdependence"'. When the network is defined according to spatial scale, interaction becomes more hierarchical than sequential in nature. Scale and spatial hierarchies have been given much greater attention in geography (eg Paddison, 1983; Taylor and Thrift, 1983; Taylor, 1984) and in other fields of study such as development and planning (Stöhr and Taylor, 1981; Martins, 1986). 'Regional' is taken by such writers to refer to an intermediate scale between national and local and is used here in this sense. Martins observes (1986, p.3), 'the concept of region is a mental construct associated with a scale of political space: a scale which is greater than a single local authority and smaller than the State'. Paddison (1983) recognizes considerable variations exist between countries with regard to their regional divisions.

Most tourism research has involved studies at a single spatial scale, from local to international, but attention has also been directed to multi-level research and synthesizing phenomena at different scales. The notion of a spatial hierarchy is central to a number of models which underpin the geography of tourism (Pearce, 1987a), notably those concerning structural aspects (Hills and Lundgren, 1977; Britton, 1982) and tourist flows (Miossec, 1976; Pearce, 1981; Lundgren, 1982). Pearce (1987a, 1990a) has analysed different scales of tourist travel patterns, showing how flows at one scale are linked to another, with resultant implications for the impacts which tourism may generate. Mathieson (1985, p.17) argues that greater attention should be given to 'the scale of impact for the spheres of influence of tourist development vary and their consequences may be viewed differently depending upon whether they are assessed from a local, regional, national or international perspective'. Likewise, the goals and strategies of tourism plans vary from the local to the international scale (Pearce, 1989).

Other activities can also be expected to vary from scale to scale. Product development is essentially undertaken on the ground at a local scale where visitor facilities are provided in the form of individual hotels, attractions and so forth. Some of these may have a regional or national role, for example an international airport. Much of the marketing effort will occur away from the destination where economies of scale and the need to develop strong images will encourage regional or national initiatives, especially in competitive overseas markets. Successful development will require these different activities to be closely matched and co-ordinated. Conversely, concentration on a single spatial scale may result in key functions being overlooked or ignored. Murphy's (1985) advocacy of a 'community approach', for instance, emphasizes local concerns and participation but fails to show how small communities can effectively market their product to the wider world and thereby achieve the benefits sought from tourist development.

The nature of tourism thus calls for the use of an interorganizational framework which embraces the concept of scale and recognizes the different functions which tourist organizations might undertake in the pursuit of various goals. Basic questions then arise relating to which functions are most appropriately undertaken at which scale by which organization to achieve which goals. The nature and direction (top down, bottom up, or horizontal) of the interactions which occur among the organizations in the network also become fundamental research issues.

Tourist organizations and their environments

The network of tourist organizations is set within a broader environmental context. A major component of this is the tourism sub-environment which shall be considered in more detail below. Of the many other environmental factors which might be examined, the broader political-economic framework is particularly significant when adopting a multi-scale approach and focusing on the functions of public or semi-public destination organizations. As Paddison (1983) stresses, power is distributed geographically, with the manner in which the function of governing is divided within a state between national and sub-national governments varying along a continuum of countries from those with a markedly centralist system to others which are federal in structure. As Paddison (p.14) also points out:

> There is a more fundamental difference between these levels than that of scale alone. Decentralization to local government, for example, usually involves the running of services that it is considered more suitable to operate locally but within legislative guidelines determined by the central government. Regional-level government . . . can be distinguished by the involvement of more far-reaching 'balance of power' questions between the national government and the regions, in which the sub-national governments may have legislative competence in their own right and hence wider powers of autonomy. These state-regional questions are paramount in federal countries. In countries that have been more centralized, the substantial shifts of power from the central authority to the region implicit in this form of government have been avoided.

As tourism is a relatively recent and in many places a far from dominant sector of the economy, it is likely that the tourist organization network will heavily reflect established political and administrative frameworks, boundaries and divisions of power. In addition, the goals and functions of tourist organizations, particularly public sector ones, will be influenced by broader government policies, the 'political culture' of the country and general economic conditions in the same way that other aspects of tourism are structured by the political economy as Britton (1982) has demonstrated in small peripheral nations. The extent to which the state favours interventionist or free-market policies, for example, will impinge on the goals which tourist organizations pursue and the ways in which their activities are carried out. The state of the economy will affect the resources available to them. In these respects tourist organizations will behave like other organizations and will interact with the broader environment in the ways outlined by Dawson (1986) and others earlier, seeking to extract resources, return inputs, all the while being regulated by the environment. The nature and extent of these exchanges constitute a major field of inquiry.

At the same time, tourist organizations in their structure and activities will reflect the more specific tourism sub-environment in which they exist or indeed may be seen to serve. Of particular importance for the interorganizational network will be the degree of spatial homogeneity or diversity as characterized by the following attributes:

- the scale and economic and social significance of tourism,
- the composition of the tourist industry: scale and type of operations, nature of ownership,
- the type of tourism: coastal, alpine, urban, rural, the nature of the attractions (natural/man-made, active/passive, formal/informal), circuit versus destination, short versus long visits,
- the pattern of growth: expansion, contraction or stability, a long or short history of development, planned or spontaneous growth,
- the type of markets: domestic or international, short-haul or long-haul, independent or organized, diversified or narrowly based, mass or independent.

Many of these attributes will have been conditioned by the broader environment.

Interaction will occur between the network of tourist organizations and the tourism sub-environment viewed at a range of scales. The organizations will again be seeking resources from the environment in the form of funds, membership, and information in return for which outputs will be provided such as marketing campaigns, development plans, tourism statistics and so forth. The organizations may also be seeking to shape and improve the tourism environment in a variety of ways from regulation through physical development to stimulating market potential.

A temporal perspective

Environments change over time. Tourism develops and as it develops the attributes outlined in the preceding sector evolve – changes occur in the nature and composition of the industry and of the markets, with resultant changes in the various impacts which tourism generates (Pearce, 1987a, 1989). Given the environmental–organizational interactions which occur, changes might thus be anticipated in the interorganizational network and in the goals and functions of tourist organizations. Further insights into tourist organizations should therefore result from incorporating a temporal perspective in their study. For graphical purposes such a perspective is depicted in Figure 1.1 by cross-sections at different times (T1, T2, T3 . . .). In practice, however, it may be more useful to trace the different changes over a period of time for rarely will all elements in the system change simultaneously and it may be the examination of the processes that leads up to the set of structures and interrelationships at any one time that sheds the greatest light on the forces at work. In research on tourist organizations this requires much additional effort for there are few earlier studies to draw upon.

A comparative approach

Changes in both environmental settings and interorganizational networks will occur not only through time but also across space. In this initial phase of research on tourist organizations where there is little scope yet for synthesis, comparative cross-national studies hold promise for advancing knowledge in this area. The case for comparative studies is well made in the planning field by Masser (1981) who emphasizes the extent to which comparisons may stimulate the development of theory and the practical value of such studies and the benefits of learning from others. In his review, Masser cites Feldman (1978, p.287) on comparative public policy:

The introduction of comparison into the analysis of public policy promises to expose the range of choice available to societies whose perception of choice may be bound by institutions, economic, social structure, and culture. It promises insight into the role of institutions by exposing parallel institutions operating in other systems. And it promises embracing theory for politics, as well as for policy, beyond the boundaries erected by the details of systems because comparison helps establish norms for judgement and helps distinguish the essential from the trivia.

Substitute organizations for institutions, environments for systems, tourism for politics and this argument applies readily to the study of tourist organizations.

The comparative approach has yet to emerge as a distinctive, readily recognizable methodology in tourism research despite its application to a wide variety of problems during the 1970s and 1980s (Pearce, 1991). However, comparative studies are widely established in the organizational literature where they commonly take the form of a series of case studies or involve the use of more quantitative methods as in the Aston studies.

Chapter outline

Drawing on the ideas discussed throughout this chapter and using Figure 1.1 as a conceptual framework, the next seven chapters are devoted to the systematic analysis of tourist organizations in six countries: the USA, the Federal Republic of Germany, the UK, the Netherlands, Ireland and New Zealand. This selection has been based on a number of considerations. In order to achieve some measure of 'control through common features' (Masser, 1981), the countries are drawn from developed Western nations rather than from a mix of industrialized, socialist and developing states. At the same time, in order to explore the influence of environmental factors the selection includes a range of political systems: two federal (the USA and Federal Republic of Germany), three unitary or

centralized (the Netherlands, Ireland and New Zealand) and one intermediate case, the UK, classified by Paddison (1983) as compound unitary. Practical considerations also played a role as original fieldwork was needed to obtain much of the necessary information. Such considerations influenced not only the choice of countries but also the nature and extent of the analysis within each. Clearly coverage of the United States is achieved less readily than of Ireland and in this and other cases analysis of the sub-national organizations has been selective. Consequently, the emphasis in the different countries is on particular regions once the general national framework has been established. In the United States the focus is on Hawaii; in Germany, on Bavaria; in the UK, on Scotland.

Much of the fieldwork was carried out in 1989 and consisted of in-depth interviews with current and former personnel in the focal organizations and, where possible, in other organizations as well as the tourist industry of the region concerned. Field visits also enabled a greater appreciation of environmental factors and some evaluation of policies and projects. A wide variety of documentation was also collected and subsequently examined: annual reports, policy statements, plans, audits, promotional material, statistical data, research reports, and so on. The emphasis throughout was on the goals and functions of the organizations and on interactions within the interorganizational networks and between them and their environments.

Chapters 2 to 8 begin with a brief overview of the environmental attributes of the country concerned, emphasizing in particular its political structure. The characteristics of tourism in each country are then outlined and the nature and structure of the network of tourist organizations examined. Attention is then directed to the different functions performed by the network and the interactions which occur as these are carried out. Differences in emphasis and treatment do occur from chapter to chapter but the common approach adopted does generate a comprehensive body of comparative material which enables more general findings to be drawn out and reviewed systematically in the final chapter.

2

United States of America

The United States of America is the largest and most complex of the national case studies. The issues discussed in Chapter 1 and conceptualized in Figure 1.1 are dealt with in different ways and at two different levels. This chapter covers the country as a whole, focuses on official tourist organizations and attempts to provide an overview of these. Following Figure 1.1, the first two sections set the scene, outlining the broad environmental factors and reviewing tourism in the USA. Emphasis then shifts to the three different scales at which tourist organizations are examined: federal policies and the United States Travel and Tourism Administration (USTTA), the state travel offices and local government. The interaction between organizations at these scales is then examined. Of necessity, these sections deal with general issues, that on states for example draws heavily on the common source material provided by the surveys of state travel offices and briefly illustrates patterns found there with the experience

of specific states. With the big picture established by Chapter 2, Chapter 3 turns to a more detailed analysis of interorganizational relationships in a particular state, Hawaii. This focus enables the inclusion of a variety of organizations and enables a closer examination of state and sub-state linkages.

Environmental factors

Of the many broad environmental factors that impinge upon US tourist organizations, three are particularly important in the context of this study: size, federalism and political culture. The United States is the fourth largest country in the world (9 160 450 sq km), has the single largest economy (1986 GDP $4 195 billion) and in 1989 had a population of 248 239 000. The sheer size of the United States has resulted in considerable internal diversity: physical, economic, social and cultural. The many physiographic regions (mountains, plateaux and lowlands) are complemented and compounded by numerous socio-economic regions from the more traditional (Yankee North/Confederate South/Settled East/Frontier West), through the cultural (classifications by Zelinsky, Garreau, Gastil) to the recent and broader Rustbelt/Sunbelt divisions (Knox et al, 1988). Sheer size and internal diversity are also general factors which have tended to favour more decentralized government as 'through more localized policy-making, political decentralization can cater for a wider variety of policy decisions' (Paddison, 1983, p.44).

Federalism is a dominant form of political decentralization in which two levels of government are considered equals constitutionally. Under the US constitution sovereignty is shared between the federal government in Washington DC and the state governments, now fifty in number, with their own bicameral legislatures. While certain guarantees are given to the states (equal representation in the Senate, territorial integrity, a republican form of government, protection against invasion and domestic violence) and certain tasks are clearly federal in nature (foreign affairs, defence, aspects of economic policy) much ambiguity concerning policy areas remains (McKay,

1990). Over the last fifty years the federal government has assumed increasing responsibility in a range of domestic matters.

Under the 10th Amendment 'the powers not delegated to the United States by the Constitution, nor prohibited by it to the States are reserved to the States respectively or to the people'. By default, tourism – not an issue to the Founding Fathers – would seem to be primarily a state function though aspects of foreign affairs may impinge on international tourism and other interstate activities such as transportation have increasingly come into the federal domain. The state framework might therefore be expected to dominate the structure of tourist organizations in the United States with the considerable diversity of the fifty states in terms of size, economy and political culture being reflected in their tourist organizations.

Each state also has some influence on the responsibilities and organizations of local authorities which may be established at a lower level in each state, primarily to deliver public services such as primary and secondary education through locally raised taxes (Johnston, 1988). Significant variations are to be found among the fifty states in the degree of state–local centralization (Stephens, 1974; cited by Paddison, 1983).

Considerable regional diversity also occurs in terms of political culture. Johnston (1988, p.85) drawing on the earlier work of Elazar (1966) identifies three basic elements of political culture in the United States, between which some conflict may occur:

- the culture of *individualism*, characterized by 'minimal government', free enterprise and the 'culture of the marketplace',
- *moralistic culture*, 'which promotes the concept of government for the common good. The American government serves the US population as a whole, not segments within it',
- a *traditionalistic* element where 'the assumption is of a fixed social structure in which the relatively small group at the peak of the hierarchy sees its role as undertaking the functions of government in order to ensure maintenance of the existing social order'.

According to Elazar, the South has been dominated by a traditionalistic culture, many north-eastern states by an individualistic culture while the New England and Great Lakes states have been dominated by a moralistic culture. For tourism, however, it is the free enterprise minimal government involvement philosophy which has generally been the most significant.

The relationships between the three levels of government – federal, state and local – can be examined in a variety of ways, one useful measure being the share of the taxes each collects. Table 2.1 shows that the federal government collects over half

Table 2.1 *Travel generated tax receipts in the USA (1987)*

Level of government	All tax receipts %	Travel generated tax receipts		Travel generated tax all tax %
		$ billions	%	
Federal	57	18.5	55.1	3.4
State	26	11.2	33.1	4.5
Local	17	3.9	11.6	2.5
US total	100	33.6[1]	100.0	3.6

Note: [1] Plus $1.8 billion in foreign visitor generated taxes of which 55% to federal government.

Source: After US Travel Data Center (1989a)

of all taxes while the states receive about one-quarter. In terms of travel generated tax receipts, however, the states' share is significantly greater (33 per cent) while the local authorities' percentage drops. Consequently the states as a whole derive proportionately more of their taxes (4.5 per cent) from the travel sector compared to the federal (3.4 per cent) and local (2.5 per cent) governments. Considerable variations occur from state to state (US Travel Data Center, 1989a). In terms of the federal-state-local travel generated tax take, the states' share of receipts in 1987 exceeded that of the federal government in six states (Mississippi, 52.3 per cent; Kentucky, 51.1 per cent; West Virginia, 50.8 per cent; Vermont, 49.4 per cent; South Carolina, 48.5 per cent, Hawaii, 47.5 per cent). Likewise, states vary in their dependence on these receipts (in Nevada travel generated taxes amounted to 39.5 per cent of all state tax receipts; Vermont, 14.7 per cent; New Hampshire, 11.2 per cent; Florida, 10.6 per cent . . . Montana, 2.7 per cent; Alabama, 2.5 per cent; Oregon, 2.2 per cent; Alaska, 1.5 per cent). These figures are indicative of the ways in which the broader political economy of the United States and its internal diversity may impinge on tourist organizations there.

Tourism in the USA

The size and diversity of the USA have provided a varied resource base upon which the United States tourist industry has developed. The country's many national and state parks contain a range of outstanding natural features and offer abundant opportunities for outdoor recreation. Then there are the gentler landscapes of regions such as New England, the beaches of New Jersey, Florida and Hawaii, the ski-fields of the Rockies and Vermont, and so on. These natural attractions are complemented by historic sites and monuments, for example in Washington DC, and by many purpose-built attractions, including in Disneyland and Disneyworld some of the most successful of their kind in the world. US tourism is also characterized by the importance and dynamism of its large

modern urban areas – New York, Chicago, Los Angeles, San Francisco. While sightseeing, entertainment and visits to friends and relatives are all important here, so too are business travel and the very large convention industry. Van Doren and Gustke (1982) report that business travellers constituted 43 per cent of the market for US hotels in 1978, followed by tourists (32 per cent) and conference participants (17 per cent).

Size has not only endowed the country with this diversity, but also made visiting 'the United States' difficult if not impossible. It is much less easy to conceive of a visitor 'doing the USA' than it is many small European countries; rather one is clearly forced to be selective, to visit for example the West Coast or even just California, the major urban areas or to concentrate on attractions of specific interest. This has implications for marketing tourism and for tourist organizations.

The US travel industry is comprised of a mix of a very large number of small businesses and a small number of very large firms. Some 98 per cent of the country's 336 000 firms deemed to be in the travel industry are classified as small businesses. The absolute number of these should not disguise the role played by a handful of large enterprises in key sectors. Half of the 2.82 million hotel rooms in the USA are controlled by the top twenty-five hotel companies while eight carriers held 95 per cent of the domestic air market in 1988 (US Travel Data Center, 1989b). At the same time, much travel, particularly domestic travel, is very informal and independent in character, with travel by private car being by far the most dominant mode.

According to the United States Travel and Tourism Administration (USTTA, 1987a), the US travel industry

- is the nation's third largest retail industry following food stores and automotive dealers,
- is the country's second largest private employer,
- is one of the top three employers in thirty-nine states,
- directly employs 5.5 million Americans,
- generates more than $58 billion a year in wages and salaries.

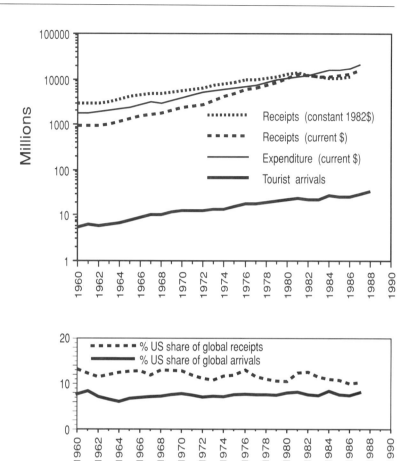

2.1 Evolution of international tourist arrivals and international tourism receipts in the USA (1960–88) (Data source: USTTA 1986, 1987a)

Domestic travellers and foreign visitors are estimated to have spent a total of $313 billion on travel in the USA and its territories in 1988; all but 5.75 per cent of this sum was generated by domestic travellers (US Travel Data Center, 1989b). In 1988 Americans took more than 1.2 billion person trips within the United States to places 100 miles or more away from home. Foreign visitors to the USA totalled 33.7 million in 1988 while Americans took 41 million trips to foreign countries.

The dominance of the domestic market in the USA largely results from the interplay of the broader environmental factors outlined in the previous section. First, the size and affluence of the United States' population has created a very large market. Second, the country is well endowed with a wide range of tourist resources. Third, use of these resources by the American population is classified as domestic tourism as this travel occurs within US borders whereas much comparable travel in the world's other large market, Europe, is deemed international due to the existence there of many small coterminous nation states whose frontiers are readily crossed. The USA has only two international borders – with Canada and Mexico.

Figure 2.1 shows a generally steady increase in US visitor arrivals and receipts since the 1960s, although some downturn occurred in the early 1980s (in constant dollar terms annual receipts for 1982 to 1986 all fell below the 1981 peak). Overall, the trends in Figure 2.1 broadly follow global ones, with the result that the US market share has remained virtually unchanged over this period,

Table 2.2   Regional distribution of travel generated expenditure in the USA (1986)

	a US and foreign visitor expenditure		b US travel expenditure		c Foreign visitor expenditure		d $\frac{c}{a}$	per capita total visitor expenditure
	$ billions	%	$ billions	%	$ billions	%	%	$
Pacific West	49.4	18.4	44.3	17.5	5.1	33.3	10.3	$1 384
Mountain West	24.5	9.1	23.5	9.3	1.0	6.5	4.5	$1 884
West North Central	16.8	6.3	16.5	6.5	0.3	2.0	1.2	$956
West South Central	25.6	9.6	23.9	9.5	1.7	11.1	6.6	$953
East North Central	32.2	12.0	31.3	12.4	0.9	5.9	2.8	$771
East South Central	9.8	3.7	9.6	3.6	0.2	1.3	2.0	$645
South Atlantic	52.9	19.7	49.8	19.7	3.1	20.3	5.9	$1 293
Middle Atlantic	42.2	15.7	39.9	15.8	2.3	15.0	5.5	$1 132
New England	14.8	5.5	14.1	5.6	0.7	4.6	4.7	$1 163
USA	268.2	100	252.9	99.9	15.3	100	5.7	$1 113

Data source: US Travel Data Center (1989a)

ranging from 7 to 8 per cent of global arrivals and 10.5 to 13 per cent of international tourism receipts. An international travel 'deficit' is recorded throughout the period, with expenditure by outgoing US tourists exceeding international receipts in every year but 1981. USTTA estimates indicate that the neighbouring countries of Canada (41.9 per cent of arrivals in 1987) and Mexico (22.6 per cent) are the major foreign markets, with the remaining visitors being drawn from a wide range of overseas countries including the United Kingdom, France, Germany and Japan.

Significant geographic variations occur throughout the USA on these different measures. Table 2.2 shows the distribution of travel generated expenditure is far from uniform. In absolute terms the three top-ranked regions for all travel expenditure in 1986 were the South Atlantic, Middle Atlantic and Pacific West. However, the Pacific West attracts a far greater share of foreign visitor expenditure (33 per cent), with spending from this market accounting for 10.3 per cent of the region's total compared to the national average of 5.7 per cent. Conversely the Mid-West (West

and East North Central) and the South (West and East South Central) receive proportionately less foreign visitor expenditure and their overall per capita receipts are substantially below the national average. Total per capita receipts are highest in the Mountain West, Pacific West and in the regions along the Atlantic coast.

Figure 2.2 shows that significant statewide variations in domestic travel generated expenditure occur within these broader census regions and that different spatial patterns of absolute and relative (per capita) expenditure are found at this level. In absolute terms California is followed by Florida, New York, Texas, New Jersey and Pennsylvania – states with large populations. On a per capita basis, however, tourism is more important in Nevada, Hawaii and New England. Only two states – Florida and New Jersey – feature in the leading ten on both measures. USTTA figures for 1987 show major differences are also to be found in the regional distribution of foreign visitors. Mexican arrivals are concentrated in the four border states from California to Texas. Northern states depend most heavily on Canadians – Washington (78.8 per

2.2 Distribution of domestic travel generated expenditure in the USA (1987) (a) total expenditure (b) expenditure per capita (Data source: US Travel Data Center 1989a)

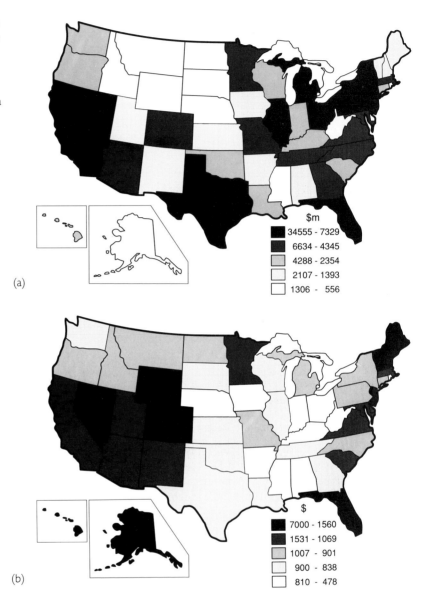

(a)

$m
	34555 - 7329
	6634 - 4345
	4288 - 2354
	2107 - 1393
	1306 - 556

(b)

$
	7000 - 1560
	1531 - 1069
	1007 - 901
	900 - 838
	810 - 478

cent), Michigan (75 per cent), Vermont (95 per cent) and Maine (96.5 per cent) – but in absolute terms Canadians are most numerous in New York and Florida. The gateway states of California, New York, Florida and Hawaii were leaders in terms of absolute numbers of overseas arrivals but in relative terms the overseas component was highest in Hawaii (85.6 per cent), Louisiana (81 per cent) and Illinois (76.7 per cent).

Few comprehensive figures are available on domestic travel patterns in the USA but much demand would appear to be either intra-state or intra-regional. Smith's (1983) analysis of the 1977 National Travel Survey, for example, suggested a variety of functional regions in the United States based on flows between adjoining states, underlain by a strong north–south pattern. Californians account for over 50 per cent of all travel and tourism revenues in California (Doube, 1985). Over half of New Jersey's travellers in 1987 came from the Mid-Atlantic with a further 18 per cent from the South Atlantic (New Jersey Division of Travel and Tourism, 1988).

Federal policies

For its size, the USA has a very small national tourist organization with a limited range of functions. In 1991, the United States Travel and Tourism Administration (USTTA) had a base budget of $14.6 million and a staff of ninety-five, of whom fifty-one were in overseas offices. While the Bush administration has been somewhat more supportive, the USA almost saw its NTO disappear altogether during the 1970s and 1980s (Airey, 1984; Richter, 1985; Ronkainen and Farano, 1987). This is perhaps not surprising in a country which has never had a strong national tourism policy and where the virtues of private enterprise have long been extolled. As Richter notes, 'the Eisenhower administration specifically considered and rejected the proposal that the federal government become involved in tourism promotion'. The US Travel Service (USTS), the forerunner to the USTTA, was established under the Kennedy administration by the International Travel Act 1961 but support for tourism through the 1960s was limited and fragmented. The federal government's role in tourism was debated extensively during the 1970s with first the study of the Tourism Resource Review Commission and then the National Tourism Policy Study which highlighted the need for a broad, national tourism policy. Bills to establish a national tourism policy and a restructured national travel and tourism agency were vetoed by President Carter in December 1980. Finally, in October 1981, despite the new administration's lack of enthusiasm, President Reagan signed the National Tourism Policy Act which created the USTTA.

In commenting on the final passage of this Act, Airey (1984, pp.278–9) underlines the influence of broader environmental factors on tourism and tourism organization:

The 1981 National Tourism Policy Act and the resulting administrative structure for tourism in the USA is the outcome of the interplay of various forces. In part it is the outcome of an Administration which at best has seen a federal involvement in tourism being confined to the promotion of international tourism for balance of payments purposes and at worst has seen no explicit role for the federal government in tourism. In part it is the outcome of a Legislature who have seen a much stronger role for federal government in tourism and one which is more broadly based, at its fullest extent to encompass recreation as well as tourism, and all aspects of tourism both domestic and international. And in part it is the outcome of a tourism industry which has maintained an effective lobby for government support for tourism and particularly international tourism.

In the end, the final product clearly illustrates the outcome of these three major influences. The broad sweep of the National Tourism Policy and the seniority of the head of USTTA is the product of the various studies and proposals of Congress; the narrowing down of the legislation onto tourism (excluding recreation) is in line with the effective lobbying of the tourist industry; and the final concentration on international promotion, and the meagre resources is a product of a hostile Administration. . . .

Despite all the efforts, the end result is not radically different from that which went before.

Passage of the 1981 Act did not end the debate as President Reagan subsequently called repeatedly but unsuccessfully for the USTTA to be eliminated. Ronkainen and Farano (1987, p.3) summarized his administration's attitudes in this way:

Administration officials believe that the private sector can better safeguard America's share of the world tourism market than can a bureaucratic agency. In fact, they do not deem tourism promotion as an appropriate federal activity. Further, they do not want the general public to pay for programs which benefit specified segments of society. Finally, the President contends that tourism promotion has little impact in inducing increased receipts from foreigners. At the heart of their position, the Administration officials do not believe that it is possible or beneficial for the USTTA to attempt to unify the diverse range of travel and tourism firms into a single industry.

These arguments are contested by Ronkainen and Farano (1987), who argue that 'Travel firms operate in a micro framework, maximizing their share of the existing U.S. tourism market' rather than seeking to increase the United States' share of the world market. Indeed, Figure 2.1 showed there has been no increase in US market share since 1960. Ronkainen and Farano also claim the USTTA 'has demonstrated a remarkable return on taxpayers' dollars' and that their efforts have been 'wholeheartedly embraced' by the private sector.

Whatever the merits of these respective arguments there is little doubt that the USTTA and its forerunner, the USTS, have always operated in a lean if not openly hostile environment, a factor which has curtailed the functions of the country's NTO and lessened its chances of achieving its stated goals.

The USTTA

The USTTA is an agency of the US Department of Commerce headed by an Under Secretary of Commerce for Travel and Tourism. Its principal mission, which it inherited from the USTS, is

> to develop travel to the United States from abroad as a stimulus to economic stability and to the growth of the US travel industry, to reduce the Nation's travel deficit, and to promote friendly understanding and appreciation of the United States.

Its principal goals are 'to increase the US share of worldwide tourism receipts and to increase this Nation's real earnings from tourism' (USTTA, 1987a).

However under the 1981 Act a dozen other goals were established. These include those which make explicit reference to both tourism and recreation, namely to

- optimize the contribution of the tourism and recreation industries to economic prosperity, full employment and the international balance of payments of the United States,
- make the opportunity for and benefits of tourism and recreation in the United States universally accessible to residents of the United States and of foreign countries.

Provision is also made to pursue broader cultural goals and to develop travel and finally to

- assist in the collection, analysis and dissemination of data which accurately measures the economic and social impact of tourism to and within the United States to facilitate planning in the public and private sectors,
- harmonize, to the maximum extent possible, all federal activities in support of tourism and recreation with the needs of the general public and the states, territories and recreation industries, and to give leadership to all concerned with tourism, recreation and national heritage preservation in the United States.

The emphasis given to these different goals is reflected in the structure of the USTTA, which has offices for policy and planning, research, tourism marketing and management and administration. These lie under the Office of Under Secretary, which has overall responsibility for the policies and directions of the USTTA (Edgell, 1984). Regional offices are maintained in Toronto, Mexico City, Tokyo, London, Paris, Frankfurt, Amsterdam, Milan, Sydney and Miami (for South America). Paris also has the International Congress Office. The emphasis is clearly on international tourism with little if any explicit support for recreation despite its inclusion in the goals cited earlier.

The under secretary also serves as vice chairman of the Tourism Policy Council and as an *ex-officio* member of the Travel and Tourism Advisory Board, two related organizations set up under the

1981 Act. The council's role is 'to assure that the national interest in tourism is fully considered in Federal decisionmaking'. Among other things, the council is mandated to

> coordinate the policies and programs of member agencies that have a significant effect on tourism, recreation, and national heritage preservation,

and

> seek and receive concerns and views of state and local governments and the Travel and Tourism Advisory Board with respect to Federal programs and policies deemed to conflict with the orderly growth and development of tourism.

However, as is underlined in the 1st *Program Report* of the USTTA (1982, p.4):

> The Council is *not* empowered to coordinate State, local or private sector policies, but only those at the Federal level.

The fifteen members of the Travel and Tourism Advisory Board, on the other hand, shall be selected 'so as to provide as nearly as practicable a broad representation of different geographical regions within the United States and of the diverse and varied segments of the tourism industry'. Moreover, 'at least one shall be a representative of the states who is knowledgeable of tourism promotion'. The role of the board is to advise the under secretary regarding the National Tourism Policy Act and the assistant secretary for tourism marketing with respect to the preparation of the annual marketing plan, one of the specified 'duties' of the USTTA.

The Travel and Tourism Advisory Board meets two or three times a year. During its meetings in 1987 it reviewed: USTTA's fiscal year 1987–88 international marketing plan, a tourism industry crisis management plan, visa waiver status, National Tourism Week, Pacific Basin tourism programme, USTTA marketing initiatives, USTTA fee

proposals and the 1994 World Cup Soccer proposal.

The Tourism Policy Council normally meets four times a year. In 1987 it addressed some topics also considered by the board (eg the World Cup proposal, visa waiver status and the crisis management plan) but generally focused on other inter-agency issues, some general, others more specific. These included cross-border problems affecting US and Canadian bus tour operators, USTTA's proposed facilitation fee, the feasibility and advisability of establishing a consolidated passenger inspection fee at air and sea ports of entry, an expected increase in foreign visitor arrivals, AIDS and impediments to travel.

The USTTA itself is concerned primarily with marketing, particularly with facilitating the marketing efforts of others in the absence of its own budget for large-scale direct mass media advertising. In terms of advertising the emphasis has been on encouraging co-operative advertising because (USTTA, 1986, p.10) such techniques 'are particularly effective in tourism marketing because the "product" being sold is never a single-item purchase but always consists of a group of related components – a destination, means of getting there, lodging and dining, and enjoyable things to see and do'. The 1987 annual report notes (USTTA, 1987a, p.7) an 'historic first-time effort between USTTA, a geographic U.S. region [six New England states] and a major US air carrier, promoting tourism from a foreign market', involving in this case a joint television campaign in the United Kingdom whereas previous co-operative efforts had essentially been limited to the print media. In 1988 the USTTA matched its entire budget ($13 million) with co-operative advertising funds (Ahmed and Krohn, 1990).

Other facilitation is done through the on-site marketing services of the regional offices which supply information directly to consumers and also provide support to foreign travel wholesalers and retail agents, for example conducting workshops and organizing familiarization ('fam') trips. Logistical support to tourism industry trade shows is also important, with the USTTA co-ordinating

Table 2.3   Key accomplishments of the USTTA in marketing (1987)

Item	
Travel trade enquiries serviced	188 255
Trade contacts initiated	44 442
Number of shipments of travel brochures and maps to foreign travel outlets	70 810
Workshops or seminars conducted for tourism industry personnel	130
Attendees at workshops and seminars	27 449
Number of major travel wholesalers inspecting US sites	1 128
Number of consumer enquiries answered	546 055
Travel missions co-ordinated	80
Travel mission participants assisted	931
Travel shows organized or participated in	44
Foreign journalists to USA on product inspection trips	889
Future international congresses obtained for US venues	42
Attendees expected at future congresses	56 600
Exchange earnings anticipated from future international congresses	$82 Mil
International congresses held in US in FY 1986	30
Attendees at FY 1986 congresses	30 000
Estimated exchange earnings from FY 1986 congresses	$48 Mil
Co-op ad programme partners	1 143
Co-op ad programme partner funds	$4 178 106
Co-op marketing programme partners (other than advertising)	2 833
Co-op marketing programme partner funds	$7 162 206

Source: USTTA (1987a).

the US presence in such events. Other technical assistance includes providing liaison between foreign wholesalers and agents and regional state and city tourism interests in the USA as well as supplying the US tourist industry with up-to-date marketing intelligence. Through its media services programme the USTTA stimulates the demand for information on the USA by organizing familiarization trips for journalists and placing US tourism stories in foreign media. The USTTA's marketing activities for 1987 are summarized in Table 2.3.

Despite the existence of the research division, research is not reported on directly in the annual reports of the USTTA, being included in passing under the provision of marketing intelligence. Wynegar (1984, pp.183–4) provides some interesting comments on the research implications of the rundown of the agency in the early 1980s:

Essentially what we want to get out of these [new evaluation] studies is to determine what our competitive position is. We have been out of the marketplace promotionwise for the five-year period due to budgeting constraints. We want to determine among the potential travellers in those countries what are the images, attitudes, perceptions, the main things they look for when selecting their travel destination. . . . We also, after an absence of about four years, are beginning to issue some data from a secondary source, the Immigration and Naturalization Service, on the volume of travel from individual countries of residence. *We simply have been flying blind for the past four years without any basic data on the volume of inbound travel.* These studies are going to be issued quarterly. [emphasis added]

The USTTA facilitates not only tourism marketing but also international travel itself in the sense of 'simplifying the movement of people and things across and through international borders'. This takes several forms, from making, in association with the Tourism Policy Council, recommendations on visa waiver legislation for temporary visitors, advising travel trade segments on new procedures to administering a corps of multilingual receptionists at twelve gateway airports.

In none of these areas are the activities of the USTTA particularly distinctive, with the general exception of the modest scale with which they are carried out. While the agency may be doing its best with the resources available to it, Figure 2.1 clearly suggests that throughout the 1980s the USTTA has been unable to achieve its principal goal of increasing the US share of worldwide tourism receipts. Efforts at the federal level, however, have to be seen alongside the states' involvement in tourism.

State travel offices

State government participation in tourism in the USA has been much more substantial than the relatively limited federal involvement. Each of the fifty states has a state travel office (STO): Hawaii and Texas have two, the combined proposed budgets of which totalled over $317 million for fiscal year 1988–9 (US Travel Data Center, 1989b). Five states that year – New York, Illinois, Texas, Hawaii and Pennsylvania – had travel office budgets which exceeded that of the USTTA ($13 million). This section reviews the development of

the STOs, analyses differences in their budgets and examines their various functions.

Development

By 1946, twenty-six of the forty-eight states had become involved in travel advertising and promotion in anticipation of the postwar surge in domestic travel (Doering, 1979). While many STOs were established in the early 1940s, other states such as Pennsylvania (Shih, 1981) had become involved before the Second World War and the territorial legislature of Hawaii had voted $15 000 for the work of the Joint Tourism Committee as early as 1915 (HVB, 1967). Texas, on the other hand, did not establish a state tourist agency until 1963, and then with a modest appropriation of $80 000. All fifty states had travel offices by the early 1970s (Doering, 1979). Although California and Maine temporarily abolished theirs in 1976, the 1970s generally appear to have been a period in which state support for tourism firmed as economic growth in more traditional industrial sectors slowed:

> Today the role of tourism in stimulating State economic development is increasingly accepted as a legitimate and proper one for State government. Over the last decade many States have created state travel and tourism programs to complement their industrial development programs. (O'Neill, 1979, p.iv)

However, a survey of STO officials in 1979 also suggested a lack of widespread support, with only twenty-four of forty-seven states reporting 'above average interest and support from the governor' and thirteen, 'above average support from the legislature' (Council of State Governments, 1979).

The expansion of STO budgets nevertheless testifies to a continuing state commitment to tourism during the 1980s, with the combined STO budgets growing from $77.7 million in 1978–9 to the proposed $317 million in 1988–9. Morrison (1987) attributes part of the growth in STO budgets to a 'bandwagon effect' brought about by the success of neighbouring states which had increased their travel budgets, particularly the aggressive 'I Love New York' campaign. Launched in 1977, the 'I Love New York' campaign was designed 'to improve the composite picture across the State, rather than singling out any specific area or type of activity' (Murphy, 1979). The campaign was made possible by a greatly expanded tourism appropriation ($4.3 million in 1977 compared with $600 000 in 1974), obtained after a determined drive, apparently led by a state assemblyman, to attract greater state funding. A major argument in this bid was the cumulative loss of travel dollars to New York which would result from state growth rates lagging behind the national average (Council of State Governments, 1979; New York State Dept of Economic Development, 1988b).

The economic development rationale for the states' promotion of tourism is evidenced by the US Travel Data Center's (1988) survey which shows thirty-seven STOs functioned as divisions of larger departments of commerce, economic development, industry and trade or some combination thereof. In other cases, the STO was part of a broader department of parks, recreation and tourism, local affairs and highways. Eight of the offices were autonomous cabinet level tourism agencies or commissions, with the Hawaii Visitors Bureau (HVB) being an independent bureau contracted to the state (see Chapter 3).

The Tennessee Department of Tourist Development was established in 1976 as the first cabinet level state tourism promotion organization. It is mandated to

> promote new investment in the tourist industry, provide comprehensive services to existing tourist enterprises, promote in other states the attractions of Tennessee, distribute Tennessee information publications and supervize the system of welcome centers in the State. (Tennessee Department of Tourist Development, 1989, p.77)

Advantages of full department status are seen to be direct access to the governor, the state's highest official, and greater clout in dealings with the state legislature (Blanton and Jackson, 1979).

Budgets

STOs vary not only in structure but also in size and function (US Travel Data Center, 1988). In 1988–9 STOs averaged 36 full-time staff, with members ranging from 3 to 145. The average budget for 1988–9 was $6.3 million; New York budgeted $24.3 million, Kansas, $1.1 million. Almost half the total $317 million was accounted for by the top ten states (Table 2.4). On average the STO budget represented $1.28 per state resident, ranging from $20.53 in Alaska to 19c in California. State general revenues were the sole funding source for just over half of the STOs; in the other cases supplementary revenue came from lodging and other tourism-dedicated tax receipts, membership dues, lottery funds and occasionally private sources.

STO budgets differ markedly in size but little systematic variation is to be found. Table 2.5 shows some correlation between the size of STO budgets and other absolute measures – state population, travel generated expenditure, state tax receipts and travel generated tax receipts – but the relationships are not very strong, reinforcing a pattern found by earlier studies (Council of State Governments, 1979; Doering, 1979; Hunt, 1990). In relative terms – STO budgets related to per capita travel generated expenditure and per capita travel generated tax receipts – no statistical relationship exists at all which is perhaps even more surprising.

While certain leading states in terms of their STO budgets also have large populations and economies, for instance Texas, the lack of statistical correlation in Table 2.5 appears in part to be influenced by the anomalous behaviour of certain key states (Figure 2.3). California, the leading state in terms of domestic travel generated expenditure, has traditionally had only a modest STO budget.[1] As Doering (1979, p.312) noted:

> Apparently, the prevailing sentiment in California is that since the state is already the nation's leading trip destination, there is little reason for additional state travel marketing. . . . Moreover, tourism advertizing and promotion for California is reinforced by

Table 2.4   State Travel Office budgets (1988–9)

State	1988–9 Proposed budget		1976 Budget	1988–9 Per capita budget	
	$	rank	rank	$ c	rank
New York	24 331 900	1	2	1.36	25
Illinois	23 903 900	2	29	2.05	14
Texas	18 294 770	3	24	1.07	37
Hawaii	16 040 119	4	4	14.42	2
Pennsylvania	14 058 755	5	3	1.17	33
Michigan	11 600 000	6	7	1.25	29
Alaska	10 820 100	7	16	20.53	1
Florida	10 634 907	8	1	0.84	42
Virginia	9 924 352	9	10	1.63	20
Tennessee	9 859 500	10	5	2.00	17
Massachusetts	9 530 058	11	19	1.61	21
New Jersey	8 841 000	12	34	1.14	35
Colorado	8 095 000	13	26	2.44	9
Georgia	8 041 868	14	8	1.25	30
South Carolina	7 522 000	15	12	2.14	12
Minnesota	6 777 100	16	28	1.56	23
Oklahoma	6 656 271	17	15	2.06	13
North Carolina	6 407 469	18	6	0.98	39
Wisconsin	6 400 000	19	20	1.31	27
Nevada	6 114 891	20	38	5.58	4
Missouri	5 655 998	21	18	1.10	36
Ohio	5 612 553	22	36	0.51	47
California	5 500 000	23	47	0.19	50
Arizona	5 451 200	24	23	1.53	24
Alabama	5 332 772	25	17	1.29	28
Kentucky	5 017 000	26	11	1.35	26
Maryland	4 913 012	27	27	1.05	38
Montana	3 911 750	28	31	4.85	5
Louisiana	3 747 445	29	14	0.86	40
Utah	3 695 087	30	13	2.16	11
Wyoming	3 552 245	31	47	7.48	3
Iowa	3 364 406	32	40	1.18	32
Maine	2 870 394	33	47	2.35	10
Arkansas	2 757 890	34	40	1.15	34
Washington	2 599 367	35	39	0.55	46
Rhode Island	2 561 000	36	47	2.57	8
New Mexico	2 454 600	37	25	1.61	22
Connecticut	2 454 000	38	42	0.75	43

Table 2.4   State Travel Office budgets (1988–9) (continued)

State	1988–9 Proposed budget		1976 Budget	1988–9 Per capita budget	
	$	rank	rank	$ c	rank
South Dakota	2 400 000	39	22	3.36	7
West Virginia	2 245 234	40	47	1.21	31
Mississippi	2 115 000	41	21	0.84	41
Indiana	2 100 000	42	30	0.38	49
Oregon	2 097 000	43	33	0.74	45
Idaho	2 073 300	44	32	2.04	16
Vermont	1 937 300	45	37	3.42	6
New Hampshire	1 915 207	46	41	1.73	19
Delaware	1 382 200	47	44	2.05	15
Nebraska	1 190 763	48	43	0.74	44
North Dakota	1 187 000	49	35	1.80	18
Kansas	1 166 278	50	45	0.46	48

Data source: US Travel Data Center (1989a)

Table 2.5   Strength of relationship between projected State Travel Office budgets (1988–9) and selected state variables

	R^2
Population	0.323
Travel generated receipts 1987	0.254
Travel tax 1987	0.273
State tax 1988	0.295
Per capita travel receipts 1987	0.005
Per capita travel tax	0.003

Data Source: US Travel Data Center

the state's frequent unsolicited exposure in motion pictures, television and other media, and by the work of local groups.

This may be an appropriate strategy for in terms of dollars spent on the STO to total domestic travel generated expenditure (and ignoring that some STO expenditure goes on overseas promotion) California has by far the most favourable ratio (1:4374 in 1987 compared to the state average of 1:909).

Conversely, Figure 2.3 also shows two other large states – New York and Illinois – are 'overspenders' relative to their populations but this is especially the case with Alaska and Hawaii whose per capita STO budget, at respectively $20.53 and $14.42, is far above the state average of $1.28. In these four states tourism would appear to enjoy a higher level of political support which, in the cases of Hawaii and Alaska, may be related to the relative importance of tourism to these states and the limited range of other avenues of development. Hawaii and Alaska ranked respectively second and eighth in terms of per capita domestic travel generated expenditure in 1987. Nevada, the top ranking state for per capita travel generated expenditure, had only the twentieth largest STO budget – tourism based on gambling would appear to be less expensive to promote. Florida, second ranked in terms of total receipts and fourth ranked in per capita receipts would, like California, appear to benefit from some natural advantages and an established image for it has only the eighth largest

2.3 Relationship between State Travel Office budgets and state populations

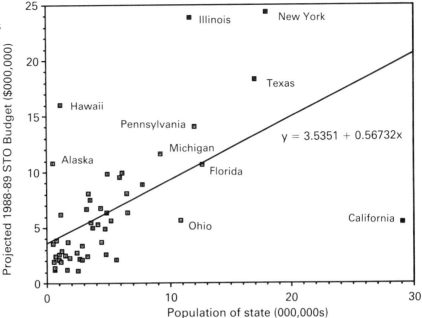

STO budget. Of course variations in rankings on different measures could also reflect how effectively budgets are spent but this can not be determined in the absence of other data such as those on domestic and international promotion, international expenditure, and all other promotional expenditure.

The generally weak statistical relationships, however, may be underlain by stronger geographical groupings (Doering, 1979). The ten largest STO budgets for 1988–9 were to be found in the Mid and South Atlantic and East North Central regions along with Texas, Hawaii and Alaska (Figure 2.4a). In per capita terms (Figure 2.4b), two distinct regional clusters emerge in the Mountain West and in New England; Hawaii and Alaska again feature in the top ten. Further work is required here but these geographical patterns may reflect a regional bandwagon effect or be common responses to similar conditions and perceived opportunities. In any event, the general lack of commonality in the ten leading states on the basis of total and per capita STO budgets further testifies to the diversity of STOs in the United States and perhaps suggests that those states making a greater effort on a per capita basis may nevertheless still be handicapped by the

comparatively small size of their final budgets. Only where the per capita contribution becomes very marked – Alaska and Hawaii – is the gap bridged.

Table 2.4 indicates that there is a certain amount of stability in the ranking of STO budgets but change is also evident. Though comparisons for any two years must be viewed cautiously given the annual fluctuations which occur, a Spearman rank-order correlation of 0.6713 was derived for the budget rankings of 1976 and 1988–9. States such as New York, Hawaii, Pennsylvania, Florida and Tennessee were already among the leading ten in 1976; others such as Illinois and Alaska are more recent additions to the list (Texas had been ranked third in 1975). Other significant gains were made by New Jersey (34th to 12th), Nevada (38th to 20th) and by California and Maine, both of which had had their budgets restored. Conversely, several states which ranked in the bottom ten in 1976 remained there in 1988–9: Kansas, Nebraska, Delaware, New Hampshire. Significant declines were registered by North Carolina (6th to 18th), Kentucky (11th to 26th), Utah (13th to 30th), Louisiana (14th to 29th) and Mississippi (21st to 41st).

Hunt (1990), in another longitudinal analysis,

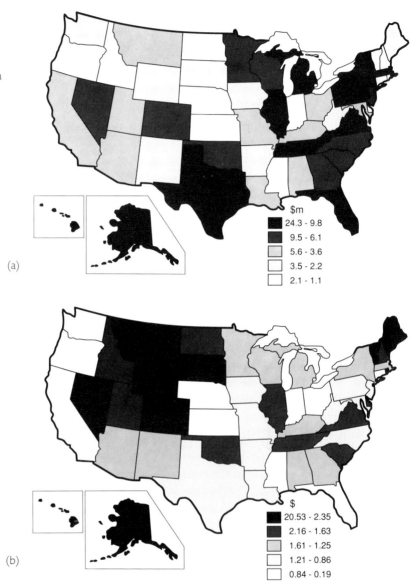

2.4 Projected State Travel
Office budgets (1988–9)
(a) total budgets
(b) budgets per capita
(Data source: US Travel Data
Center 1988)

(a)

$m
24.3 - 9.8
9.5 - 6.1
5.6 - 3.6
3.5 - 2.2
2.1 - 1.1

(b)

$
20.53 - 2.35
2.16 - 1.63
1.61 - 1.25
1.21 - 0.86
0.84 - 0.19

tentatively concluded that there was a relationship
in the level of budget increase over time and
change in market share; the more aggressive states
generally increased their market share but not all
such states conformed to this pattern.

Annual variations in STO budgets appear to
reflect broader economic changes and varying levels
of political support, tourism budgets being one of

the first items cut in harder times. Waters (1990,
p.15) notes:

When states must make reductions in
government spending because of budget
deficits, the budget for tourism promotion is
often reduced at a time when there is an
increased need to increase tax revenues. While

this may seem shortsighted, it happens at both state and city levels of government. In the past year both New York City and Boston wiped out their total contributions to their convention and visitors bureaus. The states of New York, Texas, Florida, Massachusetts, Maine and Nevada made substantial reductions in the budgets for their travel offices.

Functions

The functions of the STOs are well summarized by their budgets. Tables 2.6 and 2.7 highlight the emphasis given in the United States to marketing and promotion. If personnel and other administrative costs are assumed to be evenly spread, then this general category would account for 80 to 90 per cent of the average STO budget. Just under 40 per cent is allocated to advertising alone, with the bulk of the remainder going on associated activities: printing and production,

inquiry fulfilment, promotion, press and public relations (PR) and the Matching Funds Program by which marketing costs are shared with the private sector, local authorities or sub-state tourist

Table 2.6 Summary of average State Travel Office projected budgeted expenditures by category (1988–9)

Personnel & other administration	$1 262 823	(48)
Advertising	$2 448 717	(50)
Printing & production	$460 541	(46)
Inquiry fulfilment	$366 797	(42)
Promotion, press and PR	$355 838	(45)
Matching Funds Program	$747 510	(36)
Welcome Center Operations	$443 435	(33)
Research	$113 214	(37)
Other	$759 157	(37)
Total budget	$6 342 479	(50)

Note: Number of states reporting is given in parenthesis.
Source: US Travel Data Center (1989a)

Table 2.7   Projected budgeted expenditures by category of the ten leading US State Travel Offices (1988–9)

	Total Budget	Personnel & other adminis- tration	Advert- ising	Printing & produc- tion	Inquiry fulfil- ment	Promotion, press & PR	Match- ing Funds Program	Welcome Center Opera- tions	Research	Other
	$	%	%	%	%	%	%	%	%	%
New York	24 331 990	12.0	49.7	6.1	6.3	1.7	23.4	–	0.4	–
Illinois	23 903 900	6.9	48.1	3.0	[1]	5.2	5.3	[2]	–	31.3[2]
Texas	18 294 770	17.1	41.9	8.3	[1]	4.7	–	2.5	1.2	24.2[4]
Hawaii	16 040 119	31.4	24.9	–	3.1	35.2[2]	–	–	5.3	–
Pennsylvania	14 058 755	2.0	30.9	7.2	9.5	2.1	46.2	–	2.0	–
Michigan	11 600 000	23.3	30.2	12.9	7.8	2.6	8.6	–	0.9	13.8[3]
Alaska	10 820 100	15.2	47.8	8.0	5.5	5.4	3.6	1.3	3.3	9.7[1,6]
Florida	10 634 907	39.4	45.7	1.2	3.3	7.4	–	1.3	1.4	0.3
Virginia	9 924 352	21.0	41.7	1.0	1.6	2.8	–	10.9	0.9	20.0[7]
Tennessee	9 859 500	13.8	25.9	5.4	3.3	1.3	2.3	43.7	0.7	3.5

Notes: [1]   Included in Printing
       [2]   Included in Press, promotion and PR
       [3]   Direct and special grants
       [4]   'Texas Highways' Magazine
       [5]   Includes all marketing expenses other than advertising
       [6]   Foreign marketing
       [7]   Includes ad agency fees and international marketing

Data source: After US Travel Data Center (1989a)

Table 2.8   Foreign advertising allocations of selected State Travel Offices (1988–9)

	All reporting states (27)		Florida		Hawaii (HVB)		Virginia	
	$	%	$	%	$	%	$	%
Japan	2 964 250	36.9	150 000	6.2	1 700 000	82.1	87 250	13.2
Canada	1 436 960	17.9	660 000	27.4	121 336	5.9	–	–
United Kingdom	797 630	9.9	–	–			240 250	36.4
Germany	628 650	7.8	–	–			217 250	32.9
Europe			708 000	29.4	106 560	5.1	105 250	16.0
Latin America	2 213 300	27.5	485 000	20.1			–	
Other			407 000	16.9	142 646	6.9	10 000	1.5
Total	8 040 790		2 410 000		2 070 542		660 000	

Data source: After US Travel Data Center (1989a)

organizations. Some of the 'other' category also includes separate funding for international marketing and advertising agency fees. Visitor servicing, expressed here through the operation of Welcome Centers, accounts for around 6 per cent of the average budget, while research averages less than 2 per cent. The absence of any direct intervention in development is particularly noteworthy.

States vary in the emphasis they give to these activities, though part of the variation reflects the way in which individual budgets are structured (Table 2.7). Advertising is almost always the dominant category. States such as Pennsylvania and New York also accorded importance to matching funds, with a consequent reduction in the personnel and administration category. Thirty-three states reported funding Welcome Center operations, a function that assumes a significant role in states such as Tennessee. Hawaii has long led the way in carrying out research.

Given the patterns outlined earlier (Table 2.2), it is not surprising that the domestic market appears to be the paramount focus of the STOs' activity, accounting for perhaps as much as 90 per cent of their marketing effort. Some thirty-two states in 1988–9 reported specific advertising expenditure overseas, nine indicated none while the remainder

had yet to determine their allocations or made no comment. The thirty-two states budgeted a total of approximately $10 million, just over 8 per cent of the total advertising budget. Most domestic marketing is through media advertising. Eleven states operate out-of-state information centres; the Hawaii Visitors Bureau has five mainland regional offices while a number of New England states are represented in New York. Thirty-one states specified they were taking part in domestic travel shows, a similar number to those participating abroad (others did not differentiate between shows).

Twenty-seven states operate tourist information centres overseas, primarily in Japan, Canada, the United Kingdom, Germany and Belgium. These first four countries were also the major specified overseas markets in terms of advertising, though emphasis varies from state to state as the budgets for the three leading states which detailed their overseas expenditure shows (Table 2.8).

Matching Funds Grants are seen by many states as a way of stimulating and co-ordinating state marketing and promotion efforts with those at a local, county or regional level. Thirty-six states had such a programme in 1988–9, though funds allocated to this varied significantly (Table 2.7). Many funds are matched on a 50:50 basis but

2.5 Tourism regions within Tennessee

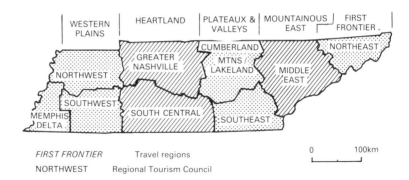

FIRST FRONTIER — Travel regions
NORTHWEST — Regional Tourism Council

0   100km

higher and lower ratios are also to be found.

The State Matching Funds Program in New York was introduced by the Tourism Promotion Act 1978 with the objective of stimulating increased tourism traffic, cultural and convention activity (New York State Dept of Economic Development, 1988a). To participate, each county was required to designate a 'tourism promotion agency' (TPA), the resultant network of local, county and regional tourism organizations being credited with greatly improving co-operation and co-ordination. The programme has subsequently expanded in terms of funds available and uses to which these can be put. In Tennessee the Department of Tourist Development makes available a $25 000 Matching Funds Grant to an approved chartered non-profit tourist promotion organization, regional tourism councils, in each of the nine regions defined by the State Planning Commission.

Regionalization may be important not only from an organizational perspective, in terms of mobilizing and co-ordinating local and regional interests, but also in presenting and promoting the state. Particularly for the short-haul domestic market it may be necessary to identify and depict distinctive tourism regions in order to highlight the diversity which is offered and to facilitate travel to particular areas bearing in mind that the whole state is not usually visited by individual tourists. Thus six tourism regions are promoted in New Jersey: Gateway, Skylands (ski areas), the Delaware River (cross-roads of America's history), Greater Atlantic City (gaming), The Shore and the Southern Shore. Each of these has a corresponding regional council.

In Tennessee, on the other hand, five 'travel regions' are promoted but nine regional tourism councils exist (Figure 2.5). Co-ordination becomes particularly important where overlapping boundaries occur.

Visitor servicing through the operation of state Welcome Centers is more significant and widespread than indicated by Tables 2.6 and 2.7 as these are often jointly funded by the STO and some other agency, usually the highways or transportation department. In some cases, as in New York where 92 centres are reported, the STO may provide no funding at all. Altogether there are about 500 state Welcome Centers in 46 states. The Tennessee Department of Tourist Development, for example, operates ten Welcome Centers at the inter-state highway entrances to Tennessee. These offer a free reservation system. Useful marketing information is also obtained by recording visitor numbers and through visitor registrations (Tennessee Dept of Tourist Development, 1989).

While most STOs engage in research, the resources allocated to this activity are generally rather modest (Tables 2.6 and 2.7), although they may be boosted by research undertaken in other divisions, as in Florida. The case for state travel research by Cook (1987) and Taylor (1987) outlined in Chapter 1 is well made also by Shih (1981, p.363) of the Pennsylvania Bureau of Travel Development:

An adequate, renewable data base will not only permit the state tourism organization to more intelligently assess the travel market and pinpoint promotional opportunities, but also provide a base for elected officials to make rational decisions in resource allocation.

These arguments are borne out by the 1988–9 Survey of State Travel Offices which showed the major types of studies undertaken were: economic impacts (36 states), advertising effectiveness/conversion studies (32), state visitor profile (31) and consumer attitude/awareness/image studies (25). The economic impact studies help establish more clearly the significance of tourism to the state in terms of jobs created, and revenue and taxes generated, thereby strengthening the case for state support (eg Ohio Office of Travel and Tourism, 1986; US Travel Data Center, 1989c). This purpose is stated quite explicitly in the Georgia economic impact studies, where it is noted (Davidson-Peterson Associates, 1990, p.1) that

> The intent of these studies is to measure the economic benefits derived by Georgia residents and Georgia governments from the dollars spent in Georgia by tourists who visit the State.

Furthermore (p.ii)

> The estimates of economic impact . . . are used:
> To *document the importance* of tourism as a key segment of the Georgia economy today and as an integral part of economic development efforts;
> To *underscore the need* to continue to support the expenditure of time, effort and dollars to promote tourism growth; and
> To *track* the results of Georgia's tourism marketing effort.

While recognized as important, STO research has been hampered by a number of constraints (Cook, 1987), the most serious and frequent being

- budget constraints,
- limited staff/time,
- complexity of factors affecting travel industry today,

- lack of research training among staff members,
- lack of reliable travel research methods,
- lack of a workable data collation system.

Shih (1981) called for regional co-operation in travel research but there is little evidence of this yet.

Planning is not recorded as a separate budgetary item in the survey of STOs but data in the research section provide some indication of the nature and extent of planning activity. Thirty-two states reported they had either a travel development plan and/or policy statement, nine had none and nine made no comment. Many states appear to have primarily marketing plans (eg Tennessee Department of Tourist Development, 1989) while a smaller number have more comprehensive plans, such as the Tourism Master Plan of New York State (New York State Dept of Economic Development, 1988a, 1988b).

The New York plan was released in March 1988 by the state's Department of Economic Development (the full agency, not just its Division of Tourism) under legislation passed in 1985 which called for the formulation and annual amendment of a five year comprehensive plan for 'the balanced development and coordination of adequate tourism programs and facilities, and tourism promotion activities and campaigns designed to attract tourists'. The plan (New York State Dept of Economic Development, 1988a, p.1)

> reaffirms the Department of Economic Development as the primary focus of State efforts to strengthen the tourism industry, as an advocate for the industry, and as an active partner both with other agencies of State Government and the private sector.

Areas covered in the plan include many of those mentioned above, namely advertising, marketing and promotion, matching funds, tourism information systems, research and education. Its most distinctive element in the United States context, however, is the support given to tourism business development through the Regional Economic Development Partnership Program

(REDPP), the aim of which 'is the creation and retention of permanent private sector jobs, especially in economically-distressed regions of the state'. Inclusion of tourism in the REDPP reflects a belated recognition that tourism is not merely a local retail activity but 'part of the State's export base' and one for which 'a properly-targeted State tourism development program can help offset market inequities and imperfections'. The emphasis is on developing attractions and facilities through providing incentives for the development of projects which will 'contribute significantly to tourism destinations' and encouraging investment in areas 'where a shortage of tourism facilities has deterred business growth and where new facilities would spark increased overall business activity'. While the sums involved are not yet large – the 1988–9 REDPP appropriation makes $1.25 million available for tourism destination programmes – the New York initiative in this area may yet parallel its earlier innovation with the 'I Love New York' campaign.

Local government

The third tier of government tourist organizations, those associated with city government, has attracted little attention yet available evidence suggests that in monetary terms they may be as important as the STOs. In a 1978 survey of cities with a population of over 100 000, expenditure on tourism, travel and convention programmes and promotion totalling almost $54 million was reported from 102 cities (US Travel Service, 1978). By comparison, the total STO budget for 1976 was $53 million. Other recent individual state and city figures support this pattern. The Atlanta Convention and Visitors Bureau alone had a total budget of $8.1 million for the year ended 30 June 1988, 61 per cent of which came from a public room sales excise tax; the Georgia Tourist Division had a 1987–8 budget of $7 million. Travel advertising expenditure surveys show that in 1988 states spent $71.5 million compared with $58.5 million from other domestic destinations. Together, they accounted for 12 per

cent of all travel advertising in the USA, compared to 9 per cent for foreign destinations advertising in the USA and 64 per cent for all airlines (Waters, 1990).

The US Travel Service (1978) survey remains the most comprehensive source of information on city government involvement in travel and tourism. It also highlights the diversity which is to be found at this level. Of the 142 cities reporting (out of 168 contacted), about half indicated they contracted out all their tourism activities to a variety of agencies such as convention and visitors' bureaux and chambers of commerce. Approximately 16 per cent handled these activities internally through staff, offices or units with special responsibilities in this field; a similar proportion had both their own unit and contractual arrangements and 16 per cent indicated their city was not involved in promoting tourism.

The most commonly reported activities undertaken by cities in the field of tourism were the production of information materials, the administration of speakers' bureaux and the construction and maintenance of public facilities. National and regional advertising, promotion and public relations constituted a second set of activities. Convention planning and technical assistance were also areas of major involvement, particularly in the larger cities, many of which had convention hall/civic centre projects. Some cities also have a hotel/motel reservation system and carry out tourism research. About half of the cities surveyed reported participating jointly with the private sector in such activities as advertising and promotion, arranging familiarization tours and developing tour packages.

The emphasis given to each of these activities varies according to the nature of the destination and the maturity of the city's visitors' bureau. Co-ordination and developing a sense of common purpose is particularly important in the beginning as Frank (1985, pp.139–40) notes:

The Santa Monica Bureau has spent its first two years pulling the community together and heading them in the right direction. It has worked with various organizations to develop brochures, services and teaching them the proper tourism 'language'. Now we will really start to focus on what our markets should be. As part of the Greater Los Angeles Community we are able to pick from a wide range of markets but clearly we cannot go after all of them. We plan to home in on one segment of a variety of markets.

In contrast, the larger and well established Greater Los Angeles Visitors and Convention Bureau (Drake, 1985) has well developed departments for travel development (trade shows, sale blitzes, familiarization tours and travel industry relations), convention marketing (with a $1 million plus budget for marketing and registration), administration (liaison with the mayor's office and the state, publications and merchandising) and membership development.

City governments have also played a major development role with tourism being incorporated in urban revitalization projects in cities such as Baltimore, Philadelphia, Boston, Charleston, New Orleans and San Francisco (Ford, 1979; Law, 1985). Law concluded (p.527):

Public initiatives and investment are important if tourism possibilities are to be realized, a point accepted in this most free enterprise of countries. Planning and urban renewal agencies can co-ordinate the resources required to create facilities which will attract visitors. However, the success of the tourist industry will depend on the extent to which private investment is stimulated.

There is also a reminder in the US Travel Service (1978) study that American cities are to some extent creatures of the states. States become involved in local tourist development in three ways:

1 by passing enabling legislation which allows for the collection of taxes (eg hotel/motel occupancy taxes, mixed-drink taxes, entertainment taxes) to support local promotion activities;
2 by providing matching funds;
3 by undertaking activities jointly with cities, for example joint programming of promotion and public relations.

The capacity of particular cities to fund tourist activities is thus dependent to some extent on individual state policies. Sixty-three cities in the 1978 city survey indicated that they funded all or part of their tourism promotion and convention development activities with a hotel/motel occupancy tax. The variation in State Matching Funds programmes has already been noted. These programmes also of course give rise to some double counting in the figures for state and city expenditure on tourism outlined above. The cities in the 1978 survey saw further funding and assistance with promotion and advertising as the main areas for more state involvement with their own activities.

Interorganizational interaction

Various forms and levels of interorganizational interaction exist among official tourist organizations in the USA which reflect in part the country's federal structure and its free enterprise philosophies. The previous section, for instance, noted some state involvement in local tourist development as a consequence of the general dependence of local government on the states, but in general the local offices operate quite independently from the STOs. Where the state input has been less forthcoming greater effort from the local level has been called for, such as from the Big Four in California (Drake, 1985, p.142): 'In past years, California State Office of Tourism really didn't have the dollars or the staff to market too extensively so the San Francisco, Los Angeles, Anaheim and San Diego Bureaus developed a California promotional plan'.

States too essentially act autonomously in the field of tourism as no strong mandated links exist between the STOs and the USTTA. The USTTA nevertheless provides technical assistance to the states and local government as well as the private sector, particularly in terms of research, market intelligence and co-operative marketing (see below). The USTTA also developed a 'model State Tourism Policy' to assist states to adopt legislatively comprehensive state tourism policies (Edgell, 1985). This follows the efforts of its forerunner with the major local government and state reviews cited earlier being prepared for the US Travel Service (USTS, 1978; Council of State Governments, 1979).

The existence of fifty separate STOs has given rise to considerable diversity in the range of activities and support provided for these, with each state pursuing tourism strategies which it sees as appropriate (Tables 2.7 and 2.8) or which reflect broader state policies. Nevertheless, the fifty STOs do not act in isolation from each other. Indeed, there appears to be a growing 'bandwagon' effect, with the activities of one STO flowing on to others. This was well evidenced by the competitiveness engendered by the success of the 'I Love New York' campaign which resulted in the general growth in STO budgets and a blossoming of other state slogans. Evidence that STOs are indeed conscious of other states' marketing efforts is also to be found in their various reports which include data on state travel budgets (eg Ohio Office of Travel and Tourism, 1988; Michigan Travel Bureau, 1989). For example the Michigan Travel Bureau's argument that 'If Michigan's investment in travel promotion does not remain competitive, the growth of the past few years cannot be maintained' is supported by data showing stability in Michigan's funding at a time of substantial increases to the budgets of other leading states. Such arguments, bolstered by the economic impact studies, are used to extract further resources for the STOs. The combined effect of these factors was the marked expansion in STO expenditure during the 1980s, a trend not paralleled by an equivalent USTTA response to the activities of other NTOs. On the contrary, state participation in tourism increased at a time when the USTTA was being threatened with closure.

Increasing competitiveness at home has been accompanied by growing co-operation between states in terms of joint marketing efforts, particularly abroad. Co-operative marketing at a regional level, bringing together the joint efforts of two or more states, is not a new idea but it is one which has seen growing interaction between not only STOs but also STOs and the USTTA, as well as private sector bodies and local organizations. In December 1985 the USTTA began to develop three to five year international marketing plans with regional tourism organizations; by 1987 forty-six of the fifty states were involved (Seely, 1987). 'Ultimately, USTTA's marketing plan for any given country will consist of a series of individual, cooperative promotional campaigns for several US regional groups, predetermined by these groups themselves' (USTTA, 1987b, p.1).

Factors encouraging regionalization and benefits from a regional marketing programme are seen (Seely, 1987; USTTA, 1987b; Ollendorff, 1988) to include:

- a regional visitation pattern in which foreign tourists usually visit two or three states during a vacation in the USA,
- segmenting a large country into areas of manageable size helps groups of states to develop a stronger image and to demonstrate the diversity of the USA, factors which may lead to extended stays,
- pooling regional resources may make it possible to carry out promotional programmes which are cost-effective and big enough to make an impact in international markets,
- joint marketing enables greater participation in marketing efforts by firms and organizations which would/could not otherwise get involved,
- regionalization makes USTTA facilitation easier and more effective through concentrating co-ordinating efforts on fewer bodies,
- regionalizing helps focus and measure the economic benefits of tourism more efficiently.

Several types of regional tourist organization are to be found within the USA; some are made up of state travel directors, others consist entirely of industry representatives while a third group brings together a mix of public and private sector members (USTTA, 1987b). Travel South USA and Foremost West, for example, are regional organizations which bring together contiguous states (Arizona, Colorado, New Mexico, Utah and Wyoming in the case of the Foremost West) in which the state travel directors have 'agreed to band together to leverage increased marketing impact and legislative support for program expenditures' (USTTA, 1987b, p.9). In contrast, the Southeast Tourism Society was established as a private sector group with representatives from seven south-eastern states, and membership (300 by 1986) on an invitation only, dues-paying basis. Membership was subsequently extended to STOs in the south-east on a non-dues-paying, non-voting basis. The Old West Trail Foundation (Montana, Nebraska, North Dakota, South Dakota and Wyoming) was chartered in 1964 as a non-profit corporation to promote tourism through a working partnership between private industry and governmental bodies.

These organizations may undertake both international and domestic promotional campaigns but the emphasis has been on the former where the advantages of a regional effort outlined above are often more readily appreciated and achieved. Even here, however, the overall significance of combined efforts should not be overstated in the total marketing drive of the states, local governments and the private sector (Table 2.3). Nevertheless, regionalization may be a growing trend. Morrison (1987, p.16) reports on a survey which indicates that while the majority of state travel directors were in favour of increased inter-state cooperation they are also faced with a difficult paradox:

> their neighbouring partners are also usually a major source of tourism business. . . . It seems difficult to join forces with someone who is at the same time trying to 'steal' your state residents and encouraging its own residents not to visit you. Living with these anomalies requires a high degree of sophistication in marketing and a recognition that trade offs are necessary to achieve objectives.

Morrison also raises the question of defining regions for promotional purposes. He notes the lack of correspondence between the twelve regions clustered for promotional brochures of the USTTA in 1985, the eight regions established by the Discover America Travel Organizations (DATO: now the Travel Industry Association of America – the national private sector umbrella organization for the tourist industry) and the nine US Census Bureau regions which form the basis for many statistical series (Table 2.2). Earlier Smith (1983) had drawn attention in his analysis of domestic travel to the lack of correspondence between his 'functional' regions and the formal ones of the National Travel Survey (apparently based on the eight DATO regions). The question also arises as to whether groups of states that are functional regions for domestic travel also cluster in the same way for international visitors. This may be the case in smaller, traditionally identifiable regions such as New England, but the boundaries of other regions may be more fluid. One pragmatic response to this is representation in several regional tourist organizations: Virginia is represented in the Southeast Tourism Society, Travel South USA and George Washington Country. Further analytical work is required here to match spatial patterns of supply and demand with the co-operative needs of the STOs, sub-state organizations and the private sector.

Note

1   The California Office of Tourism received no funding for the months of July and August 1988. Its total $5.5 million allocation therefore covers only ten months of fiscal year 1988–9.

3

Hawaii

The small, remote, sub-tropical multi-island State of Hawaii contrasts with the rest of the USA characterized by its size, diversity and continentality (Chapter 2). These features combine to produce a distinctive set of conditions which, while not dissimilar to those of other island destinations (Pearce, 1987a, 1990a), are unique in the American context. Thus although identified in the preceding chapter as a leading state on most of the measures of tourism and STOs, Hawaii in many ways is atypical of the rest of the union. However, the general effect of these conditions is often to throw many of the issues discussed in Chapter 2 into sharper relief, thereby making Hawaii a useful state case study which may highlight areas to be explored in subsequent research in other states. The next two sections set the scene by reviewing broad environmental factors and outlining the nature of tourism in Hawaii. Attention then turns to the activities of the state tourist organizations, the emergence of sub-state bodies and the interactions between these, particularly with regards to marketing.

Environmental features

The 50th state is 47th in terms of land area and consists of eight main islands, in order of size: Hawaii (the Big Island), Maui, Oahu, Kauai, Molokai, Lanai, Niihau and Kahoolawe (Figure 3.2). These islands, all volcanic in origin, make up over 99 per cent of the total land area (16 642 sq.km); the remainder is made up of smaller offshore islands and the North-western Hawaiian Islands. These latter islands, together with Molokai, Lanai, Niihau and Kahoolawe, will not be considered further as over 99 per cent of all visitor accommodation and the majority of the population are found on the four largest islands.

With a 1989 population of 1 112 000, Hawaii ranked 39th in the USA. The population has grown rapidly since 1940, most of the growth occurring on Oahu which today accounts for three-quarters of the state's residents (Hawaii 11 per cent, Maui 8.5 per cent and Kauai 4.5 per cent). Hawaii is characterized by its ethnic diversity, no one ethnic group being a majority (Armstrong, 1983).

Traditionally the Hawaiian economy depended on the export of tropical products, particularly sugar and pineapples. Such commodities were surpassed in the 1960s by federal expenditure (initially on defence, with non-defence items such as welfare and civil service spending overtaking this later on) and the growth of tourism (Farrell, 1982; Armstrong, 1983). Tourism accounted for 9 per cent of the gross state product in 1963, 18 per cent in 1973 and 24 per cent in 1983 (DPED, 1986). Visitor industry receipts in 1980 were estimated at $3 billion. By the mid-1980s, the visitor industry accounted for over one-third of all civilian jobs in Hawaii and a third of total personal income. Most of the economic activity is on highly urbanized Oahu, which in 1990 had an estimated 77 per cent of all civilian employment (Hawaii, 9.4 per cent; Maui, 9.1 per cent; Kauai, 4.5 per cent). Per capita income levels are also highest on Oahu, followed by Maui, Kauai and the Big Island. The latter two islands in particular have remained more rural,

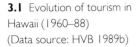

3.1 Evolution of tourism in Hawaii (1960–88) (Data source: HVB 1989b)

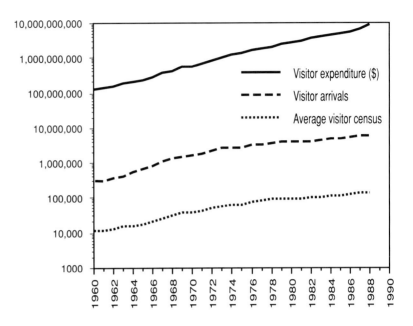

their economies being hit by the agricultural downturn.

The small surface area, the growth of population with its consequent demand for new housing and highways, the desire to protect agricultural lands and conserve areas of natural beauty and significance, the emergence of native land claims and the expansion of tourism have combined to create substantial pressure on the land, land use conflicts and the implementation of planning and protective measures.

The small size and insular nature of Hawaii have also contributed to it being the most centralized state in the union. Only a single level of local government exists below the state, that of the four counties; the mayors are mayors of counties rather than cities. Hawaii also has a unified statewide school system (Armstrong, 1983).

The roles and interrelationships of the federal, state and county governments in Hawaii are reviewed in some detail by Farrell (1982), particularly with regard to land use and development. He notes (pp.114–15):

The physical framework for tourism was always there, trade relations with the United States created a fascinating plural society, while federal activity resulted in recreational reserves and open agricultural spaces both of critical importance to tourism.

And elsewhere (pp.113):

The state, for its part, exerts a general degree of control; sets guidelines; attempts to maintain a statewide perspective; encourages redistribution and a balance of population and economic activity; coordinates overall planning; influences development through taxation; allocates capital improvement project funds; maintains relations with the mainland; and, above all, within broad areas, says where urban development should and should not take place. The state, through land-use decisions, may encourage the development of a particular island or region and, by withholding its authorization, may prevent development in otherwise attractive areas.

As for the counties (p.137):

It could be claimed that the state sets the tone and the county through personal contact, attention to detail, policing, leading, persuading and cajoling, gets the work done. The county, too, receives the reaction of the community if what is done is not to its liking. An attempt is made to bridge the gap between State and county by having county representatives on most of the governor's advisory committees.

Farrell then goes on to argue:

> Though the counties are mentioned after the state in the organizational hierarchy, this should not indicate an inferior status. Whereas the state may appear aloof and the federal government remote, the county government is closely identified with the people.

However, in terms of resources, particularly financial resources, the counties are undeniably inferior to the state, with an ongoing battle by the mayors to extract more revenue from the governor. In terms of travel generated tax revenue in 1987, for example, the state took 47.5 per cent, the federal government 46.9 per cent and the counties 5.6 per cent, making the state's and counties' shares respectively among the highest and lowest in the USA (US Travel Data Center, 1989a). On the other hand, the Hawaiian counties perhaps have a stronger identity than many on the mainland due to their insular nature.

Tourism in Hawaii

Tourism in Hawaii shares many characteristics of other small tropical island destinations. The state is largely dependent on the sun-sand-sea market; its climate and beaches are its major resources. These are complemented by a range of other natural and artificial attractions. On Oahu these include the National Memorial Cemetery of the Pacific (Punchbowl) and the Arizona Memorial (the two sites which record the largest attendances), the Polynesian Cultural Center, Sea Life Park, Waimea Falls Park and circle island tours. On the Neighbour Islands spectacular scenery draws many

visitors on day and side trips: on the Big Island, Hawaii Volcanoes National Park; on Maui, Haleakala National Park and the coastal road to Hana; on Kauai, the Waimea Canyon and cliffs of the Na Pali Coast. Golfing has also been developed as a major attraction, particularly on Maui and the Big Island.

While these attractions have drawn visitors to Hawaii since the end of the nineteenth century, significant increases in visitor arrivals were dependent on improved accessibility which did not occur until the introduction of jet services in the 1960s. Cruise ships still bring some passengers but virtually all arrivals today are by air from distant markets (Los Angeles, 3 862 km; Tokyo, 6 196 km). Hawaii differs markedly in this respect from the mainland states which primarily draw on the intra-state and neighbouring state domestic markets, with travel overwhelmingly by private car. Hawaii also depends on major inter-island transfers by air, for although there are now mainland flights direct into the Big Island and Maui, most traffic into the state enters through Honolulu International Airport. Fortunately the Neighbour Islands had the legacy of a good network of military airports which has provided the basis for the development of an effective inter-island service.

The development, composition and distribution of tourism in Hawaii are depicted by Figures 3.1 and 3.2 and Tables 3.1 to 3.4. Figure 3.1 shows a steady increase in visitor arrivals through the 1960s and 1970s, with generally lower rates of growth in the 1980s. An absolute decrease in arrivals was reported for 1980 (-0.7 per cent), with no change the following year. A total of 6.1 million visitors was recorded for 1988. Growth rates for the average daily census (the average number of arrivals in Hawaii on any given day) have also fluctuated during the 1980s but at levels below those for visitor arrivals due to the increasing proportion of shorter stay eastbound visitors (31 per cent in 1988, 22.5 per cent in 1980).

Hawaii has the highest foreign : domestic ratio of visitor arrivals for all states, a reflection of its mid-ocean position. In 1988 one-third of all arrivals were from abroad and two-thirds from the mainland (Table 3.1). One out of every five visitors

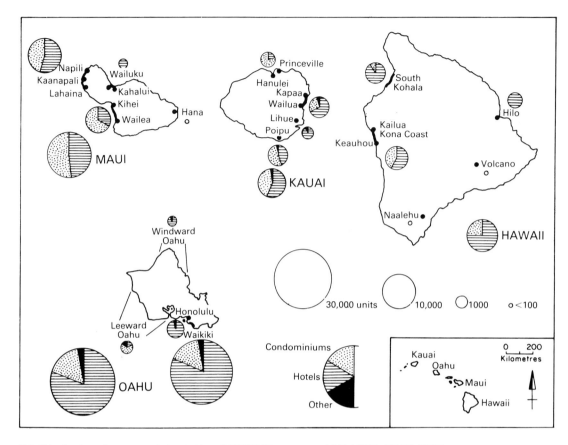

3.2 Distribution of accommodation in Hawaii (1989) (Data source: HVB 1989b: DBED 1987)

Table 3.1   Origin of visitors to Hawaii (1988)

Country/Region	Eastbound	Westbound	All visitors	%
USA	598 730	3 438 380	4 037 110	65.7
Japan	998 470	218 300	1 216 770	19.8
Other Asia	94 210	33 710	127 920	2.1
Canada	26 610	221 560	248 170	4.0
Australia	53 020	116 090	169 110	2.8
New Zealand	35 470	55 520	90 990	1.5
Europe	58 220	169 350	225 570	3.7
Other	12 960	13 820	26 780	0.4
All visitors	1 877 690	4 264 730	6 142 420	100

Source: After Hawaii Visitors Bureau (1989a)

Table 3.2 Distribution of westbound visitors to and beyond Hawaii (1960–88)	1960	1970	1980	1988
Total westbound Visitors	293 584	1 174 705	3 046 132	4 264 730
Visitors to Hawaii %	72.8	84.8	89.3	91.5
Visitors beyond Hawaii %	27.2	15.2	10.7	8.5
Visitors to Hawaii	%	%	%	%
Oahu only	23.9	37.8	29.6	30.6
Oahu and other islands	54.8	62.2	50.5	37.8
Neighbour Islands only	1.2	19.9	31.6	
Undecided	20.1			
Visitors beyond Hawaii	%	%	%	%
Oahu only	71.0	87.9	84.0	84.9
Oahu and other islands	11.2	12.1	12.5	10.7
Neighbour Islands only	0.6		3.5	4.4
Undecided	17.2			

Source: Hawaii Visitors Bureau (1989a and mimeoed statistics)

was from Japan. Canada remained Hawaii's second largest foreign market, followed by Australia and New Zealand. Europeans constituted almost 4 per cent of all visitors. The dominant mainland markets were California and Washington, followed by New York, Illinois and Texas.

As a mid-ocean group of islands, Hawaii is visited both as a destination in its own right and as part of a larger circuit, the sole destination function becoming relatively more important as access has improved (Table 3.2). By 1988 only 8.5 per cent of westbound visitors (who constituted 80 per cent of all arrivals) were travelling beyond Hawaii compared with 27 per cent in 1960. Marked differences occur in the spatial behaviour of visitors travelling to and beyond Hawaii. Those who make Hawaii their sole destination have shown an increasing propensity to venture off Oahu. The greatest proportion continue to combine a visit to Oahu with visits to other islands but by 1988 there were as many people intending to visit the Neighbour Islands only as stay solely on Oahu. In contrast, those visitors travelling beyond Hawaii are largely constrained to Oahu itself. Their stays are on average only half as long as the destination visitors (five compared with ten days).

Oahu, with Honolulu International Airport and Waikiki, remains the most important island in the group in terms of both accommodation capacity and expenditure, but its share on both these measures decreased substantially during the 1970s and 1980s due to developments on the Neighbour Islands (Table 3.3). The most dynamic growth in the 1970s was on Maui and although more rooms were added there in the 1980s the most rapid rates of growth in that decade were on Kauai. In many respects the Big Island did not capitalize on its early position as Neighbour Island leader although in the late 1980s the opening of the Hyatt Regency Waikoloa heralded a new resurgence. Factors accounting for this dispersion include improved accessibility, reaction to the concentration on Waikiki, the attractiveness of the Neighbour Islands, changing market demands and development initiatives.

The island profiles in Table 3.4 show significant differences occur in the character and extent of tourism in Hawaii, particularly between Oahu and the Neighbour Islands. Oahu has over half of the total accommodation capacity but it has proportionately more units in hotels than condominiums (condos). In part this represents the age of the Oahu plant – condos being a more

Table 3.3   Evolution of tourism in Hawaii by island (1960–88)

Accommodation capacity

	1960		1970		1980		1989	
	units	%	units	%	units	%	units	%
Oahu	5 716	83.8	21 217	70.6	34 173	61.3	36 467	53.6
Maui	291	4.2	2 720	9.1	10 521	18.9	15 439	22.7
Hawaii	581	8.5	3 486	11.6	6 299	11.3	8 161	12.0
Kauai	237	3.5	2 609	8.7	4 707	8.5	7 398	10.9
State	6 825	100	30 032	100	55 700	100	68 034	100.0

Visitor expenditure[1]

	1970		1980		1986	
	$ millions	%	$ millions	%	$ millions	%
Oahu	442	74.3	2 097	73.0	3 444	62.6
Maui	54.5	9.1	400.6	13.9	1 195.5	21.7
Hawaii	53.4	9.0	187.6	6.5	343.8	6.3
Kauai	45.1	7.6	189.3	6.6	516.9	9.4
State	595	100	2 875	100	5 500	100

Note: [1] Inter-island airfares have been distributed on a pro rata basis. Expenditures by eastbound visitors have been included with Oahu. Excludes expenditures by Hawaii residents.

Sources: Farrell (1982); HVB (1989a); DBED (1987)

recent development – and the greater share of shorter stay circuit travellers the island attracts. Oahu also has a significantly greater share of budget accommodation, again reflecting Waikiki's maturity. Occupancy rates are highest on Oahu, the 85 per cent annual occupancy reflecting the 'at capacity' situation which now exists for much of the year and the subsequent pressure to develop the other islands. The higher occupancy rate and the far greater share of the higher spending Japanese visitors that Oahu attracts offsets to some extent its lower average daily hotel room rate and accounts for the difference in the shares of capacity (53.6 per cent) and expenditure (62.6 per cent) shown in Table 3.3. Maui is the most upmarket of the islands, with a much greater share of luxury and first-class accommodation and an average room rate nearly $50 higher than the state average. It is also the only Neighbour Island to attract a significant percentage of staying Japanese visitors. Condo development too has been much greater on Maui. The Big Island and Kauai constitute an intermediate level between Maui and Oahu but have lower occupancy rates than both.

Differences between the islands, however, transcend these raw figures. Oahu is the established destination, with far greater name recognition in Honolulu and Waikiki, than any of the Neighbour Islands – indeed Waikiki is arguably the world's best known beach. It is also now a highly urbanized

Table 3.4   Distribution of tourism in Hawaii by island

		State	Oahu	Maui	Hawaii	Kauai
Accommodation						
Capacity (1989)						
Hotels	no.	155	76	27	31	18
Hotel units	no.	47 474	29 346	7 470	6 143	4 179
	%	100	61.8	15.7	12.9	8.8
Condos	no.	256	53	112	42	44
Condo units	no.	19 140	5 919	7 936	2 018	3 034
	%	100	30.9	41.5	10.5	15.9
Total units[1]	no.	68 034[2]	36 467	15 439	8 161	7 398
	%	100	53.6	22.7	12.0	10.9
Class[3] (1989)						
Luxury	%		23.6	37.1	34.2	31.5
First class	%		45.1	51.9	46.3	50.1
Budget	%		31.3	11	19.5	18.4
Average daily hotel room rates (1988)	$	87.94	75.66	134.26	87.15	94.04
Occupancy rate (1988)	%	70.1	85.4	61.8	55.2	53.1
Visitors						
Average visitor[4] census (1986)	no.	132 910	72 870	34 330	9 870	14 840
	%	100	55.6	25.8	7.4	11.2
Westbound visitors[5] (1988)	no.	4 264 730	3 013 860	1 884 050	782 360	1 043 710
	%		70.7	44.2	18.3	24.5
Japanese visitors[5] overnight & longer (1988)	no.	1 216 770	1 188 810	207 800	66 680	89 450
	%		97.7	17.1	5.5	7.4
Convention visitors (1986)	no.	250 703	171 893	48 859	19 435	10 449
	%		68.6	19.5	7.8	4.1

Notes:
[1]   Also includes apartments and cottages.
[2]   Also includes 559 units on Molokai and 10 on Lanai.
[3]   Classifications based on property self-assessment. Distributions represent responses from 84% of the total state inventory.
[4]   All eastbound and northbound visitors have been allocated to Ohau.
[5]   Includes visits to more than one island.
Sources: HVB (1989a, 1989b); DBED (1987)

destination with a greater range of night life and shopping than the other islands. At the same time maturity and urbanization have brought difficulties, ageing plant has led to the need for major refurbishment programmes, congestion and overcrowding are problems. In contrast, the more modern facilities of the Neighbour Islands are complemented by good stretches of less crowded beaches and high quality golf courses, an air of relative tranquillity replaces the hectic activity of Oahu, and the spectacular natural scenery has been joined by the new fantasy resorts of the Kauai Westin and the Hyatt Regency Waikaloa. Different islands therefore appeal to different market segments. For the Japanese a trip to Hawaii is more a visit to America than to a tropical island – Waikiki and its shopping therefore appeals. Waikiki also attracts stopover circuit travellers, first time mainland visitors and budget-conscious Australians and New Zealanders. The Neighbour Islands, particularly Maui, appeal more to the discerning upmarket mainland visitor seeking peace and tranquillity in the sun, a romantic honeymoon destination, a quality golfing experience or a fantasy escape.

These inter-island differences have implications for Hawaii's tourist organizations. So too does the tightly clustered pattern of tourist accommodation on individual islands (Figure 3.2). This spatial concentration is most pronounced on Oahu, where 90 per cent of the island's units are found at Waikiki – a massive 32 800 rooms on a one square mile site. On the other islands there are two to four major resort areas. On Maui, 60 per cent of the units are found along the Kaanapali coast between Lahaina and Napili, with 36 per cent along the stretch from Kikei to Wailea. The Big Island has three clusters: at Hilo (15 per cent) and on the Kona (50 per cent) and Kohala (34 per cent) coasts. On Kauai, accommodation is less concentrated: two major clusters at Poipu (30 per cent) and between Wailua and Kapaa (37.6 per cent) are complemented by developments in and around Lihue (notably the 850 room Westin Kauai) and at Princeville-Hanalei.

Farrell (1982) provides further details on each of these areas, especially on their development up

until 1980. He identifies two major types of tourist development in Hawaii – small scale and large scale. These categories are based not on the absolute number of units but on the process of development for Farrell includes Waikiki as small scale along with Poipu, Wailua-Kapaa, Hilo and Kailua-Kona. Such development (p.54) is characterized by

> numbers of single individual or corporate operators running hotels and condominiums often on minimally sized lots. Frequently there are significant areas of buildings cheek by jowl all presenting a mishmash of unplanned heterogeneity. Each individual development is planned . . . but no complex is planned in relation to its neighbours and, overall, the entire district usually lacks manageable coherence.

In contrast (pp.54–5)

> The large-scale development occupies an extensive area as a single unit . . . from several hundred to several thousand acres or more. Planning is characterized by a grand all-encompassing design-coherence and theme in landscaping, circulation and the placement of buildings. Most projects are presented to local governments as planned unit developments. . . . Once underway, it is possible for the developer to keep control of every aspect of development.

Kaanapali, begun in the early 1970s, was the first major master planned resort in Hawaii; other examples include Wailea (Maui), Keauhou (Big Island), Princeville (Kauai) and, more recently, Ko Olina on Oahu. Such resorts clearly reflect the broader historical and economic context in which they have been developed. Their scale and unity have been made possible by the existence of large tracts of former plantation or ranch land held under sole ownership. The developers have usually been 'venerable old' Hawaiian companies and landowners: Amfac (Kaanapali), Alexander and Baldwin (Wailea) and the Kamehameha Development Corporation (Keauhou).

Each of these examples is a complex of hotels

3.3 Network of tourist
organizations in Hawaii (1990)

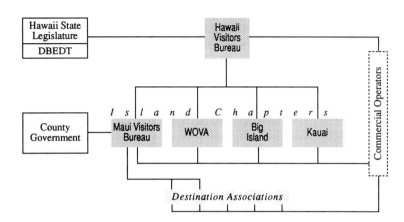

and condos. In other cases, notably along the
Kohala Coast, large (300 plus rooms) hotels with
associated golf courses constitute virtually self-
contained resorts in themselves, for example the
Mauna Kea, Mauna Lani and Royal Waikoloan.
This is especially so with the 1 200 room Hyatt
Regency Waikola which comes complete not only
with golf course but also with its own monorail and
complex of water facilities including a dolphin pool
and canal system.

Growing Japanese investment in the 1980s is
another trend to be noted. By 1987 Japanese
investors owned approximately 60 per cent of
rooms in first-class, de luxe and luxury hotels
statewide (Kenneth Leventhal & Coy, 1987).

Tourist organizations

The development of tourism in Hawaii has been
supported by a distinctive interorganizational
network (Figure 3.3). In effect there are two
organizations at the State level, the official State
Tourism Office (STO), a part of the Department of
Business, Economic Development and Tourism
(DBEDT) and the Hawaii Visitors Bureau (HVB).
While DBEDT's predecessors (DPED and DBED)
were the official funding channel for state funding
to the HVB for many years, a specific Office of
Tourism does not appear to have been established

as a separate unit within the department until 1976.
In 1984 departmental restructuring saw it become
the Tourism Branch of the Business and Industry
Development Division and in 1987 part of the
Industry Promotion Division. These and other
changes are detailed later, the generic term STO
being used throughout for the part of the
department responsible for tourism. The HVB, a
non-profit corporation, was established as early as
1903 and has received the bulk of its funding over
this time from first the territorial and then the state
government. At the sub-state level HVB chapters
have emerged on each of the main islands, with
island tourism also being supported in varying
degrees by the county governments. Distinctive
destination associations have also arisen, reflecting
the developmental characteristics of tourism in
Hawaii.

This section begins by tracing the history of the
HVB, outlining its functions and examining the
changing relationships between the HVB and the
STO. The development of the HVB chapters and
the destination associations is then explored.
Finally, the interactions between these different
levels of organization are examined, with particular
emphasis on marketing.

The Hawaii Visitors Bureau

The HVB is reputed to be the oldest state tourism
organization in the USA, tracing its origins to 1903

when the Joint Tourism Committee (later that year becoming the Hawaii Promotion Committee) was created by the Chamber of Commerce and Merchants Association to advertise the Territory (HVB, 1967). Half of the first year's budget of $30 000 came from a territorial government appropriation for tourism promotion, the bulk of the remainder coming from private subscriptions. Some $16 000 in the first year was spent on advertising and printing. This early pattern of public/private contributions and an emphasis on advertising has become entrenched although ratios and relationships have evolved.

The name Hawaii Visitors Bureau was adopted in 1944. In 1949 the legislature agreed to match dollar-for-dollar $250 000 from the business community for tourism promotion in 1950 and 1951, giving the state a million dollar budget for the two year period. The HVB separated from the Chamber of Commerce in 1959 and was chartered as a non-profit corporation to 'promote travelling by the public to and among all the Hawaiian Islands, and to maintain a continuing interest in the well-being of visitors in Hawaii'. That same year the first state legislature passed a law empowering the state agency charged with tourism development, the Department of Planning and Economic Development (DPED), to enter into a contract with the HVB for the promotion and development of tourism; previously funds were appropriated directly to the HVB. Putting the relationship on a contractual basis through a state agency, it was argued, would give the State greater control over the funds appropriated to the HVB.

While some internal changes in structure and emphases in activities have occurred from time to time, the basic organization and functions of the HVB remain much as they were on incorporation in 1959. In 1988, the HVB had a staff of 89 and a membership of 2 745, consisting of businesses, associations and individuals, both in Hawaii and on the mainland and overseas. The Board of Directors is comprised of up to 35 elected and appointed directors who represent various interest groups and geographic areas of the state. The HVB is led by an executive committee which includes the three Neighbour Island chapter chairmen. In addition, there are standing committees covering areas such as marketing, market research, membership and visitor satisfaction.

The HVB has its offices in Waikiki, with chapter offices on the Big Island (at Hilo and Kailua), Maui (Kahului) and Kauai (Lihue). Regional sales offices are located in Los Angeles, San Francisco, Chicago, New York and Washington DC (meetings and conventions) and there are international offices or representatives in Tokyo, London, Vancouver, Hong Kong, Frankfurt, Auckland and Sydney.

Table 3.5   Evolution of Hawaii Visitors Bureau income (1950 to 1988–9)

	Total income	State appropriations		Private subscriptions		Other	
	$	$	%	$	%	$	%
1950	500 000	250 000	50	250 000	50	–	–
1957–8	666 554	500 000	75	166 554	25	–	–
1967–8	2 014 000	1 439 000	71	575 000	29	–	–
1977–8	2 723 700	1 852 000	68	700 000	25.7	171 700	6.31
1986–7	8 464 391	6 969 391	82.3	1 400 000	16.6	95 000	1.1
1987–8	13 665 000	12 270 000	89.8	1 300 000	9.5	95 000	0.7
1988–9	14 346 259	13 046 259	90.9	1 300 000	9.1	–	–

Sources: HVB (1967) and annual reports

Table 3.6   Allocation of Hawaii Visitors Bureau expenditure

Major budget items

	1979–80 %	1986–7 %	1987–8 %	1988–9 %
Administration	18.4	15.1	10.1	6.2
Marketing	61.0	74.9	68.2	69.5
Research	8.7	5.7	4.3	4.8
Visitor satisfaction	3.2	1.8	1.8	2.6
Membership	2.9	1.7	1.2	1.4
Special events/promotions	4.0	0.7	–	5.2
Expo	–	–	3.0	6.6
Information systems	–	–	–	3.6
Contingency fund	–	–	11.4	
Other	1.8	–	–	
Total expenses	$3 077 760	$8 464 391	$13 665 000	$14 346 259

Marketing budget 1988–9

	$	%
Advertising	3 935 000	39.5
Literature	500 000	5.0
Public relations	534 915	5.4
Meetings/conventions	761 400	7.6
Marketing services	458 050	4.6
Trade shows	229 000	2.3
Movie	25 000	0.3
Mainland offices	720 940	7.2
Neighbour Island offices	479 065	4.8
Chapter Co-op	780 000	7.8
Asia/Pacific	1 428 624	14.3
UK/Canada	117 900	1.2
Total	9 969 894	100

Source: HVB annual reports

The HVB's budget was reasonably stable or grew only slowly during the 1960s and 1970s, with the state appropriation making up about 70 per cent of its total income during this period (Table 3.5). Some expansion occurred in the mid-1980s, with the major increase in the state appropriation coming in 1987–8, after introduction of the transitory accommodation tax. As a result, the HVB now derives 90 per cent of its income from the state and only 10 per cent from its members.

The marketing thrust of the HVB is emphasized in the budget breakdown in Table 3.6. Particularly noticeable is the operation of the mainland and Neighbour Island offices and the Asia/Pacific emphasis, both a reflection of Hawaii's geography and market opportunities and conditions. Other activities such as advertising, the production of literature, public relations and participation in trade shows is typical of other STOs as discussed in Chapter 2. These activities are also supported by expenditure on special events and participation in world Expos in 1988 and 1989.

As noted earlier, Hawaii also stands out in the research effort which underlies its marketing activities. HVB research is primarily directed at monitoring the tourist traffic and accommodation plant (Tables 3.1 to 3.4), deriving visitor profiles, measuring visitor expenditure and determining levels of visitor satisfaction. Much of this research is facilitated by the greater control and ease of measurement which exists when virtually all arrivals are by air to a limited number of entry points. Detailed information on westbound arrivals has generally been obtained more readily through surveys undertaken with the co-operation of carriers from the mainland but data on eastbound arrivals have recently improved.

Visitor servicing is the function of the HVB's Visitor Satisfaction and Community Relations Department, which operates an information office in Waikiki (a second at the Ala Moana Shopping Center was closed in 1990), handles visitor complaints, and has an important community relations role. The primary goal of the Membership Development Department is 'to maximize financial support from business and the community at large'. Budgeted private subscriptions from members remained stable in the period 1986–7 to 1988–9 at around $1 300 000. Benefits of HVB membership include the right to display brochures at HVB offices and participate in HVB co-operative promotional activities and access to HVB's data base, promotional materials and publications.

HVB–DPED/DBED/DBEDT

As state appropriations for tourism have grown and the ratio of public to private funds has increased (Table 3.5), so the legislature's interest in acquiring greater control over these monies has expanded, with budget provisos becoming more numerous and specific. A major management audit of the HVB

and the state's tourism programme drew attention to and was critical of a number of areas of HVB activity and organization as well as the nature of the HVB–DPED relationship (Legislative Auditor, 1987). The audit noted in regard to the HVB (p.97):

> The bureau enjoys the operating freedom of a private organization with virtually guaranteed, substantial state funding but with no need to produce profits, unhampered by the reviews and controls of a regular state agency, and accountable to no one for organizational effectiveness.

As for the HVB–DPED relationship (p.63):

> Hawaii is unique among the states in relying on a private organization to implement the State's tourism promotion program. The hoped-for benefit in this arrangement is to have a system in which the State can manage an overall tourism program while the private sector retains the flexibility and freedom to promote tourism in the most efficient and effective manner, without being hampered by official rules and requirements.
>
> However, what has happened is that HVB, with its long-standing, strong reputation in tourism, has preempted the State in many ways. The existence of HVB has allowed the State to evade its responsibility for clarifying its own role in the state tourism program. Instead of HVB being one instrument in the state tourism program, it has become almost the entire state tourism program. The failure of DPED to clarify its responsibilities and its relationships with HVB has had an impact on its management of the HVB contract. This has generally been ineffectual and misguided.

This criticism is perhaps not surprising given that the tourism branch of DPED, the STO, had only a couple of staff in the early 1980s.

The audit's authors also pointed out (p.64) that:

> the interests of HVB are not synonymous with those of the State. The bureau is a private organization administered by a board consisting of representatives of the visitor

industry. . . . Their primary objective is to maintain the profitability of the visitor industry. The State's interests are much broader and reflective of the State's residents as a whole.

These broader interests, it was argued, called for a more wide-ranging role from the state, one which would include (Legislative Auditor, 1987, p.39) 'coordinating infrastructure needs, monitoring the industry and its impact on the community, and ensuring the quality of the visitor industry generally' but the audit found (p.38) 'the State's actual role in the visitor industry has been minimal'. Attention was drawn to the large number of studies and plans that had been prepared over the years, the fate of which were aptly summarized in a 1978 DPED observation that 'More often than not, plans are produced and never implemented . . . new studies are requested and prepared without adequate review of what has already been done'.

In 1976 DPED was mandated to develop a ten-year master plan for tourism as one of twelve state sector plans. A massive five-volume technical study was produced in 1978, the State Tourism Study. The plan itself went through several phases (Farrell, 1982) and was finally approved by the legislature in 1984 as the State Tourism Functional Plan (DPED, 1984). This set out policies for promotion, physical development, employment and career development and community relations. Increased funding for marketing and promotion was encouraged and the convention market emphasized. Physical development policies encouraged a well designed and adequately serviced visitor industry which considered the needs of Hawaii's people.

A 1989 audit of the State Tourism Office (Legislative Auditor, 1989) reported the legislature's support for these policies, noting the successive increases since 1984 in annual appropriations for tourism promotion, the specific targeting of the Asia/Pacific markets and the creation of the Tourism Impact Management System (TIMS). It also recalled that the 1987 audit resulted from the legislature's concern with assessing the outcome of the expenditures for tourism promotion, especially as appropriations had increased.

The mid-1980s were thus a period in which significant changes started to occur, with the state beginning to give more direction to the visitor industry and the State Tourism Office emerging from the shadow of the HVB to assume a greater leadership role. While the 1984 plan and the 1987 audit set the direction, further changes followed from a new governor's administration.

DPED, the parent department, became DBED, the Department of Business and Economic Development. The STO was moved, along with films and ocean resources, into a newly created Industry Promotion Division whose mission is 'to ensure the stability and growth of preferred industries in Hawaii through planning, development and promotional activities' (DBED, 1989). Further recognition of the growing role of tourism came in 1990 when the department was renamed the Department of Business, Economic Development and Tourism (DBEDT), with the Office of Tourism now being headed by a deputy director reporting directly to the Director of DBEDT. With the increased funding and calls for greater accountability, the STO has been mandated to produce an annual report.

In its first such report, that for 1988 (DBED, 1989), the STO lists as its three main objectives:

- to enhance the effectiveness and efficiency of the State Tourism Program,
- to provide for the optimum level of maintenance or growth in visitors and visitor expenditures which are most beneficial to Hawaii,
- to ensure that a longer term and more comprehensive perspective provides for the foundation of tourism development in Hawaii by

    serving as the central agency which provides leadership and direction of tourism marketing activities

    monitoring the impacts of tourism on residents,

    assisting in the formulation and prioritization of State tourism policies.

The 1988 report highlights the major activities of the STO and the new directions which are emerging. Marketing is now being guided by a new Strategic Marketing Plan (DBED, 1988), which was required by a 1987 Act before 25 per cent of the marketing funds could be expended. This restates the importance of tourism to Hawaii, finds that the state should not attempt to 'manage' the tourism sector of the economy but recommends that 'the State should take an active and increased role in determining what kind and amount of tourism is best for Hawaii' and that 'the State should work more with the private sector and community to win their cooperation with those policies'. The State Tourism Functional Plan is now seen to provide a basis for general guidance but more emphasis is to be put on the strategic plan for marketing and assisting the industry.

The strategic plan also signals a change in marketing focus for the state with the recommendation (p.6) that

Public funds should not be primarily directed toward maintaining core markets. State resources should be used where needed to complement the private sector's efforts and to assure a healthy industry. They will be directed toward:

- Identifying and targeting new markets.
- Creating good policy and decision-making systems.
- Managing impacts of tourism on the environment and society.
- Protecting the industry against threats, contingencies and fluctuations.
- Creating positive and supportive conditions to retain and attract industry and services.

These changes are seen in the growing emphasis given to the Asia/Pacific and other new markets, funding of a study on the siting and development of a new convention centre, the commissioning of an analysis to identify and profile Hawaii's major 'sunshine destination' competitors, promotion of special events and participation in the 1988 and 1989 Expos.

Progress is also being made with the development of the Tourism Impact Management System (TIMS) which was initiated in 1986. The major components of TIMS are attitudinal surveys of residents and focal groups, compilation of a Tourism Data Book, publication of a *Community Journal on Tourism* and intermittent special studies. The *Community Journal on Tourism*, the first issue of which appeared in 1989, is 'a multi-volume collection of documents, positions, opinions and perspectives focusing on resident, business, and civic groups regarding the impact of tourism' (Deloitte, Haskens and Sells, 1989, p.3). While attitudinal surveys on tourism's impacts are reasonably well established, most have been one-off studies by academics (Liu and Var, 1986; Pearce, 1989). In TIMS, an ongoing monitoring system has been set up by an STO, a significant innovation and one indication of the broadening of the STO's role in Hawaii even if the sums involved are not a large item in the overall budget.

The broadening of the STO's activities is shown well by the allocations in its 1988–9 budget (Table 3.7). General marketing still receives three-quarters of total appropriations but the remaining 25 per cent allocated to other activities represents a considerable diversification. Moreover, while the HVB was contracted to carry out virtually all the general marketing, contracts to other bodies were let by the STO for most of the additional activities, so that the HVB received 77 per cent of the total appropriations. Coupled with the tightening of the general contractual basis between the STO and the HVB, this constitutes a significant change from the position at the beginning of the decade. Furthermore, the 1987–8 and 1988–9 budgets contain specific allocations for the HVB island chapters (under Field Offices): this represents the most recent stage in a long history of substate activity which will now be considered.

Neighbour Islands

At the sub-state level the trend has been towards stronger island organizations engaged more and more in their own marketing efforts. This development parallels the growth and dispersal in visitor numbers depicted in Tables 3.2 and 3.3, with the multi-island geography of Hawaii leading to stronger and more distinctive identities for each

Table 3.7   Hawaii State Tourism Office budget (1988–9)

Account title	Total appropriation		STO	HVB
	$	%	$	$
General tourism marketing	12 111 259	75.6	250 000	11 861 259
Strategic planning	230 000	1.4	230 000	–
Tourism Impact Management System	140 960	0.9	140 960	–
Community and industry relations	1 050 000	6.6	1 050 000	–
World expositions	1 606 617	10	1 086 617	520 000
Sports events	560 000	3.5	560 000	–
Programme administration	341 283	2.0	341 283	–
Total appropriation	16 040 119	100	3 658 860	12 381 259

Source: After DBED (1989)

of the major islands than is perhaps possessed by regions within mainland states and a consequent call for action by each respective island. This same geography has also resulted in a long explicit recognition of the need or desirability to spread the tourist traffic, as in the HVB's stated purpose on incorporation of promoting travel 'to and among all the Hawaiian Islands'.

HVB offices were first established on Maui, Kauai and the Big Island in 1950. They were staffed initially by a secretary to service the Neighbour Island HVB committees and maintain visitor information offices. Full-time island managers were appointed in 1967, their chief responsibilities being 'to work with community and governmental agencies in promoting tourism projects, managing the HVB committees and offices; and promoting the Neighbour Islands as a series of visitor destination areas' (HVB, 1967, p.2). Neighbour Island representatives also sat on HVB committees and the advice of County Advisory Committees on Tourism was sought when contracts between DPED and the HVB were established. That for 1965, for example, directed the HVB *inter alia* to 'place special emphasis on the development of the Neighbour Islands as a visitor destination area' (HVB, 1967, p.49).

While the traffic to the Neighbour Islands grew during the 1960s and 1970s (Table 3.2 and 3.3) it is difficult now to assess fully the role of such contracts and HVB activity in this process. However, it is instructive to note the HVB chairman's comments in the 1979–80 annual report:

One major problem we must address is the widening divergence between the HVB and the Neighbor island groups. The Neighbor Islands historically seem to feel that the HVB is generally dominated by the Oahu interests and that marketing activities we engage in are not sufficient to adequately promote their islands. The Executive Committee of the HVB will have to make a concerted effort to continue to work even more closely with the Neighbor Island travel people to make certain everyone is working in concert for greatest benefit to the State as well as individual island destinations.

The situation appears to have deteriorated on Maui in particular with the HVB there closing in the 1970s and an independent Maui County Visitors Association (MCVA) forming in 1973 to market the island successfully (Table 3.3). Given their different conditions and markets (Table 3.4), this push for more direct intervention by each island is not surprising.

The HVB eventually responded by amending its byelaws in 1983 to authorize Neighbour Island chapters to be formed with their own boards and the ability to raise their own funds. Some modest grants for island marketing were also provided. The Big Island chapter was formed in 1983, that on Kauai in 1984 and the MCVA, after protracted negotiations, became the Maui HVB chapter in 1985. The Maui chapter has 350–400 members; that on Kauai about 300.

Establishment of the chapters and the granting of specific sums for island marketing has enabled the islands to extend their existing functions of visitor servicing, hosting 'fam' trips, co-ordinating participation in trade shows and, in particular, to develop more substantial and aggressive marketing campaigns. At first the direct allocations for marketing were modest – $10 000 in the first year – but as more pressure has been brought to bear on the legislature, appropriations to the island chapters (above administrative costs) have become increasingly significant. For the financial year 1988–9, the Kauai HVB Chapter was allocated $175 000 for destination marketing, the Maui HVB Chapter, $305 000 (including $100 000 for Molokai), and the Hawaii County HVB Chapter, $200 000 (DBED, 1989). Further significant increases were anticipated the following year. Such funds must be used for marketing programmes which fulfil state goals and complement the overall marketing mission of the HVB.

County governments may also make major contributions to the island chapters. In 1989 the Maui HVB Chapter derived half of its funds from DBED, 20 per cent from the county and 30 per cent from the private sector.

Maui has a longer established tradition of aggressive marketing, especially to the upper end of the market, finding particular niches in the golfing, honeymoon and Japanese markets. However, with the recent growth in quality plant on the other islands, Maui's position is being increasingly challenged. Kauai has capitalized on its desirability as a film location to promote the island. It has

recently prepared a series of vacation planners and is extending into new markets in Australia, Canada and Europe as well as Japan. The confusion of Hawaii the state with Hawaii the county has presented the latter with an identity problem which the island chapter is trying to overcome by developing a stronger consistent image of the 'Big Island of Hawaii' (previously some seven different names had been in use, eg the Orchard Island, the Volcano Island). Niches are also being sought through promoting the diversity of the island. In addition, visits to the Big Island are being promoted in association with island products such as Kona coffee, papayas and macadamia nuts.

The implications of the growth in the Neighbour Island traffic, the campaigns of the MCVA and some of the destination associations and the emergence of the new chapters were not lost on some of the Waikiki operators. While others may have seen the HVB's efforts as favouring Oahu and Waikiki, in effect no separate organization existed to promote them specifically. Moreover, by the early 1980s Waikiki's image had become jaded with some plant and infrastructure becoming rundown. Discussions were held in 1982 and 1983 between several of the leading hotels and a marketing consultant with the result that the Waikiki Beach Operators Association (WBOA) was formed 'to promote Waikiki/Oahu as the world's preeminent resort destination by *reestablishing and reasserting* its image through the use of advertising, public relations and promotions' (WBOA, 1988, p.4; emphasis added). In 1988 the state appropriated $100 000 for a specific WBOA promotion. However, with the emergence of the HVB chapters on the Neighbour Islands, questions were now raised as to why there was not an Oahu chapter. In 1989, WBOA became the official Oahu Chapter of the HVB as WOVA, the Waikiki/Oahu Visitors Association, but retained some degree of autonomy (its executive director is not an HVB employee but is under contract).

By 1989, WBOA's/WOVA's budget had increased to $625 000, some 90 per cent of it being spent on marketing, particularly advertising, with an active public relations and promotions programme also being maintained. The 1988 annual report claims 'as a result of our efforts, approximately 400 million people heard, read about or saw Waikiki and the island of Oahu as a whole'. Oahu average occupancies increased from 74 per cent in 1981, to 81 per cent in 1984 and 85 per cent in 1988.

WOVA also explicitly fosters community and government relations, seeing itself as 'a partnership of tourism professionals able to speak as a single, unified voice on behalf of the leading visitor destination in the islands, and in the world today'. With the Waikiki Improvement Association, WBOA supported the Kalakaua Avenue block party held on 29 July 1988. Attracting 100 000 people, this appears to have been a promotions exercise as much as an exercise in community relations and has since become an annual event.

With the establishment of WOVA and the increase in direct appropriations to the HVB chapters, a significant tier of sub-state organizations had been established by the end of the 1980s, each promoting tourism on its respective island within the framework of the overall state plan.

Destination associations

At the local level, two sets of destination associations occur in Hawaii, each of which reflects the broader pattern of large- or small-scale development noted earlier. The most distinctive are the tightly structured, limited membership associations which essentially function as the marketing arm of the master-planned resorts, notably the Kaanapali Beach Operators Association and the Wailea Destination Association on Maui and the Keauhou Visitor Association on the Big Island (Figure 3.2). These associations vary in detail but all were basically set up by the master developer to promote a specific resort, membership being limited to operators and developers within that resort who are contractually obliged to become members on a first year, five year or ongoing basis. Membership from adjoining areas, for example, Lahaina and Napili in the case of Kaanapali and other parts of the Kona Coast in the case of Keauhou, is specifically excluded. Half a dozen major properties are involved at Wailea and Keauhou, with the latter having a number of

smaller members, such as rental car firms and sightseeing operators. The Kaanapali Beach Operators Association brings together some 5 000 rooms, with the association's structure giving the marketing director much tighter control over the plant than usually exists with destination associations. The emphasis is wholly on marketing, particularly in the early years of establishing name recognition of the resort within the context of the respective island and Hawaii. Kaanapali, the most established of the three, is now challenged with maintaining its position in the face of growing competition from recent growth in quality products elsewhere in the state.

The second set of destination associations in Hawaii are typical of those to be found in many parts of the world, bringing together on a voluntary and reasonably loose basis a range of big and small operators to promote and develop tourism in a particular area. In Hawaii these have emerged in several areas characterized by what Farrell (1982) called small-scale development, for example the Hilo Hawaii Visitors Association on the Big Island and Poipu Beach Resort Association on Kauai. In other such areas, for example Lahaina and the Kona Coast, associations have not yet developed or have come and gone. The large resorts of the Kohala Coast appear to function independently of each other.

The most active of this second group is the Poipu Beach Resort Association. This is a non-profit corporation, governed by a board of directors and managed by an executive director. It was established in the early 1980s on the initiative of the person who subsequently became director. In the absence of a major developer, and at a time of new facilities expanding capacity and falling occupancy rates, she saw a need to co-ordinate efforts to promote Poipu and began by getting five of the largest operators to set aside money to jointly advertise the area. By the late 1980s, membership had increased to 160 (compared with 16 at Kaanapali). The association 'works to better the economy of the South Shore and the businesses affected by the South Shore's tourism trends'. This is done by developing awareness that Poipu, Kauai, is an attractive visitor destination, a goal that is pursued by co-operative advertising, participation in trade shows and other similar activities. Local guides and directories are also published. A secondary purpose, and one which reflects the representativeness of the broad membership base, is to become involved in local and regional issues related to the maintenance and improvement of the district. This involves sitting on various county and state advisory commissions and lobbying for support for improvements to roading, signage, harbours, parks and beautification.

With the exception of the shortlived Waikiki Beach Operators Association which metamorphosed into the Oahu HVB chapter as WOVA, destination associations have not developed on Oahu, the off-Waikiki hotels being limited in number and dispersed in location (Figure 3.2). However, in the Waikiki Improvement Association (WIA), Waikiki has an important related association which has played a significant development and lobbying role. In considering the activities of the WIA, it is necessary to recall that Waikiki is not only a well established resort area, accounting for some 32 000 units in 1989 (47 per cent of the state's total, Figure 3.2), but also an important residential area, being home to about 30 000 residents. Over 100 000 people – tourists, residents and employees, are estimated to be in Waikiki on any given day, on a site about one square mile in area.

Established in 1967 with the support of the HVB, the WIA is a non-profit organization, consisting in 1989 of 350 members, both corporate and individual. It has as its major objectives (HVB, 1967, pp.39–41) to

- develop and maintain Waikiki as an attractive visitor destination area, and as a place of rest and recreation for Hawaii's residents,
- enlist the interest and support of individuals and firms for the development and improvement of Waikiki,
- promote and encourage rehabilitation of Waikiki's blighted areas,
- co-operate with public agencies and other

organizations in the orderly planning and development of the Waikiki area,
- promote conditions conducive to the economic and cultural good and betterment of the entire community with particular reference to the Waikiki area.

During the 1980s the WIA has been particularly concerned with lobbying for the upgrading of deteriorating plant and infrastructure in Waikiki. The president noted in the 1989 annual report that 'Much of our work has been to provide our elected officials the information necessary for them to make decisions that positively affect Waikiki'. The report also records a certain measure of success, for example a $10.6 million state and city funded Kalakaua Avenue Safety and Beautification Project; the passing of city council ordinances relating to pedicabs, visitor publication dispensers and hand-billing activities; and the passing of legislative measures for beach restoration, bridge repair, a freeway access study and funding for a planning conference. The 1989 report also refers to the Kalakaua Avenue block party, transportation meetings, electoral forums, community safety activities and the Return Witness Program. The latter aims at reducing crime by assisting victims and witnesses to return to Hawaii to testify in visitor-related hearings.

The proactive role of the WIA is well-demonstrated by the Waikiki Tomorrow Conference which it sponsored in October 1989, with funds obtained from the state. The conference was organized around four major themes: economic trends, social and cultural issues, the physical environment and transportation. Pre-conference meetings and position papers identified major issues in each of these areas which conference participants were involved in ranking. This process produced a list of prioritized problems and projects which could subsequently be presented to the legislature and elsewhere as broadly agreed areas for future action (WIA, 1990). At the same time, the WIA was appointing someone to work with the legislature.

Interorganizational marketing activity

Formal aspects of the interaction between these different levels of organization have been examined in preceding sections, notably the changing relationships of DPED/DBED and the HVB and links between the HVB and the island chapters and the related activities of WOVA and the WIA. This section considers interorganizational activity in marketing, the dominant function of the tourist organizations from the HVB to the destination associations.

Expanding resources and the emergence of stronger sub-state organizations have increasingly enabled each island to pursue its own marketing strategies and cater for its own particular needs. However, co-operative ventures in advertising and promotion are the general rule as organizations combine forces in various ways to stretch their limited funds. The island chapters tend to use their budgets to lever further marketing dollars out of the destination associations, the county governments and the private sector, particularly the carriers, in order to develop co-operative advertising campaigns and to facilitate travel show participation and other promotions.

About three-quarters of the Big Island's chapter funds go on chapter initiatives (which may involve other partners) and about a quarter are undertaken in association with the HVB. On Kauai, three destination associations, the Kauai Visitors Bureau and the Kauai County joined forces to develop a co-operative advertising campaign in 1989, contributing respectively $150 000, $200 000 and $200 000 as their share of a 50 : 50 deal with United Airlines. The marketing director of one of the Maui destination associations indicated approximately 50 per cent of their dollars were spent on programmes with airlines, 25 per cent in association with the Maui Visitors Bureau and other Maui operators, 15 per cent with the HVB and only 10 per cent on their own.

The airlines not only are 'natural' partners in such ventures given Hawaii's dependence on air travel, but also provide an essential network of contacts and access to travel agents and reservation systems, with the islands and destinations being unable to establish their own ongoing presence in the market. Typical co-operative ads combine the image of the island or resort with the sales message of the particular airline (Plate 3.1). A small survey in 1983 of airlines serving Hawaii indicated significant sums were being spent on advertising, with 70 per cent being spent on promoting Hawaii as a destination, rather than the firm's specific product (Liu, 1983). The airlines may take the initiative, as in the early 1970s when United made a conscious thrust in association with the counties to promote the Neighbour Islands. More often their role is passive, reacting to the proposals put forward by the various organizations in terms of their own budgets and assessments of market opportunities in what is 'at best a dynamic process'. Dealing with the organizations has advantages for the airlines, as working with the HVB or the chapters is less labour intensive and creates some economies of scale compared to working with many individual operators. Co-operative ventures with organizations would, however, appear not to be without their problems. The regional marketing director of one of the major airlines concerned noted 'Organizations are only as effective as their members' desire to step outside their own agendas' while a second observed that for co-operative ventures to be successful the organizations 'have to buy in emotionally and strategically'.

While different sub-state organizations may differ over the emphasis given – and the creation of the Neighbour Island chapters was in large part a reaction to the perceived dominance of Oahu – there appears now to be a genuine recognition at all levels of the need to first establish Hawaii in the market-place, with the role of the island chapters being to attract their share of visitors to each respective island where the destinations associations in turn then attempt to carve out their own niches (Plate 3.2). The HVB and the island chapters have played a particularly important role in opening up new markets in Asia, Australasia and Europe, with the smaller destination associations being especially active on, but not limited to, the US mainland.

The central direction and co-ordination

3.1 Co-operative advertising: local and island tourist organizations join forces with an airline to promote particular destinations within Hawaii.

provided by the state's Strategic Marketing Plan becomes particularly significant in the light of the expanding activities of these organizations. While the plan is binding only for the state appropriations and thus virtually excludes the destination associations as well as the private sector, the degree of co-operative advertising and promotion means its influence and direction is felt even there. Some perspective on the sub-state organizations is provided by Table 3.6, which shows the HVB chapter appropriations constituted only 7.8 per cent of the HVB's marketing budget (augmented to some extent by private sector and county contributions).

Further research is required to establish levels of satisfaction with the existing network and channels of interorganizational influence. However, it would appear, for example, that the sheer volume of plant commanded by the Kaanapali Beach

Operators Association is a not insignificant factor when programmes for Maui are established and that the past success of Maui campaigns means the Maui voice is listened to on the HVB marketing committee.

It is also important to recognize that interorganizational interaction involving other agencies and affecting other aspects of tourism, particularly development, also occurs. The differing but interrelated aspects of physical planning undertaken by federal, state and county agencies discussed by Farrell (1982) have already been alluded to earlier. The Governor's Ocean Resources Tourism Development Task Force (1988) identified as a key issue the need to 'reconcile overlapping agency jurisdictions to minimize business costs and to be able to deal more effectively with user conflicts'. For instance, some eleven agencies (seven divisions of three state

3.2 Resort brochures set particular destinations within the broader context of their respective island and of Hawaii

departments and four county departments) are involved directly or indirectly in the management of Hanauma Bay, a popular but now seriously polluted snorkelling and swimming area on Oahu. Reconciliation of their various jurisdictions is seen as a necessary step in the solution of physical problems there. Rivalry between the state and the city and county of Honolulu was particularly evident in 1989 in their support for separate convention centre projects.

Conclusions

Following the general overview of United States

tourist organizations in Chapter 2, the more specific focus of this chapter has enabled functions and interactions within one state, Hawaii, to be examined in much greater detail. This research has highlighted the need for detailed research at this scale to complement the summary, comparative data presented in the annual reviews of STOs. Closer examination has enabled many of the underlying processes to be elucidated and the particular characteristics of the state to be presented. The interorganizational network which has emerged in Hawaii clearly reflects the influence of specific features of tourism there, notably its scale and concentration in particular areas within a mid-oceanic multi-island state. While these features may be peculiar to Hawaii, the general approach adopted might now usefully be applied to other states in order to flesh out some of the broad patterns identified in Chapter 2, to account for some of the differences identified there and, in general, lead to a greater understanding of the role of tourist organizations at different scales within the United States.

4

The Federal Republic of Germany

The Federal Republic of Germany provides a second example of the development of tourist organizations within a federal system. Although Germany and the USA share similar political structures, the patterns of tourism within the two countries are quite distinct. For much of the 1980s Germans constituted the world's largest outbound market in terms of expenditure; in 1988 they took second place behind the Americans. Germans who take their main holiday abroad now outnumber their domestic counterparts by two to one. Within Germany the domestic demand nevertheless still exceeds that from inbound international tourists.

Developing a nationwide picture of tourist organizations in Germany is more difficult than in the USA due to the lack of a comparative data base on regional tourist organizations such as that provided by the STO surveys used in Chapter 2. Consequently, a more selective approach has been adopted here. Once the scene has been set in the next two sections, policies and organizations operating at a federal level are examined. Attention is then focused on the interaction of tourist organizations in Bavaria, the most important *Land* in terms of tourism. Throughout, reference to postwar Germany is to the Federal Republic of Germany prior to reunification in 1990 but inclusive of West Berlin.

Environmental factors

The Federal Republic of Germany is a wealthy industrial nation with the largest population (61 million in 1987) and economy (1989 GNP, DM 2 260 400 million) in Europe, although in surface area (248 708 sq km) it is exceeded by several other countries. Three broad topographical areas can be recognized from north to south: the North German Plain, the Central German Uplands (Mittelgebirge) and the Alpine Foreland. While the population is distributed unevenly, with major conurbations in the Rhine-Ruhr, Rhine-Main and Rhine-Neckar areas, the German urban system is more balanced than in many other European countries. This results from historical developments, the truncation of the urban hierarchy brought about by the division and separation of Berlin and the country's decentralized federal system.

Germany has a long history of federalism. The present federal structure was imposed by the occupying powers after the Second World War to lessen the possibility of the re-emergence of a strongly centralized totalitarian state. The new Federation (*Bund*) consisted of ten states or *Länder*, largely determined on the basis of zones of occupation as well as traditional boundaries (as in the case of Bavaria). West Berlin had a special status but for all practical purposes was treated as the eleventh *Land*. Sovereignty is vested in the Federation; the *Länder* have no right of secession but each has its own constitution, government, administrative agencies and independent courts.

Under the constitution authority is divided between the Federation and the *Länder*, making the two mutually dependent (Kloss, 1976; Blacksell, 1987). Most of the legislative power is vested in the federal government, the *Länder* participating in the legislative process through the *Bundesrat* (Upper House). The *Länder* have legislative authority for everything not expressly reserved in the Basic Law to the federal government (eg foreign policy, fiscal issues, defence); education, cultural affairs, local government and local government are matters for the *Länder*. However, most of the administrative responsibility lies with the *Länder* who enforce not only their own laws but also federal ones. The *Länder* also have the right to tax to raise their own income.

In economic matters the federal government has essentially been non-interventionist, pursuing a policy of *Sozialemarkwirkschaft*. According to Blacksell (1987, p.232):

> Rather than 'social market economy' it [*Sozialemarkwirkschaft*] is better translated by the phrase 'socially responsible market economy', implying, as is in fact the case, that although state intervention should be kept to a minimum, it should certainly not be eschewed at the expense of public welfare. The key to West German domestic economic policy has been the belief that a steady reliance on the principles of the market economy, linked to improvements in the social services, will guarantee the successful reconstruction of the economy as a whole.

The *Länder* vary in size from the city states of Bremen (400 sq km, population of 654 000, 1987) and Hamburg (800 sq km, 1 567 000) to the larger *Länder* of Bavaria (70 000 sq km, 11 043 000) and North Rhine-Westphalia (34 000 sq km, 16 672 000). However, regional economic variations are not particularly marked (gross monthly earnings in 1987: FRG average, 3 884 DM; Schleswig-Holstein, 3 494 DM; Hamburg, 4 149 DM) and Blacksell (1987, p.231) concludes 'notwithstanding its federal political structure, West Germany is basically a homogenous society'.

The *Länder* also determine the structure of local government (Kloss, 1976: Wild, 1981). The larger *Länder* are subdivided into intermediate administrative regions, *Regierungsbezirke*, which today have a limited administrative role and also

function as federal planning regions. Local authorities, *Gemeinden*, have the power to regulate all local responsibilities as of right. Small *Gemeinden* may cede those functions they are unable to undertake to a larger county unit, the *Kreis*. The local authorities also administer various federal and *Länder* laws.

The degree of decentralization in Germany can be measured to some degree by the distribution of public funds and employment in the public sector:

	Distribution of public funds	Employment
Federal government	43%	1.2 million
Länder	29%	1.9 million
Local authorities	28%	1.2 million

Federal principles are now well entrenched in all aspects of German society. According to the Parties Act, political parties must have a regional structure such that individual members can exert appropriate influence on opinion-forming within their party. A wide range of economic and cultural activities is also organized on a federal basis, with employers, employees, farmers and sportsmen for instance being grouped in regional associations, each having a central body at the federal level. It is scarcely surprising, therefore, that tourism is also organized along these lines.

Tourism in Germany

Geography and history have endowed Germany with a varied but in some respects restricted resource base for tourism. In the north, Germany's North Sea/Baltic coastline is limited in length and subject to unreliable summers, factors which reduce its appeal to foreign visitors and make it primarily a domestic destination. Likewise in the south, the German Alps are limited in extent and the country's ski-field capacity is far exceeded by that of its Alpine neighbours. Many of Germany's recreational opportunities are to be found in the uplands of the Mittelgebirge, the Black Forest and the foothills and lakes of Bavaria. Rivers such as the Rhine, Moselle and Danube are popular for cruising. The country's cultural landscape also appeals to visitors, both domestic and foreign, from the castles of Bavaria and the Rhine to the historic buildings and towns of the Romantic Road, and to Cologne's splendid cathedral. Germany's cities also draw visitors, both for special events such as the trade fairs of Hannover and Frankfurt, Munich's Oktoberfest and Bayreuth's Wagnerian festival and as attractions in their own right (Hamburg, Munich, Berlin). Roth and Wenzel (1983) suggest that Germany's decentralized development has been not only the basis of the country's economic and social progress but also 'a great chance for tourism'. However, economic and industrial development have also brought problems of congestion, overcrowding and environmental problems, for example extensive damage to the country's forests through 'acid rain', problems which have encouraged the outbound traffic.

In terms of accommodation, about two-thirds of the formal capacity[1] (in establishments of more than eight beds) is available in the hotel sector where establishments average a modest thirty-one beds, ranging from fifty-five beds for hotels proper to twenty-one for guest houses (Table 4.1). Much hotel development since the 1970s has come from domestic and international chains, particularly at the upper end of the market in the major cities (Agel, 1987). The largest hotel group in Germany is Steigenberger, with 30 hotels and 5 000 rooms. Agel reports an oversupply of hotel capacity in the mid-1980s. Table 4.1 also shows a significant para-hotel sector. Spa facilities have long been important in Germany while large-scale development of holiday centres and holiday parks occurred in the 1970s (Becker, 1987). Camping is also popular in some areas, with a total of 16 million bednights recorded in 1988 (Flachmann, 1989).

Much travel by foreign visitors is independently organized. Inclusive tour travel constitutes around or below 20 per cent of most European markets and that of North America (Agel, 1987). While a massive package tour industry exists in Germany, most tour operators are oriented to the outbound

market, serving sun-lust destinations in the Mediterranean and farther afield. In contrast, much of the inbound traffic is by car from neighbouring countries.

Growth in the outbound market followed the postwar expansion of the German economy. By 1987 an estimated 69 per cent of Germans aged 14 and over were taking their main holiday outside the country, a total of 21.6 million holidays, compared with only 31 per cent in 1960 (Dundler, 1988). Nevertheless, for much of this period the number of domestic holidays continued to expand slowly due to an increase in net travel propensity (1960, 28 per cent; 1987, 64.6 per cent). By 1980 the number of main domestic holidays had peaked at 10.2 million, with slight decreases being experienced throughout the 1980s (1987, 9.5 million). This trend in main holidays has been offset to some extent by an increase in supplementary holidays, many of which are spent within Germany (Becker, 1987). Hiking and walking are the most popular recreational activities with domestic holidaymakers.

Development of inbound international tourism in to Germany in the postwar period has been rather erratic (Roth and Wenzel, 1983). After a rapid expansion of foreign bednights in the 1950s came a period through to 1975 in which years of slow growth alternated with years of stagnation. Substantial increases occurred in the late 1970s. The 1980s were again a period of slower growth but by 1988 almost 30 million bednights were recorded in establishments of more than eight beds.

In the period 1960–88 the Dutch replaced the Americans as the single largest market, both in terms of bednights and recorded receipts (Table 4.2). The other major markets are all European, particularly neighbouring countries. Some variation occurs in their relative importance depending on whether the measure is bednights or receipts; Austria is much more significant in terms of receipts.

Despite this increase in inbound tourism, the domestic market remains overwhelmingly dominant. In 1988, German guests accounted for 87 per cent of the 234 million bednights recorded (90 per cent in 1980).

Table 4.1   Distribution of supply and demand by type of accommodation in the Federal Republic of Germany (1988)

	Units no	Beds no	Beds %	Beds/ unit	Bednights no (000s)	Bednights %	Bednights % foreign	Average length of stay days
Hotels	10 009	549 815	30.9	55	72 713	31	22.8	2.2
Inns	11 592	243 528	13.7	21	20 026	8.6	12.7	2.4
Guesthouses	6 089	138 251	7.8	23	16 622	7.1	5.9	6.3
Bed and breakfast	10 181	245 429	13.8	24.1	30 899	13.2	16.6	2.2
Sub-total	37 871	1 177 023	66.2	31	140 260	59.9	18.0	2.6
Rest and holiday homes[1]	2 087	159 901	9.0	76.6	22 733	9.7	3.3	5.3
Holiday centres[2]	29	24 639	1.4	850	3 340	1.4	34.9	6.4
Holiday apartments[3]	5 605	196 906	11.1	35.1	20 021	8.5	8.7	9.5
Huts and youth hostels	1 001	94 133	5.3	94.0	10 156	4.3	10.2	2.7
Sub-total	8 722	475 579	26.7	54.5	56 250	2.4	8.3	5.3
Sanatoriums/spa hotels	902	126 677	7.1	140	37 821	16.1	0.5	28.1
Total	47 495	1 779 279	100	37.4	234 331	100	12.9	3.6

Notes:
[1] Erholungs-und Ferienheime, Schulungsheime
[2] Ferienzentren
[3] Ferienhäuser-wohnungen
Source: Statistiches Bundesamt (1988)

With these national patterns and trends outlined, attention can now be directed to regional patterns of demand and supply as summarized in Table 4.3. Domestic demand is largely determined by the population potential of each *Land* (columns b and c). North Rhine-Westphalia is the single largest domestic market, Bavaria generates fewer domestic holidays than expected and Lower Saxony more. On the other hand, the importance of each *Land* as a domestic destination (column d) is influenced by the availability of resources, with the coastal *Länder* of Schleswig-Holstein and Lower Saxony assuming prominent positions along with Bavaria and Baden-Württemberg (the Black Forest). When domestic

demand is measured in bednights, however, some changes in ranking occur (column f). Bavaria is still the leading *Land* followed by Baden-Württemberg, while the populous industrial region of North Rhine-Westphalia assumes third position through increased business and other travel, while seasonal Schleswig-Holstein with many private rooms sees its share drop.[2]

Bavaria leads in terms of foreign bednights although with a greatly reduced percentage (20 per cent of foreign bednights; 29 per cent of domestic). The importance of urban destinations to the foreign visitor is seen in the greater shares held by North Rhine-Westphalia, Hesse and the city states

Table 4.2 Evolution of foreign bednights and international receipts in the Federal Republic of Germany (1960–88)

	1960[1]		1970[1]		1980[1]		1988[2]	
	Bednights %	Receipts %	Bednights %	Receipts %	Bednights %	Receipts %	Bednights %	Receipts %
USA	15.5	38.4	18.2	22.6	12.6	11.7	13.0	9.8
UK	12.8	7.5	10.3	4.5	9.7	4.6	8.6	4.9
Netherlands	12.2	3.7	14.7	11.5	23.8	17.6	19.1	15.6
France	8.7	10.7	7.8	10.2	5.5	12.2	4.9	8.8
Bel.-Lux.	6.9	3.5	5.8	4.2	5.7	6.2	4.3	4.1
Switzerland	6.1	8.6	4.8	6.4	4.3	6.8	4.6	4.3
Denmark	5.8	3.0	5.0	5.3	4.3	7.2	4.6	7.0
Italy	5.5	3.7	4.3	10.8	3.5	7.9	4.8	5.6
Sweden	5.3	n.a.	4.2	4.0	3.2	3.7	4.4	5.6
Austria	4.3	6.1	3.6	11.6	3.6	16.5	3.5	11.6
Other	16.9	14.8	21.2	8.9	23.8	5.6	28.2	22.7
Total	11 358 000	DM2 020m	16 376 000	DM4.853m	22 700 000	DM10 600m	29 779 408	DM14 888m

Sources: 1 Roth and Wenzel (1983); 2 DZT (1989)

of Hamburg, Bremen and Berlin as well as in the reduced importance of the coastal *Länder* of Schleswig-Holstein and Lower Saxony. North Rhine-Westphalia and Rhineland-Palatinate also benefit from proximity to the major markets of the Netherlands and France. Almost 30 per cent of the total Dutch bednights are spent in the Rhineland-Palatinate with 19 per cent in North Rhine-Westphalia and 18 per cent in Bavaria. Varied landscape as well as proximity is also a factor with the Dutch as the flat plains of Lower Saxony attract only 6 per cent of Dutch bednights. Bavaria accounted for one-third of all American bednights followed by Hesse (21 per cent, Frankfurt airport) and Baden-Württemburg (17 per cent, Heidelberg and the Black Forest). Different *Länder* thus depend in varying degrees on particular foreign markets. Further examples of this specialization are provided by Schleswig-Holstein and Lower Saxony which depend heavily on Scandinavian visitors. Despite the changes in the composition of the total tourist traffic noted above, the regional distribution of all foreign bednights has remained surprisingly

stable since the 1960s (Roth and Wenzel, 1983).

In terms of total bednights (column j) Bavaria is followed by Baden-Württemberg, North Rhine-Westphalia, Lower Saxony and Hesse. A comparable ranking occurs with respect to total capacity, with Hesse just being edged out of fourth position by Schleswig-Holstein. Again, the regional spread of total capacity exhibits a remarkable consistency since 1960, especially as the total number of beds nationwide more than doubled in the period through to 1988.

The two indices of tourism intensity in Table 4.3, the tourist function index (column n) and the ratio of bednights to population (column m) suggest that in relative terms tourism is more important in Schleswig-Holstein than Bavaria. In general, however, these indices are very low, indicating that at the level of the *Länder* tourism is not a particularly significant activity. Values for specific localities, of course, are likely to be much higher.

At the level of the *Kreise*, employment in tourism is particularly important in the Bavarian Alps, the Bayerischer Wald, the Black Forest, parts of the

Table 4.3   Regional distribution of tourism in the Federal Republic of Germany (1988)

	Population (1987) no.	%	Domestic Tourism (1985/86) Origin %	Dest. %	Bednights 1988 Domestic no.	%	International no.	%	Total no.	%	Beds in tourist accommodation 1988 no.	%	Bednights Popn (i)/(a)	Bednights T(f) (k)/(a) × 100
Schleswig-Holstein	2 612 000	4.3	3.5	17.3	16 457 070	8.1	723 603	2.4	17 180 673	7.3	166 284	9.4	6.6	6.3
Hamburg	1 567 000	2.6	4.0	0.6	2 287 285	1.1	1 168 640	3.9	3 455 925	1.5	22 372	1.3	2.2	1.4
Lower Saxony	7 198 000	11.8	15.9	13.5	24 840 975	12.2	1 863 695	6.2	26 704 670	11.4	214 830	10.1	3.7	3.0
Bremen	654 000	1.0	1.0	0.6	658 466	0.3	224 490	0.7	882 958	0.4	5 737	0.3	1.4	0.9
North Rhine-Westphalia	16 672 000	27.3	27.6	7.1	26 551 527	13.0	4 732 393	15.7	31 283 920	13.4	228 346	12.4	1.9	1.4
Hesse	5 552 000	9.1	8.9	5.2	22 083 804	10.8	4 268 948	14.2	26 352 752	11.2	187 134	9.2	4.7	3.4
Rhineland-Palatinate	3 606 000	5.9	7.0	5.2	12 840 981	6.3	3 648 821	12.1	16 489 802	7.0	148 325	8.3	4.6	4.1
Baden-Württemberg	9 350 000	15.3	14.5	15.5	32 624 011	16.0	4 568 148	15.2	37 192 159	15.9	263 003	14.8	4.0	2.8
Bavaria	11 043 000	18.0	10.8	32.4	59 936 811	29.4	7 478 526	20.1	67 415 337	28.8	501 600	28.2	6.1	4.5
Saarland	1 041 000	1.7	1.4	0.6	1 258 209	0.6	134 111	0.5	1 392 320	0.6	10 865	0.6	1.4	1.0
Berlin (West)	1 884 000	3.0	5.4	2.0	4 675 063	2.3	1 305 369	4.3	5 980 432	2.6	30 783	1.7	3.0	1.6
Total	61 170 000	100	100	100	204 214 204	100	30 116 744	100	234 330 948	100	1 779 279	100	3.8	2.9
	(a)	(b)	(c)	(d)	(e)	(f)	(g)	(h)	(i)	(j)	(k)	(l)	(m)	(n)

Data Source: Statistisches Bundesamt (1988)

Rhineland-Palatinate and coastal areas of Lower Saxony and Schleswig-Holstein. In few counties, however, does tourism generate more than 250 jobs per 10 000 residents (Statistisches Bundesamt, 1988).

In general, there has been a dearth of detailed research on the economic impact of tourism in Germany (Schnell, 1988). Schnell reports a Commerzbank estimate that 1.5 million jobs in 1986 depended on tourism, some 6 per cent of all gainful employment. A later study commissioned by the Deutscher Reisebüro-Verband (DRV, 1989) supports this estimate, deriving a figure of approximately 1.2 million full-time jobs. The DRV study also estimated that turnover from domestic and inbound international tourism created a net value added of about DM 70 million or about 4.6 per cent of the national income. Over half of the total tourism turnover was generated by day trips, day business trips and transit traffic.

Most attention has focused on Germany's so-called travel deficit. In 1988 Germans travelling abroad are estimated to have spent DM 44 000 million while visitors to Germany brought in approximately DM 14 000 million (DZT, 1989). WTO figures show that Germans ranked second that year to Americans for expenditure on international tourism (after having been world leaders earlier in the decade) and sixth worldwide for receipts (Waters, 1990). Figures for 1984 show international tourism accounted for 2.6 per cent of Germany's balance of payments earning but 7.2 per cent of expenditure (Lee, 1987). Schnell (1988) reports that the federal government is not unduly concerned about the travel imbalance, the argument being that destination countries will use the receipts from German tourists to buy German products so that ultimately, the German economy does profit from outbound tourism.

Schnell concludes (p.213):

The federal government takes a sanguine view of the future of tourism: the basic economic determinants of tourist demand – increased net income and increased leisure time – will effectively remain unchanged, while there is no apparent reason why the West Germans

should cease spending a disproportionate amount of their incomes on travelling. . . . The trend to preferring foreign destinations to those within the Federal Republic will continue. However, there are opportunities to improve domestic tourism because of the increasing participation in short-term travel, and developments such as urban tourism will continue to be important. Nevertheless it has been recognized that further research is necessary into how domestic demand for holidays within West Germany can be increased.

Federal policies

Tourism has never attained a very prominent position at a federal level in Germany, with few explicit policies on tourism being formulated and no separate ministry or department of tourism being established. All issues of tourism policy (eg the dialogue between the federal government and the Parliament (*Bundestag*), between the federal level and the *Land* level, liaison with international bodies, dialogue with the tourist industry) are the responsibility of the Ministry of Economic Affairs. The tourism policy section of the ministry had six staff in 1989. Frequently tourism is dealt with as part of broader social and economic policies, for example the regional development programme. Other ministries may also have small sections dealing with aspects of tourism (eg the Ministry of Agriculture supports a farm holiday programme).

According to Dr Feldmann (1988), founding chairman of the *Bundestag*'s Tourism Sub-Committee, 'Tourism policy was really launched in 1975 with the submission of the Government's tourism policy by Federal Minister of Economics, Friedrichs'. Under this policy (Deutscher Bundestag, 1975), the federal government's goals were identified as:

● to ensure that the necessary framework conditions are in place for a continuous development of tourism,

- to increase the performance and the competitiveness of the German tourism sector,
- to improve the possibilities for wide sections of the population to engage in tourist activities,
- to expand international co-operation.

These goals appear to have become entrenched for they are still reported as such in the OECD's 1989 survey of tourism policy (OECD, 1989). The OECD report (p.47) also noted a number of general measures had been taken:

> Essential conditions in tourism policy were made very early on: guaranteeing full freedom of movement for the citizens, free currency convertibility, free choice of destination and increasing competition in efficiency between commercial suppliers of tourism services.
>
> The level of efficiency of the tourism sector is determined predominantly by small and medium-sized enterprises in Germany. For this reason, the economic policy of the Federal Government is aimed at creating appropriate conditions for efficient small and medium-sized industries.

Feldmann (1988) notes that tourism issues were rarely debated by the plenary sessions of the *Bundestag*. It was only in May 1987 that the *Bundestag* established its Tourism Sub-Committee, thereby providing a more regular vehicle for the discussion of tourism matters (Figure 4.2). The OECD survey (1989, p.47) observes:

> In this sub-committee the Federal government reports among other things on issues of immediate interest in tourism policy, such as the effects on tourism of ecological detriments to the environment, the harmonization of international statistics on tourism, the European Year of Tourism 1990, promotion of family holidays, setting-up of reservation systems in the German tourism industry and the evaluation of such systems.

While this explicit interest in tourism is comparatively recent, the federal government has nevertheless long played an important but less direct role in the development and promotion of tourism. In association with the *Länder* governments the Ministry of Economic Affairs has funded a large number of tourism projects in regional development programmes. The federal Ministry of Economic Affairs has also been the major funding agent of the DZT, the body responsible for promoting international tourism to Germany.

Tourism and regional development

Economic policy in Germany has largely been non-interventionist and most public expenditure has not had a regional dimension. Nevertheless Germany, like most other European countries, developed regional development policies in the 1960s and 1970s with Blacksell (1987, p.250), noting 'the long-standing commitment to a uniform standard of living in all parts of the country is perhaps the prime illustration of the "social responsibility" implied in the concept of the "social market economy"'. Responsibility for regional development lies jointly with the federal and *Länder* governments, with federal government providing much of the funding and co-ordination, while the *Länder* have implemented the various policies and programmes which have been established, retaining a lot of discretion and initiative in doing so.

The most significant programme for tourism has been that for the improvement of the regional economic structure (*Verbesserung der regionalen Wirtschaftsstruktur*) introduced in 1969 (Schnell, 1975; 1988; Blacksell, 1987). Figure 4.1 shows designated tourism regions cover most of the areas of the country eligible for regional development assistance (*Gemeinschaftsaufgabegebiete*). Those in the border region receive special assistance. Regional development need, rather than tourism potential, appears to have been the major criterion in their destination. Schnell (1975, p.74) observes:

> When delimiting these areas, neither demand analyses nor landscape evaluations were made to ascertain the suitability of the areas for holiday recreation purposes. In all those regions which, for several reasons, cannot

4.1 Tourism and regional development in the Federal Republic of Germany (Source: After Deutscher Bundestag, 1985)

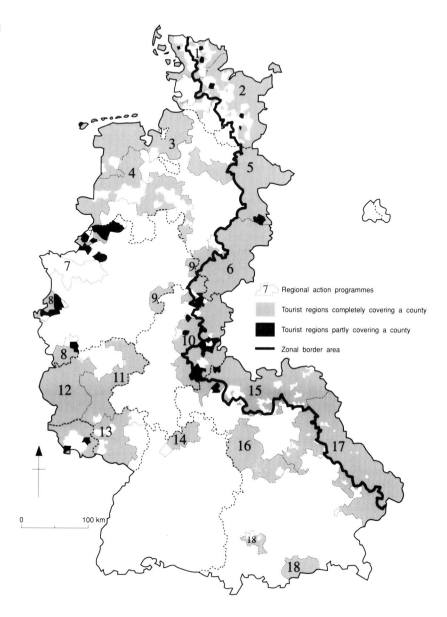

7 ⟨ Regional action programmes

    Tourist regions completely covering a county

    Tourist regions partly covering a county

    Zonal border area

0   100 km

offer attractive locations for industry, tourism was declared to be the universal remedy to stop further economic decline and other structural change.

Within these areas assistance is made available by way of grants and low interest loans for both private and public sector projects. In 1975, 12 per cent of the total programme funds were spent on tourism projects (Schnell, 1988). For the period 1985–9 the percentage allocated to tourism had dropped to 8 per cent or an average of DM 129 million per year (Deutscher Bundestag, 1985). Of this, 5 per cent was spent on the creation of new and the maintenance of existing jobs in the private sector (eg construction or improvement of accommodation, recreational facilities) and 3 per cent on public tourism facilities (eg swimming pools, golf courses, congress centres). Funding from this programme was particularly significant in the growth of holiday centres and parks noted earlier (Becker, 1987; Schnell, 1988).

Just over 40 per cent of all allocations to tourism projects in the period 1985–9 went to projects in Bavaria (compared with 23 per cent for all projects), where the proportion of programme funds spent on tourism was 14 per cent or DM 53 million per year. Distribution of funding within the *Land* is decided at this level, in this case by the Bavarian Ministry of Economic Affairs, with the district offices in the *Regierungsbezirke* also participating in the decision-making. Grants of up to DM 2 million may be made at the district level while decisions on larger amounts are referred to Munich. However, the district representatives also appear to play a major role in these latter decisions, being better informed about local conditions and needs. Tourism development programmes prepared in 1974, 1978 and 1989 (Bayerische Staatsregierung, 1978, 1989) provide some overall direction (for example the emphasis is on improving quality rather than expanding capacity, assisting small and medium-sized enterprises rather than large ones) but much of the assistance appears to be reactive with the ministry responding on a

project by project basis to specific proposals and applications.

Tourist organizations

A complex network of tourist organizations reflecting the country's federal structure has developed in Germany (Figure 4.2). The tourism policy sector within the Ministry of Economic Affairs is the country's NTA (national tourist administration) while the Deutsche Zentrale für Tourismus (DZT) functions as Germany's NTO (national tourist organization). Other tourist organizations (*Fremdenverkehrsverbände*) exist at the levels of the *Länder*, local authorities and in some cases intermediate levels (only those for Bavaria are depicted in Figure 4.3). *Länder* and local governments as well as commercial operators fund these organizations which come together at the federal level under their 'roof' organization, the Deutsche Fremdenverkehrsverband (DFV). Other sectoral organizations also exist alongside this network (Tietz, 1980; Wolff, 1983; Deutsches Fremdenverkehrspräsidium, 1988) to serve the interests of their members: DEHOGA (hotels), the Deutschen Bäderverbändes or DBV (spas) and the Deutsche Reisebüro-Verband or DRV (travel

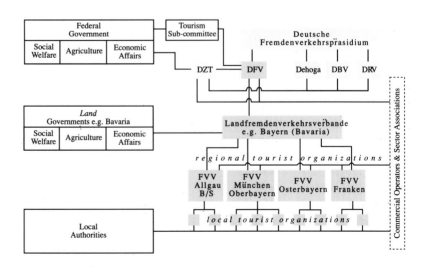

4.2 Network of tourist organizations in the Federal Republic of Germany

4.3 City marketing groups and holiday routes in the Federal Republic of Germany

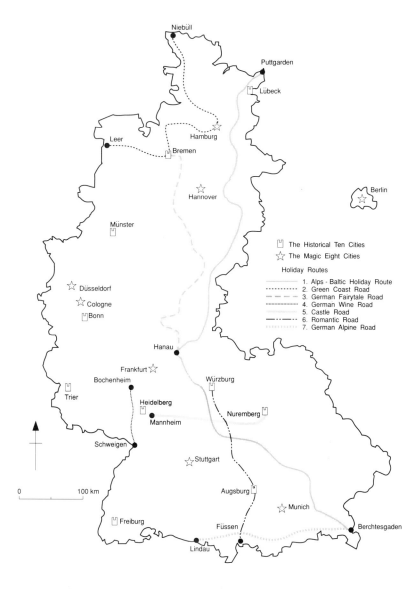

agencies and tour operators). These federal level organizations co-operate under the aegis of the Deutsche Fremdenverkehrspräsidium to promote their common interests. The following sections examine in turn the structure and function of the DZT, the DFV and the local and regional organizations in Bavaria.

Deutsche Zentrale für Tourismus

Headquartered in Frankfurt and with twenty-five overseas offices, the DZT is responsible for promoting travel to Germany from abroad. In 1989 the DZT had 180 staff in Germany and overseas and a budget of DM 44.1 million (US$23.3 million). The DZT in its present form was founded on 25 May 1948 but its prewar predecessors may be traced to the Bund Deutscher Verkehrsverein, founded in 1902, and the Reichszentrale für Deutsche Verkehrswerbung, created in 1920.

The DZT has always depended heavily on a grant from the Ministry of Economic Affairs. In

1989 this made up about 85 per cent of the DZT's budget, the remainder coming from membership fees and contributions as well as some self-generated income. Membership has grown only slightly from the ten founding members to sixteen in 1989. These are primarily national sector associations – eg Deutscher Fremdemverkehrsverband (tourism), Deutscher Bäderverband (spas), DEHOGA (hotels) – major carriers (Deutsche Bundesbahn: railways), Lufthansa, Köln-Düsseldorfer (Rhine ferries), and more recently special marketing groups of cities, namely the Historic Ten and the Magic Eight. The DZT has a nine member board, including a representative each from the Ministry of Economic Affairs and the Treasury. There is also a larger advisory council consisting of elected and *ex-officio* members which brings in representatives of federal and *Länder* governments, members of other organizations at these levels and representatives of the other members.

The DZT is concerned exclusively with promoting travel to Germany through undertaking market research, advertising, production and distribution of information material, sales promotion, press and public relations activities, participation in trade fairs, exhibitions and workshops and other related activities. It is not involved in planning (apart from its own market plans), development, visitor servicing and other possible NTO functions outlined in Chapter 1. Nor does it play a role in domestic tourism.

The marketing activities of the DZT have a fourfold aim (DZT, 1985, p.11):

- to increase the number of overnight stays by foreign visitors,
- to increase the growth of income from foreign tourism,
- to raise the market share of Germany in international tourism,
- to nurture the image of being an attractive country to travel to.

A general foundation campaign in each of the foreign markets is supplemented by individual campaigns which concentrate on target groups or special events. The central emphasis has been on promoting a romantic image of Germany – old towns, beautiful countrysides, castles and cathedrals. One way this has been done is through the promotion of various inter-regional thematic routes, such as the Romantic Road, the German Fairytale Road and the Alps–Baltic Holiday Route which runs the length of the country. The DZT has also encouraged German cities to join forces to advertise overseas. The eight largest come together as the Magic Eight while another group undertake joint promotion as the Historic Ten (Figure 4.3). These are supported in their activities by the DZT and Lufthansa. This association, however, is purely a marketing device to raise and stretch overseas marketing funds; in many other respects the cities are rivals. Northern regions have come together as the Top of Germany association to work on a marketing concept with the DZT to promote a part of the country which has been less attractive to foreign visitors. Regional and local participation is also encouraged in the many travel shows and workshops with which the DZT is associated, often as principal organizer of the German presence (Plate 4.1).

This joint promotional activity is also extended to DZT membership of international promotional organizations involving neighbouring countries with shared attractions, notably the Tourist Association of the Alpine Countries (with Austria, Switzerland, Yugoslavia and Italy), the Tourist Association of the Danube Countries (with Austria, Czechoslovakia, Yugoslavia, Hungary, Bulgaria and Romania), the International Rhine Promotion Association (with the Netherlands and Switzerland), Eifel Ardennes Promotion (with Belgium, Luxembourg and France) and International Lake Constance Promotion. The DZT also belongs to the European Travel Commission which has been particularly active in the North American and Japanese markets. The joint promotional strategies shown in Figure 4.3, together with the international co-operative efforts just mentioned, illustrate well the co-ordinating role of an NTO.

International co-operation has also been extended to market research. The DZT and NTOs

4.1 Co-ordination of international promotion is an important function of the Deutsche Zentrale für Tourismus: the DZT's stand at the 1989 World Travel Market in London brought together fifty different tourism representatives from Germany (Courtesy of the DZT)

of Austria and Switzerland, for instance, undertook co-operative market studies in South-east Asia in 1984 and in Arab countries in 1985, both distant and emerging markets. The DZT also participates with the European Travel Data Center in the European Travel Monitor as a means of obtaining continuous, up-to-date quantitative data on European market conditions to complement the DZT's own in-depth studies of particular markets undertaken on a periodic basis. Other data are obtained from official statistics on bednights produced by the Statistisches Bundesamt or by tourism research organizations such as the Studienkreis für Tourismus.

The extent to which market intelligence gathered by such research is translated into new business depends in large part on the effectiveness with which it is distributed downwards to individual enterprises. This is a role for the various regional tourist organizations, but given the mix of small and medium-sized businesses which predominate in Germany, distribution at lower levels appears to

occur rather unevenly. As a result of these difficulties and the federal government's policy of supporting small- and medium-sized enterprises, the DZT has also developed a special sales promotion section to assist 'those groups of agents who out of their own small resources or because of their lack of experience in overseas markets, are unable or only with great difficulty to become publicized' (DZT, 1985, p.27). The DZT also operates a reservations service to assist the middle-sized supplier. Reservations made through this system totalled 153 000 overnights in 1985.

Support for these activities is one area in which the DZT's operations appear to be directly influenced by federal policies. International co-operation is another. The grant from the Ministry of Economic Affairs does not come earmarked for designated promotions or campaigns in particular countries. On the other hand, the DZT annual report for 1985 (p.37) notes: 'The Board of Managers . . . is continually involved in making the requirements and the achievements of the DZT

4.4 Membership structure of the Deutsche Fremdenverkehrsverband (Source: After DFV n.d.)

clear to those of parliamentary and political responsibility', presumably to keep the budget expanding. In this some success has been achieved. The DZT's total budget increased from DM 29 million in 1980 to DM 44.1 million in 1989, with the Ministry of Economic Affairs grant going from DM 27.4 million to DM 37.5 million.

The Deutsche Fremdenverkehrsverband

The DFV is a non-profit organization, which represents the interests of lower order tourist organizations at a federal level. It has its headquarters in Bonn and a staff of three people. The origins of the DFV, like the DZT, may be traced to the formation of the Bund Deutscher Verkehrsverein in 1902, but it was re-established after the Second World War, undergoing several changes since to become primarily a lobby group for its members.

Membership is drawn basically from the tourist organizations at a *Länder* and regional level and from city tourist organizations. There are also three representatives of communal organizations who represent the smaller communities and half a dozen sponsor members (eg automobile and camping associations and the Rhine ferry company, Köln-Düsseldorfer). Figure 4.4 depicts the basic membership of the DFV and also shows the general structure of the network of *Fremdenverkehrsverbände* throughout the country. In most cases there is a *Land* organization, underlain in the larger *Länder* such as Bavaria and Baden-Württemberg by regional organizations. However, in North Rhine-Westphalia there are two *Landesverkehrsverbände* one each for North Rhine and Westphalia, while Lower Saxony has its four regional organizations and no *Land* organization. These different structures reflect the flexibility of a federal system. Many of the larger cities are members in their own right; some were founding members of the DFV, others were brought in to add regional balance.

By its constitution, the DFV is charged with

- representing the interests of its members to the federal legislature and executive
- co-operating with other federal organizations and institutions in order to look after members' interests and to represent them on the DZT,
- co-ordinating the co-operative efforts of members, education, advice and assistance in technical matters,
- public relations and marketing at a federal level,
- developing training and further education of tourism employees,
- fostering research and teaching about tourism.

These goals are largely pursued through the DFV's committee structure, with committees existing for marketing, political issues, transport, timetables, camping, and contacts with other organizations (eg DZT, DRF). Political issues reported for 1987 (DFV, 1987a) for instance, include the possibilities raised by the establishment of the *Bundestag*'s new Tourism Sub-Committee, environmental pollution (of the Rhine, North Sea and in the Alps), Europe 1992, tourism statistics (with Statistiches

Bundesamt) and planning and regional development. The transport committee followed up issues relating to various modes of transport in Germany while a special committee pursued questions of railways timetabling which disadvantaged certain holiday destinations and market segments. A major study was commissioned by the DFV on the Germany holiday market, 'Urlaub in Deutschland', which identified the following three target markets: families with children, culture and health tourism (DFV, 1987b). Such studies can provide direction but the DFV itself lacks the resources to undertake promotion, advertising and so forth. There is thus no federal equivalent of the DZT which undertakes or co-ordinates marketing activities for the domestic market. The DFV has also been exploring ways of developing and introducing a common reservation system to facilitate domestic travel.

The DFV has increasingly tried to stimulate awareness of these and other issues through producing and disseminating a series of position papers, for example on basic questions of tourism policy in Germany, tourism and transport, tourism and the environment (DFV, 1986a, 1986b, 1986c). Further awareness of the economic and social significance of tourism has been stimulated by co-operative efforts with the other organizations noted above (DEHOGA, DBV, DZT and DRV), under the aegis of the Deutsche Fremdemverkehrspräsidium (1988). The DFV has also organized the Deutscher Fremdenverkehrstag, two to three day meetings and exhibitions which bring together tourism representatives, politicians, members of the press and other interested parties.

It is difficult to assess the success of the DFV in these fields. However, it appears to provide a readily identifiable voice for tourism at the federal level, with the establishment of the Sub-Committee on Tourism and the appointment of the under-secretary for tourism providing some evidence that tourism is gaining increasing recognition in federal circles. Many of the other activities commonly associated with tourist organizations are undertaken at the level of the *Länder* and below.

Bavarian tourist organizations

The first Bavarian Tourism Association was formed in 1890. The present structure has its origins in the postwar reorganization (LFV Bayern, 1987a). Up until 1981 the Bavarian organization was administered by the Munich and Upper Bavaria regional tourist organization. However, the amount of work involved and questions of regional interest led to the setting up of a completely separate *Land* organization, the Landfremdenverkehrsverband Bayern (or LFV Bayern), with its headquarters in Munich and a staff (in 1989) of eight. It is a registered society, the five major members of which are the four regional tourist organization (Figures 4.2 and 4.4) and the Bavarian Spa Association (Bayerischer Heilbäderverband). In addition, in 1987 there were a further nineteen members, primarily Bavarian sector associations.

The LFV Bayern derives 90 per cent of its funding from the Bavarian Ministry of Economic Affairs which makes a major grant each year for promoting Bavaria and a smaller supplementary grant for personnel and operating costs. The promotion grant is made to support an annual *Land* marketing plan (*Landeswerbeplan*), with about two-thirds being allocated to the LFV Bayern and the

Bavarian Spa association (LFV Bayern, 1987a, 1987b). The remaining third is distributed by a committee of the LFV Bayern among the four regional organizations on the basis of such factors as population, bednights, and accommodation capacity (Table 4.4). In making this grant, the Ministry of Economic Affairs recognizes the importance of tourism in Bavaria, growing international competition and the need to undertake further marketing measures (LFV Bayern, 1987a).

The marketing committee meets twice a year to discuss and decide on the major measures to be taken with more regular meetings occurring between the staff of LFV Bayern and the directors of the four regional organizations and the Bayerischer Heilbäder Verband. It is nevertheless still difficult to combine the interests of a large and varied state such as Bavaria.

Much of LFV Bayern's budget goes on central advertising (DM 1 million in 1987). Participation in travel fairs, an important feature of German tourism, is another major activity (DM 450 000) in which the LFV Bayern generally acts as co-ordinator for the whole of Bavaria. Involvement in fairs and campaigns outside of Germany is invariably in association with the DZT. The

Table 4.4 Distribution of the Bavarian Ministry of Economic Affairs promotional grant (1987–8)

	1987[1]		1988[2]	
	DM	%	DM	%
Central measures				
LFV Bayern	2 680 000	57.5	3 027 800	58.8
Bayerischer Heilbäder-Verband	275 000	5.9	315 000	6.1
Regional measures				
FVV München-Oberbayern	529 650	11.4	549 900	10.7
FVV Franken	469 150	10.0	402 400	7.8
FVV Ostbayern	353 100	7.6	386 350	7.5
FVV Allgaü/Bayerisch-Schwaben	353 100	7.6	466 350	9.1
Total	4 660 000	100	5 147 800	100

Sources: 1 LFV Bayern (1987b); 2 FVV München-Oberbayern (1988)

organization also engages in a wide range of other marketing activities (production of brochures, handbooks and other publications, press and public relations, seminars). In particular, LFV Bayern has been concerned with developing a strong image of Bavaria, with consistent themes and messages (*Auf nach Bayern* – Let's Go to Bavaria) which the regional and local organizations can develop.

The four regional organizations (Table 4.4, Figure 4.4) constitute an intermediate tier between the *Land* and the local communities. The Fremdenverkehrsverband (FVV) München-Oberbayern, for instance, has a staff of eight and headquarters in Munich. It has some 200 ordinary members (FVV München-Oberbayern, 1988), essentially local tourist associations and local authorities, plus a further twenty or so other members (eg cable-car companies, local hotel associations and other sector organizations). The board is largely made up of local politicians, the chairman being the Regierungspräsident of Upper Bavaria. Many of the local associations have been in existence since the turn of the century or earlier. The membership contributes about two-thirds of the organization's budget, giving it a total income of around DM 1.5 million in 1988. The fees paid depend on the number of overnights recorded in each locality.

The regional organizations may be further sub-divided into sub-regions to facilitate administration and preserve regional identity and interests. Both the FVV München-Oberbayern and the FVV Franken have thirteen sub-regions (*Gebietsgemeinschaften*). Some of these sub-regional organizations date back to the 1920s and 1930s. The boundaries of the sub-regions may correspond to local authority divisions (eg *Landkreise*) or reflect distinctive tourist areas. For example in the Landkreis Chiemgau in Upper Bavaria there are two sub-regions due to the stronger image of Chiemsee which stands out from the rest of the region while the border of two other sub-regions runs through the Ammersee. The sub-regional associations will usually have a mix of official and private members. That for the Fichtelgebirge, for instance, had a total of 125 members in 1989, of which 39 were cities, towns and villages while the

remainder were made up of individual hotels, hiking associations and the like.

The regional organizations engage in a similar range of activities to the LFV Bayern, often participating jointly with it, but they tend to limit their activities primarily to within Germany. The FVV München-Oberbayern, for instance, undertakes advertising campaigns, with particular emphasis on the North Rhine-Westphalia market in summer and Hesse and Baden-Württemberg in winter. In 1988 it participated in seventeen travel fairs, including fairs in Brussels, Utrecht, Milan, London and Vancouver. Some of the sub-regional and local organizations also participate in these fairs, with the FVVs co-ordinating the stands from their regions. The FVVs also undertake press and public relations activities and in association with their members host familiarization trips. A variety of publications and catalogues are also produced and educational seminars held.

More localized information is produced and distributed by the sub-regional and local organizations, which may also undertake their own advertising and participate in travel fairs. Some of the sub-regional organizations, such as that for the Fichtelgebirge, will also operate a booking system and act as wholesalers for group tours, putting together packages involving round trip transport, accommodation and local activities. Visitor information services are usually provided by the local associations. Little market research is undertaken at this level but the sub-regional organizations play a role in distributing downwards information from the LFV or FFVs to their members.

Considerable variation occurs in the structure and activities of local tourist organizations as the following three local Bavarian examples show: a large city, Munich; a smaller regional city well known for its Wagner festival, Bayreuth; and a large ski resort, Garmisch-Partenkirchen.

Munich attracts many business, convention and trade fair visitors as well as those on holiday and throughout the postwar period has been the leading German city in terms of recorded arrivals (2.9 million in 1987) and bednights (6 million). Over 40 per cent of bednights in recent years have been generated by foreign visitors. Munich clearly plays a major role in Bavaria, accounting for almost 10 per cent of total bednights and a quarter of foreign bednights. Within the region of Upper Bavaria these shares are much greater, respectively one-third and two-thirds.

The Munich City Tourist Office (Fremdenverkehrsamt München) is a department of the city council with the director being responsible to it. Although opportunities are provided for exchanges with the tourist industry throughout the year there are no formal links with the private sector and no direct industry participation in the running of the office. In 1989 the Munich City Tourist Office had a budget of DM 23.3 million, over half that of the DZT. Just over 40 per cent of its income came from the city council, the remainder being self-generated. About 9 per cent of the budget was allocated directly to marketing.

The function of the office is to promote tourism to Munich in general. The Tourist Office employs 140 people and a further 150 guides and hostesses. It operates a wide range of visitor services (information offices, arrangement of accommodation, guides and coaches, concert bookings), has a convention bureau, produces and distributes promotional material, undertakes press and public relations work and is the promoter of the Oktoberfest beer festival and a number of other fairs and events. The Tourist Office also participates in travel shows, seminars and exhibitions, taking part in forty-six such events in 1988, including eighteen abroad (Plate 4.2). Munich, in association with Heidelberg, also has a representative in New York who deals with wholesalers, travel agents and the press. Under the aegis of the Munich Promotion Pool the Tourist Office also takes part in general city promotion with large local firms such as BMW and Siemens. Munich generally does not do any market research of its own but relies on information from the DZT, the federal statistical office, the LFV Bayern and other reports (eg from the Studienkries für

4.2 The Munich City Tourist Office's stand at the International Tourism Exchange (ITB) in Berlin, 1989, the largest of the many travel trade fairs in Europe at which tourist organizations participate regularly
(Courtesy of the Munich City Tourist Office)

Tourismus) as well as feedback from the local industry.

Bayreuth in Upper Franconia is perhaps best known internationally for the Wagner music festival, undoubtedly its most important event of the year. Other cultural festivals and performances, conferences and visits to the city bring in over 70 000 overnight visitors a year with 225 000 bednights being recorded in 1988.

The city tourist office, the Bayreuth Fremdenverkehrsverein, celebrated its eightieth anniversary in 1989. It is largely financed by the city but has some 350 members, particularly from the accommodation sector. The office has about forty staff and three main functions. In addition to the usual visitor servicing functions for incoming visitors (booking services, provision of guides, production and distribution of information and brochures) the office has also a travel agency which services outgoing travellers and is responsible for organizing many of the city's performances and conferences with the exception of the Wagner Festival itself which is organized and marketed by a special private group.

Garmisch-Partenkirchen is a designated health resort and the major ski resort in the Bavarian Alps, recording 3.3 million bednights in 1987. The tourism office is again a department of the municipality, with responsibility not only for local promotion and visitor servicing but also for managing a number of major facilities (eg skating rink, indoor swimming pool, ski jump, congress hall). The 1989 budget was DM 14 million, derived from operating revenue and municipal finances. All local tourism enterprises must pay the municipality a special tax (*Fremdenverkehrsheitrag*); there is also a visitors' tax (*Kurheitrag*).

These three local examples are indicative of the range of scales, functions and markets which are to be found within Bavaria. This regional diversity also brings some stresses and strains to the organizational heirarchy outlined. Munich clearly dominates tourism in Upper Bavaria if not the *Land* as a whole. In many respects the Munich City Tourist Office would appear to function independently of the broader region. The city has greater resources (140 staff excluding guides,

compared with 8 each for the LFV Bayern and the FVV München-Oberbayern), a strong distinct image and records the largest number of bednights of any destination within Germany. Munich may not need Upper Bavaria but, especially in foreign markets, the wider region draws on the name recognition of Munich and relies on its gateway role. At the same time, the rest of Upper Bavaria may appreciate the often independent line taken by Munich in preference to being dominated by it in joint activities. The degree of interaction between city and region depends in large part on the market segment concerned – greater functional linkages occur with the general holiday and sightseeing markets, while for the trade fair and congress markets, Munich has more in common with other members of the Magic Eight.

Similarly, but at a different scale, Bayreuth's markets are generally not shared with its surrounding region, the visitors to the city's festivals and conferences are not those attracted by the hills, roads, villages and outdoor recreational activities of the Fichtelgebirge. Consequently little or no interaction appears to occur between Bayreuth and the sub-regional organization, the FVV Franken and the LFV Bayern. Other destinations in the area which do not have the specific focus of Bayreuth may, however, participate more in co-operative efforts with these organizations.

Regional organizations may also join forces for particular campaigns. The FVVs München-Oberbayern and Allgäu-Bayerisch-Schwaben, for instance, have jointly promoted the Bavarian Alps in Great Britain, the name Bavarian Alps being more widely recognized than those of either the two regional associations.

Many of these issues are not peculiar to Bavaria as Becker (1987, p.527) notes:

> Aversion and resistance against more intensive cooperation between several neighbouring resort towns are deeply rooted in the German communities. There have been endless fights about the sharing of costs and the appropriate publicity of each resort. There are also traditional rivalries between resort towns. Nevertheless, regional cooperation in marketing is an absolute necessity.

Conclusions

A complex network of tourist organizations has developed in Germany which reflects the country's broader federal structure (Figure 4.2). At the same time the network is characterized by a separation of functions which may present some constraints to the growth of tourism within Germany.

At the federal level, the DZT has been given the task of promoting international inbound tourism, a task which it carries out using the usual range of measures. There is, however, no comparable federal body which now promotes domestic tourism although the DFV has a leadership role here and has recently commissioned a basic study into conditions in the domestic market. Actual advertising and developing the domestic market are the responsibilities of the *Länder* and lower level organizations as well as the tourist industry as such. These organizations appear to participate actively with each other and with the DZT in overseas promotions but much less concerted and co-ordinated attacks occur on the domestic market. While only the Bavarian example has been examined here, the consistency in the pattern of market share held by the eleven *Länder* suggests each is doing equally as well, or badly, in this respect as the others. At a national level, however, the trends have been for a rapid increase in outbound tourism, slower growth in the inbound market and stagnation or decline domestically. It will certainly take more than improved organization to counteract the pull of the Mediterranean but nevertheless there appears to be scope for more co-ordination and more concerted efforts by German tourist organizations. The DFV's concern to introduce a common booking system indicates the type of co-ordinating role which may be needed in a federal system.

These and other functions than just promotion are also important. The lobbying efforts of the DFV may start to bear fruit as awareness of the social and economic significance of tourism is increased. Governments which are not fully appreciative of their own tourist industry nor unperturbed by a massive drain on foreign exchange by growing numbers of outbound travellers can scarcely be expected to be very supportive of tourism.

One area where government at the federal and *Länder* level have provided support is that of development. Less visible perhaps than the more explicit activities of the different tourist organization, the regional development programmes containing tourist projects have nevertheless been funded more substantially. During the mid-1980s approximately four times as much was spent each year on tourism projects under the programme for the Improvement of Regional Economic Infrastructure as the Ministry of Economic Affairs annual grant to the DZT (DM 129 million compared with about DM 30 million). In Bavaria, around DM 50 million was being spent on regional development tourism projects whereas promotion grants to the LFV Bayern and the regional organizations ranged from DM 4 million to 5 million. These grants of course are being made for regional development and not tourism *per se* and while there may be a need for improving quality and increasing the range of facilities it is still questionable, as Schnell (1975) noted in the early years, whether there is much association between regional need, tourism potential and market demand. The links between the grants for development and promotion do not appear to be very strong, being made by different sections within the Ministry of Economic Affairs. Were the development grants to be more closely tied to the marketing plans then their contribution to the development of tourism might be greater. Such intervention however would be less in line with *Sozialemarkwirkschaft*. What will happen to the special border programmes remains to be seen.

At the time of writing it was also unclear what impacts reunification would have on the networks of tourist organizations (Godau, 1991). However, it would seem a federal system, where much activity is decentralized, could adapt readily to this new situation. After reunification the administrative units within former East Germany were reconstituted as five new *Länder*, each of which would presumably develop its own *Landfremdenverkehrsverband* while the DZT would extend its promotion to cover these new areas.

Notes

1   Since 1981 only enterprises with more than eight beds have been required to record visitor arrivals and bednights. The official data on capacity and bednights after this date used throughout this chapter reflect these new procedures and therefore are not fully comprehensive. This issue is examined by Schnell (1988) who noted that private rooms rented on a cash basis accounted for 28 per cent of accommodation capacity in 1980 and 19 per cent of bednights ín 1979–80. Moreover, the effects of the changes have not been experienced evenly, with up to a half of all beds in Schleswig-Holstein not being recorded subsequently. The DRV (1989) study estimated that nationwide there were 50 million bednights spent in private rooms or establishments with fewer than nine beds, from a total of 290 million.

2   See note 1.

5

Scotland

Scotland are as 'indestructible' as Queensland or Alberta, this 'quasi-federal' devolution does reflect qualities, similar to federally organized countries.

Second, in its concentration on only one part of such a state, Scotland, this case study differs from the five others which present a more comprehensive national analysis. This concentration reflects both fieldwork constraints and a desire to focus on a manageable part of the state which would illustrate well the features described above. At the same time, by drawing on the literature an attempt is made to set the Scottish example in the broader context of Great Britain (England, Scotland and Wales). First, Scotland's position within the political and geographical structure of the United Kingdom is examined in the following section before the basic characteristics of tourism in Great Britain and Scotland are presented. After a general review of the development of British tourism policies and tourist organizations, attention is focused on a range of Scottish organizations, notably the Scottish Tourist Board (STB), the Highlands and Islands Development Board (HIDB), the area tourist boards (ATBs) and the interactions between these.

Scotland constitutes a special case in the range of examples examined in this book. First, as part of the United Kingdom (Great Britain and Northern Ireland), it represents a transition from the federal states of the USA and the Federal Republic of Germany to the centralized examples which follow – the Netherlands, the Republic of Ireland and New Zealand. In the 'centralization–decentralization spectrum', Paddison (1983, p.31) classifies the UK as a 'compound unitary state' of the type

> whose federal-like practices stem from the establishment of regional governments, which are vested with legislative powers and/or functional responsibilities that in unitary states would normally be considered the prerogative of the central government. Regional devolution of this type is often only granted to parts of the state. . . . Insofar as regionally recognized units such as . . . Wales or

Environmental factors

Geographically, economically and politically Scotland is an integral part of the United Kingdom (UK) but it is also one which retains a distinctive character through strong historical, cultural and other factors. Scotland has one-third of the UK's surface area but only 9 per cent of its population (5.1 million in 1986 from a total of 56.7 million). Located in the northern part of the country, Scotland is peripheral to the major centres of decision-making and economic development in London and the south-east. This peripherality is heightened by topography. The Highlands and Islands are the most mountainous, remote and sparsely populated part of the UK. Urban and industrial development is concentrated in the Central Lowlands, an area in which three-quarters of Scotland's population live. This urban, industrial concentration is separated from the industrial regions of northern England by the farmland of the Borders and Dumfries and Galloway. On a larger scale, Scotland lies on the outer margins of western Europe.

The Scottish economy developed rapidly in the nineteenth century but with the collapse of heavy industries such as ship-building and iron and steel making in the twentieth century prosperity declined. Various attempts at industrial restructuring have been made in the postwar period, with the development of North Sea oil in the 1970s giving a further impetus to the Scottish economy. Economic indicators suggest the gap in levels of economic development between Scotland and the UK closed during the 1970s though progress was less certain and consistent during the following decade (Lythe and Majmudar, 1982; Randall, 1987). These writers also emphasize the integration of the Scottish economy with that of the rest of the UK. Moreover, as Lythe and Majmudar (1982, p.4) note: 'There is no real control within or on behalf of Scotland of taxation and of the money supply, and so the management of an economy cannot be exercised independently for Scotland.'

Much of what does set Scotland apart from the rest of the UK is the retention or development of peculiarly Scottish institutional or administrative systems. Scotland retained its own legal, educational and religious systems after the Act of Union 1707 and specific administrative arrangements for Scotland have also been made, with the Scottish Office being established in 1884 (Lythe and Majmudar, 1982; Randall, 1987). Based in Edinburgh since 1939, the Scottish Office today consists of five departments through which the Secretary of State for Scotland, a Cabinet minister, exercises responsibilities in an increasingly wide range of areas: agriculture and fisheries, education, health, local government, housing, physical planning, road and sea transport, electricity and tourism. The Secretary of State for Scotland also has responsibility for specific Scottish agencies such as the Highlands and Islands Development Board, the Scottish Development Agency and the Scottish Tourist Board.

According to Adams (1984, p.124):

There is a pretence that these [the Scottish Office and its network of 340 councils, boards and commissions] represent only an administration, but in fact they make policy and pass law by the expedient method of Orders in Council and nearly always out of the public eye. It is a very powerful system of government that is separate from the United Kingdom but obedient to the dictates of the centralized government of the unified kingdom. Put another way, Westminster governs Scotland with benign neglect, for which Scots get a form of independence at the cost of political emasculation. The Secretary of State for Scotland has great power over his own fief where he can do as much or as little as he likes but either way it must not disturb the political serenity at Westminster.

However, Lythe and Majmudar (1982, p.167) note:

in matters of macro-economic policy the secretary of state for Scotland stands in the same position as any other 'spending' minister. He can put his case to show why the Scottish Office should be treated in some exceptional way, but he has very little influence over the overall budgetary stance of the UK or over how much is to be made available to the 'spending' ministers.

Devolution of further powers to Scotland, including a proposal for a separate Scottish assembly, was the subject of much debate during the 1970s. However a 1979 referendum saw a rejection of devolution (a majority of those voting were in favour of devolution but they did not constitute the 40 per cent of the registered electorate needed to see the proposal succeed) although many of the issues underlying the earlier debate remain.

Local government in Scotland was reformed in 1973 with the establishment of a two-tier system under which local government functions were divided between 9 regions and 53 district councils (Sewel, 1987). The regions were allocated responsibility for strategic major personal services (eg education and social work) while other functions such as local planning and building control became the responsibility of the districts.

Responsibility for tourism was initially shared by the regions and districts.

Tourism in Great Britain and Scotland

Great Britain has a long established history of tourism. The spas and seaside resorts which emerged in Britain during the eighteenth and nineteenth centuries were among the first in Europe and the forerunners of today's holiday resorts. Touring abroad has its origins in the Grand Tour made by the English gentry in the seventeenth and eighteenth centuries. In the nineteenth century package tours were initiated by Thomas Cook and in 1950 the first inclusive charter tour by air organized by a British operator heralded the new era of international package tourism. The Holiday Pay Act 1935 paved the way for the popularization of holiday taking during the 1950s and 1960s as first domestic tourism then

international tourism expanded. During the 1960s and 1970s Britain in turn became a major destination for international visitors (0.6 million overseas visitors in 1950, 1.7 million in 1960, 6.7 million in 1970, 12.4 million in 1980, 15.8 million in 1988).

Despite the increase in overseas arrivals and some recent stagnation in the home market, domestic tourism remains the largest component of tourism in the UK; its relative importance varies according to the measure used (Table 5.1). The total number of domestic bednights spent in Great Britain is estimated to have declined from 530 million in 1978 to 505 million in 1988 (Anon, 1989). Changes have also occurred in the composition of domestic tourism over this decade, with holiday trips declining from 60 per cent to 55 per cent of the total, and holiday spending dropping from 71 per cent to 63 per cent of the total domestic spend. Business and conference travel increased to account for 25 per cent of the spend in 1988.

There has also been a noticeable decline in

Table 5.1   Distribution of domestic and overseas tourism in the United Kingdom and Scotland (1988)

		Domestic		Overseas		Total	
		millions	%	millions	%	millions	%
Trips/Visitors	UK	130[1]	89	15.8	11	145.8	100
	Scotland	11.0	89	1.3	11	12.3	100
	Scotland⁄UK		8.5		8.2		8.4
Bednights	UK	505[1]	74	173	26	678	100
	Scotland	52.7	80	13.3	20	66	100
	Scotland⁄UK		10.4	7.7	7.7		9.7
Expenditure	UK	£8 100	57	£6 100	43	14 200	
	Scotland	£1 211	76	£383	24	1 594	100
	Scotland⁄UK		15.0	6.2	6.2		11.2

Notes: [1] excluding Northern Ireland
Data sources: Anon (1989); STB (1989a, 1989b)

'main' holidays (of four or more nights), from 37.5 million in 1976 to 28.5 million in 1987 (Lickorish, 1988), though this trend has been offset to some extent by a growth in supplementary 'short break' trips. Lickorish sees a need for better development and marketing of the home product, noting (p.274):

> Domestic travel is poorly packaged and thus lacks the price benefit of bulk buying. Many of the major destinations, the resorts, have in recent years put less effort into product development and presentation, and, compared with foreign destinations, have a low promotion profile.

Wales in particular appears to have suffered from these changes but there was little overall variation

Table 5.2   Regional distribution of domestic bednights in Great Britain (1978–88)

Region	Bednights	
	1978 %	1988 %
Cumbria	1	2
Northumbria	3	3
North West England	8	8
Yorkshire and Humberside	6	6
Heart of England	5	6
East Midlands	5	6
Thames and Chilterns	4	4
East Anglia	9	8
London	6	6
West Country	16	17
Southern	6	8
South East England	8	8
Wales	13	9
Scotland	11	10
Total bednights spent in Great Britain (millions)	530	505

Source: After Anon (1989) from the British Tourism Survey Monthly

in the regional spread of domestic tourism in the period 1978–88 (Table 5.2).

In contrast, trends for overseas visitors have been more positive. The pattern in the 1970s and 1980s has generally been one of steady if not spectacular growth in visitors and bednights, with a slight downturn occurring in the period 1979–81, and again in 1986 (Table 5.3). The apparent increase in overseas visitor expenditure is tempered by inflation. While such spending increased by 143 per cent between 1978 and 1988, this was less than the increase in the price index (153 per cent). However, international tourism performed better in the latter part of this period as visitor spending increased by 52 per cent from 1983 to 1988 whereas the price index went up by only 43 per cent (Anon, 1989).

WTO figures show the UK ranked fifth worldwide in 1988 in terms of both international tourism receipts and international arrivals and fourth as a spender on international tourism. Expenditure exceeded receipts by US$3 504 million (US$14 555 million to US$11 051 million).

Within Britain, London has always been the major focus of overseas visitors, accounting for 40 per cent of all bednights during the decade 1978–88 but up to 60 per cent of all overseas visitor spending. About half of all overseas bednights were spent elsewhere in England (with the South East and West Country being the most popular), 8 per cent in Scotland and 3 per cent in Wales.

Heeley and McVey (1985, p.61) suggest that 'As the most northerly part of the northern half of Britain, Scotland's tourist industry can be seen as a prime victim of this spatial imbalance.' They also draw attention to the dependence of Scottish overseas tourism on the wider British market, noting that about 80 per cent of foreign tourists to Scotland are visiting other parts of Britain and that fewer than 10 per cent of foreign visitors to Scotland use a Scottish gateway. Results from the 1987–8 Overseas Visitors Survey show that the main reasons given by overseas visitors for not visiting Scotland while in England and Wales were: not enough time (41 per cent), Scotland was not part of a package tour (21 per cent) and their friends and relatives lived in England (16 per cent)

Table 5.3   Evolution of overseas visitors to the United Kingdom and Scotland (1976–88)

	Visitors			Nights			Expenditure		
			Scot.			Scot.			Scot.
			UK			UK			UK
	UK (millions)	Scotland	%	UK (millions)	Scotland	%	UK (£ millions)	Scotland	%
1976	10.8	1.0	9.3	134.2	12.5	9.3	1 768	119	6.7
1977	12.28	1.16	9.4	148.5	13.6	9.2	2 352	144	6.1
1978	12.64	1.23	9.7	149.1	13.1	8.8	2 507	145	5.8
1979	12.48	1.12	9.0	154.6	12.6	8.2	2 797	167	6.0
1980	12.42	1.13	9.1	146.0	12.4	8.5	2 961	185	6.3
1981	11.45	0.97	8.4	135.4	11.2	8.3	2 970	168	5.7
1982	11.63	1.05	9.0	136.3	12	8.8	3 188	207	6.5
1983	12.46	1.14	9.2	145	12.1	8.3	4 003	244	6.1
1984	13.64	1.22	8.9	154.5	12	7.8	4 614	275	6.0
1985	14.44	1.28	8.9	167	13.7	8.2	5 442	319	5.9
1986	13.9	1.26	9.0	158.2	12.8	8.0	5 553	360	6.5
1987	15.55	1.41	9.0	178.2	13.6	7.6	6 212	374	6.0
1988	15.8	1.36	8.6	172.9	13.3	7.7	6 146	383	6.2

Data sources: Heeley and McVey (1985); STB (D2.40, 1989b)

Table 5.4   Evolution of domestic tourism in Scotland (1984–8)

	Trips (millions)	Bednights (millions)	Expenditure (millions)
1984	13.1	62.7	£1 161
1985	12.5	57.1	£1 117
1986	11.9	55.6	£1 124
1987	13.4	58.1	£1 521
1988	11.0	52.7	£1 211

Source: STB (D2.37, 1989a)

(STB, 1988a). While 40 per cent of all domestic tourism trips originate within Scotland, Scotland also depends heavily on the English market (59 per cent of all trips, including 19 per cent from the South East and 10 per cent from the North West).

Given this dependence on the wider British market for both domestic and overseas tourists it is scarcely surprising that in recent years patterns and trends of tourism in Scotland have generally reflected those for the UK as a whole (Tables 5.1, 5.2, 5.3). The domestic : overseas ratio is identical or similar for visitors and bednights but the share of overseas visitor spending is lower in Scotland. Scotland has also experienced a decline in domestic tourism (Table 5.4) and some increase in overseas visitors. As a result, its share of the UK total has remained fairly constant at around 10 per cent of domestic bednights, 9 per cent of overseas visitors and 6 per cent of overseas visitor expenditure. A decline in the share of overseas bednights has occurred, however (9.3 per cent in 1976, 7.7 per cent in 1988).

Differences do exist in the composition of overseas visitors. Scotland is much more dependent on the North American market than the UK as a

Table 5.5 Distribution of overseas tourism to Scotland and the United Kingdom by country of origin (1988)

| | Scotland | | UK | |
	No. of trips %	Expenditure %	No. of trips %	Expenditure %
USA	25	25	17	22
FR Germany	10	7	12	7
Canada	9	9	4	9
Eire[1]	8	5	8	5
France	8	5	12	6
Australia	6	7	3	5
Italy	5	4	4	4
Netherlands	3	2	6	3
Denmark	2	2	<2	<2
Switzerland	2	3	3	3
New Zealand	2	2	<2	<2
Spain	2	2	3	4
Other EEC	5	n.a.	7	n.a.
Other Western Europe	4	n.a.	9	n.a.
Other Rest of World	10	n.a.	14	n.a.

Notes:
n.a. not available
1 Estimate
Source: STB (D2.40, 1989b)

whole (Table 5.5). Germany is the leading West European market for Scotland. In the North American and Australasian markets Scotland draws heavily on ethnic ties and visits to friends and relatives. Overall, 62 per cent of overseas visitors to Scotland in 1988 were on holiday, 20 per cent were visiting friends and relatives, 13 per cent were on business and 6 per cent came for other purposes. Respective figures for the UK were 43 per cent, 19 per cent, 26 per cent and 12 per cent, emphasizing the importance of the holiday market for Scotland. Of the 62 per cent who were holidaymakers, 45 per cent were travelling independently and 17 per cent on an inclusive holiday.

Results from the 1987–8 Overseas Visitors Survey highlight the attractiveness of Scotland's scenery to overseas visitors (STB, 1988a). Cultural features – churches, castles, museums, places of historic interest – were also seen as being particularly attractive and the Scots were perceived as being 'friendly people'. However, Heeley and McVey (1985, p.62) believe, 'While Scotland's tourist image is distinctive, the actual tourism products currently offered to overseas visitors are essentially complementary to, and inferior in scale and reputation to, those in England (and London in particular).'

Table 5.6 summarizes other aspects of domestic tourism in Scotland, and highlights the significance of short, secondary holidays, repeat visits, independent, non-touring holidays and the importance of outdoor recreational pursuits.

Tourism is not evenly distributed within Scotland (Figure 5.1). Three regions accounted for almost two-thirds of total tourist expenditure in 1988: Strathclyde (29 per cent), Lothian (18 per cent) and the Highlands and Islands (18 per cent). Overseas tourism is more concentrated, with 72 per cent of overseas visitor expenditure occurring in these three regions compared with 62 per cent of

Table 5.6   Summary of statistics of domestic tourism in Scotland (1988)

Purpose of trip

	% of all trips
Holiday	38
VFR-holiday	18
Total holiday	53
VFR-other	17
Total VFR	35
Business/conference	27
Other	4

Type of holiday

	% of all holiday trips
Main holiday	27
Main equal holiday	15
Second holiday	58
Inclusive holiday	15
Independent holiday	85
First time in last five years	23
Repeat visit	77
Touring holiday	10
Non touring holiday	90

Length of stay

	Av. length of trip (nights)
All trips	4.8
Holiday trips	5.8

Activities undertaken on trip

	% of all trips	% of holiday trips
Walking, rambling, hill walking	18	24
Swimming	8	9
Golf	5	5
Fishing	4	6
Field studies/nature studies	3	3
Sailing/yachting/canoeing	2	3
Shooting/stalking	2	2

Source: STB (D2.37m 1989a)

domestic spending. Little variation occurs in the share of domestic and overseas visitor expenditure received by the leading region, Strathclyde (particularly Glasgow), but the Lothian region attracts a greater share of overseas visitor spending as half of all overseas tourists to Scotland visit

5.1 Regional distribution of tourism in Scotland (Data source: STB 1989a 1989b)

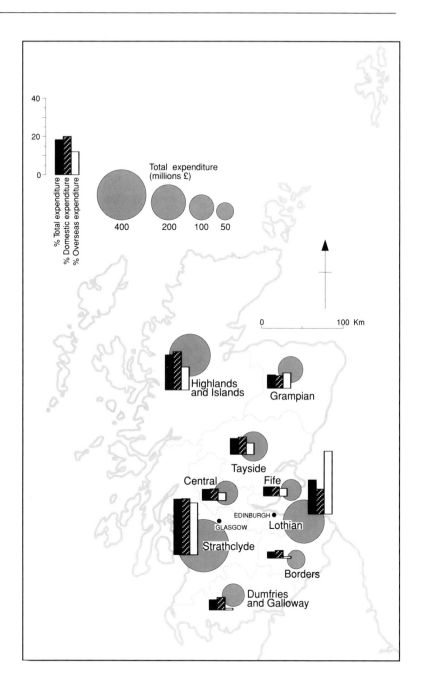

Edinburgh. Conversely, the more distant Highlands and Islands depend more heavily on domestic tourists.

In relative terms tourism is much more significant in the sparsely populated Highlands and Islands region which has only 5 per cent of Scotland's population, compared to Strathclyde's 47 per cent and the Lothian's 15 per cent. Duffield and Long (1981) provide a useful review of tourism's contribution to the Highlands and

Islands, noting (p.15):

> as much as 30 per cent of the working
> population owes its employment in one way or
> another to tourist activity. The HIDB . . . has
> estimated that tourism now earns
> approximately one quarter of the Gross
> Highland Product.

A later paper (Duffield and Long, 1984) presents a more comprehensive picture of the contribution of tourism to the Scottish economy in 1980. This again highlights the relative importance of tourism in the north of Scotland but the authors also note (pp.267–8) that the Central Lowlands 'generates more than half the total economic benefits attributable to tourist spending, be they measured in purchases, income or jobs'. In 1988, the £1.6 billion of tourist expenditure contributed around 5 per cent of Scotland's total GDP (compared with 4 per cent of the UK's GDP).

Many tourist businesses in Scotland, as in other parts of the UK , are small-scale owner managed: almost two-thirds employ no more than five people (STB, 1984a). There is a high rate of turnover, with the 1984 STB survey indicating as many as half the businesses in the accommodation sector had been established in the preceding five years. The average size of a Scottish hotel in 1988 was 19 rooms, with almost half the total room capacity being in hotels with 25 rooms or fewer (STB, 1988b). Some 20 per cent of the hotels had more than 100 rooms. The bigger hotels tend to be part of a large chain, usually owned by companies south of the border (Heeley, 1986a). Stakis is Scotland's leading hotel operator, having 20 hotels with a total capacity of 1,700 rooms in 1985. Heeley also notes (p.78):

> A critical structural weakness of Scotland's
> tourist industry is that (a) the larger tourist
> and leisure companies have so far made few
> attempts to diversify into the sector, and that
> (b) there are few (if any) equivalents to the
> private sector attractions specialists emerging
> south of the border.

Many of the scenic and cultural site attractions are provided by a range of non-profit agencies such as local authorities, trusts or the Countryside Commission for Scotland (Ewing, 1989).

British tourism policies

Despite the long history of tourism in the United Kingdom and the developments outlined in the preceding section, comparatively little attention politically has been given to tourism. Cooper (1987, p.9) notes that up until the 1980s 'the level of debate on tourism policy has been moribund; tourism was not a political issue and suffered from a lightweight image in comparison to, say, manufacturing industry'. Shaw, Greenwood and Williams (1988, p.172) state 'It is an oft-repeated dictum that government policy towards tourism in the United Kingdom is at best nebulous, in the sense that little official policy actually exists save to emphasize that tourism is a "good thing"'. The development of what policy there has been and subsequent public sector involvement through the creation of tourist organizations has been well traced in a series of papers by Heeley (1981, 1986b, 1989).

The first major piece of tourism legislation in Britain did not come until the passage of the Development of Tourism Act 1969 which created statutory tourist organizations in the form of the British Tourist Authority (BTA) and tourist boards for England (ETB), Scotland (STB) and Wales (WTB). The case of Northern Ireland had been dealt with earlier and separately by the 1948 Development of Tourist Traffic Act (NI) which led to the setting up of a Northern Ireland Tourist Board (Smyth, 1986). Up until 1969 tourism had been promoted by voluntary organizations. A 'Come to Britain' Movement which had been formed by commercial interests in 1926 (later renamed the Travel Association of Great Britain and then the British Travel Association) received a small annual grant from the Exchequer from 1929 to 1969 to promote travel to and within Britain. Voluntary tourist boards had been formed in

Scotland (1930) and Wales (1948) largely because of 'the feeling that Scottish and Welsh interests were not being adequately represented in the work of a London based "English" agency' (Heeley, 1986b, p.4).

According to Heeley (1989, p.370) the 1969 Act's 'overriding political purpose was to boost the foreign exchange earnings associated with international travel to the United Kingdom'. This followed the belated recognition of the growing economic significance of tourism resulting from the growth in overseas arrivals.

According to the Act (2.1):

It shall be the function of the British Tourist Authority –

(a) to encourage people to visit Great Britain and people living in Great Britain to take their holidays there; and

(b) to encourage the provision and improvement of tourist amenities and facilities in Great Britain;

and the English Tourist Board, the Scottish Tourist Board and the Wales Tourist Board have like functions as respects England, Scotland and Wales respectively.

However, a subsequent clause (2.3) reserved the right of overseas promotion exclusively to the BTA, leaving the country tourist boards to promote domestic tourism and foster physical development of appropriate plant. Provision was made under Section 4 for the boards to provide financial assistance to the private sector to carry out this latter function. Under Part II of the Act provision was made for hotel development grants which in the early 1970s saw a marked expansion in new hotel building in Britain. Provision was also made for hotel price notification and accommodation classification schemes but these were never implemented.

During the 1970s emphasis was given to regional policy as well as boosting foreign exchange. These two elements were confirmed by the Labour government in 1974 in what Heeley (1989, p.370) labels 'the first ever set of ministerial guidelines for tourism'. There was a clear intention here to shift the pattern of marketing and development expenditure away from London to less well known and established destinations. Although this never fully materialized the policy was later criticized by the Conservative government's Lamont review in 1983 on the grounds that it had led to 'underselling London overseas'. While little new strategy resulted from the Lamont review it did lead to a partial amalgamation of the functions of the BTA and the ETB, which came to have a common chairman and shared premises.

Further reviews followed in 1985 and 1986. Tourism was now linked directly with job creation and responsibility for it passed from the Department of Trade and Industry to the Department of Employment. Emphasis was placed on minimizing public sector obstacles to growth in tourism. However, proposals to abolish the four statutory boards and replace them with a new British Tourist Board having responsibility for all overseas tourism marketing and general oversight of domestic tourism were rejected (Cooper, 1987).

The results of another review were announced in July 1989. This saw a need for the present organization to be simplified and the industry more directly engaged (OECD, 1989). Government-supported promotion would be more sharply focused and proposals were put forward to devolve responsibilities from the BTA in London to its overseas operations and from the ETB to the regional tourist boards.

Tourist organizations in Great Britain

Figure 5.2 depicts the basic framework of tourist organizations in Britain in 1989 as established by the Development of Tourism Act 1969. The major administrative change over the two decades was the transfer of responsibility for the BTA and ETB from Trade and Industry to Employment. The STB and WTB remain respectively the responsibilities of the Scottish and Welsh Offices. Beneath the ETB and WTB a network of regional tourist boards and councils has emerged; in

5.2 Network of tourist
organizations in Great Britain

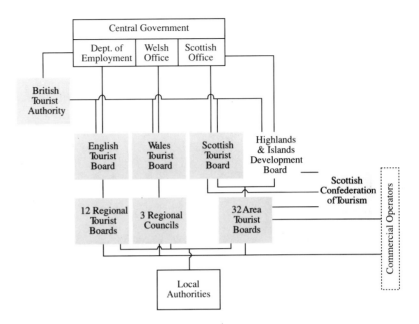

Scotland there is a lower level of area tourist
boards. In Scotland, a regional development
agency, the Highlands and Islands Development
Board, also plays an active role in tourism.

While the 1969 Act was reasonably
comprehensive – incorporating both promotional
and developmental functions and distinguishing
between domestic and international areas of
responsibility – the framework it set up was not
without its problems. Lickorish (1988, p.277), a
former director general of the BTA, reports:

> The machinery was cumbersome with
> inadequate consultative or coordination
> provision. Each tourist board was given
> basically similar powers except that overseas
> promotion was restricted to the BTA. This
> held back the necessary harmonious and
> practical joint working by the agencies for
> some time.

Co-ordination of the work of the four agencies
was not facilitated by the lack of strong central
government policies on tourism and the spreading
of responsibility among the three ministers. As
Cooper (1987) notes, the devolved administrative

arrangement led to significant disparities among the
three boards in terms of funding relative to the size
of their tourist industries, for the Secretaries of
State for Scotland and Wales enjoyed greater
freedom over tourism spending (Tables 5.2, 5.3
and 5.7). Heeley (1986b, p.9) points out though
that 'it can of course be argued that the successful
marketing and development of tourism in Scotland
and Wales requires a higher level of funding than
elsewhere in Great Britain'. Scotland also came to
obtain limited rights to promote overseas.

The BTA has essentially focused its activities on
overseas tourism even though it may develop
domestic tourism under the 1969 Act. Its
objectives, as laid out in its 1989 annual report, are:

1   To maximize the benefit to the economy of tourism
to Britain from abroad while working worldwide in
partnership with the private and public sector
organizations involved in the industry and the
English, Scottish and Wales Tourist Boards.

2   To identify the requirements of visitors to Britain,
whatever their origin, and to stimulate the
improvement of the quality of product and the use
of technology to meet them.

Table 5.7 *Government support to country tourist boards in Great Britain (1985–6)*

	Grant-in-aid (£m)	Section 4 Tourism Projects (£m)
English Tourist Board	8.8	7.9
Wales Tourist Board	5.2	2.5
Scottish Tourist Board	5.9	3.0

Source: After Cooper (1987)

3 To spread the economic benefit of tourism to Britain more widely and particularly to areas with tourism potential and higher than average levels of unemployment.

4 To encourage tourism to Britain in off-peak periods.

5 To advise government on tourism matters affecting Britain as a whole.

6 To ensure that the BTA makes the most cost-effective use of resources in pursuing its objectives.

Headquartered in London, the BTA had twenty-three offices in nineteen countries around the world. Government funding of the BTA rose from £2.9 million in 1969 to £22 million in 1987. Non-government funding for co-operative marketing ventures rose from £0.74 million to £14.4 million over this period, with non-government funding constituting two-thirds of the BTA's £24 million marketing spend in 1989. However, total BTA funding from all sources fell from 1 per cent of the overseas visitor spend in 1969 to 0.6 per cent in 1987. Despite this, Britain had risen from eighth to fifth place worldwide in terms of international tourism earnings.

Each of the three country boards has developed in its own way under the general provisions of the 1969 Act. Further information on the activities of the ETB and regional tourist boards in England is provided by ETB (1981), Heeley (1986c), Bowes (1988), Shaw et al (1987) and Shaw, Greenwood and Williams (1988). Subsequent discussion here will focus on the STB and other organizations which play a major role in tourism under the administrative system which has evolved in

Scotland, namely the Highlands and Islands Development Board and the area tourist boards. It should be noted that other agencies not considered here also may play an important role, particularly in terms of physical development, for example the Scottish Development Agency, the Countryside Commission for Scotland and the regional and district councils, whose planning schemes and development work may include tourism projects (McVey and Heeley, 1984).

The Scottish Tourist Board

As established under the Development of Tourism Act 1969, the Scottish Tourist Board is the statutory body for tourism in Scotland whose principal responsibilities are to encourage the British to take holidays in Scotland, to encourage the provision of tourist facilities and amenities in Scotland, and to advise government and public bodies on matters relating to tourism in Scotland. Under a subsequent Act the STB acquired the right to promote Scotland overseas. The STB consists of a chairman and six members appointed by the Secretary of State for Scotland, employs staff of about 120 and has its headquarters in Edinburgh. While the STB's remit extends to the whole of Scotland, the official marketing and development of tourism in the Highlands and Islands is effectively the preserve of the HIDB.

In the 1980–1 annual report the chairman stated that the STB was adopting 'a much more vigorous approach on a more limited front', an approach characterized by 'the use of aggressive promotional techniques; and a major switch of resources in favour of marketing and development'. During the early 1980s the STB pulled back from its planning activities for which it had become well known in the 1970s and from visitor servicing which came to be seen as a local function.

A fuller statement on the STB's aims and strategies is contained in its 1986 *Business Plan* (STB, 1986a, p.5):

STB's aim is to direct its resources towards the creation of stable tourism employment wherever the potential exists in Scotland. The nature of the tourist industry and the scale of our own resources combine to suggest that we can best achieve that objective by working positively alongside the trade.

While the emphasis on job creation reflects the Scottish situation – the estimated unemployment rate there in 1985 was 15.5 per cent – it also mirrors a broader government policy crystallized by the transfer of tourism (ie responsibility for the BTA and ETB) to the Department of Employment in 1985.

The *Business Plan* (p.6) also explicitly recognizes the multi-faceted nature of the tourist industry and the STB's role therein:

continued progress will be dependent on bringing into close harmony the marketing efforts, product range and quality of the multitude of public authorities and businesses that collectively make up the Scottish tourist industry. *The Scottish Tourist Board's role in achieving this is to provide leadership and act as a focal organization* [emphasis added] that provides:

i)   advice to government, public bodies, major 'carriers', Travel Trade and the private sectors in general;

ii) development of tourism facilities, including selective capital assistance under Section 4 of the 1969 Act;

iii) quality assurance programmes through classification and grading schemes;

iv) national services for visitors (eg signposting, TIC operations, press services; customer information systems, etc);

v)   a structure for collective local enterprise through Area Tourist Boards;

vi) collective national and international marketing.

Given its limited resources – a total annual budget of £10 million in an industry with a sales value of £1 400 million in 1985 – the STB's influence was seen to lie most effectively in financial leverage and in highly developed communications and leadership skills.

The STB derives around 80 per cent of its income from two grant-in-aids from the Scottish Office, a larger one for general operating costs, and a specific grant for Section 4 assistance to tourist projects (Table 5.8). Other income is derived from such activities as the sale of publications and advertising space and charges for miscellaneous services. In terms of expenditure, the STB is notable in the context of the tourist organizations examined in this book for the proportion of its budget devoted to development – over a quarter of its expenditure in the late 1980s went on Section 4 assistance to tourist projects. Nevertheless, marketing remained the dominant activity in terms of money spent, for in addition to direct expenditure on advertising and promotion, a significant share of 'other operating charges' went on associated activities such as publications, distribution, the operation of information centres and services and market research. Moreover, in the broader British context the marketing role of the BTA, which has no development functions, must also be recalled. Assistance is also provided to the area tourist boards.

One of the distinguishing features of the STB's marketing effort is the way in which responsibility for overseas promotion was for long limited by the 1969 Act to the BTA. The STB acquired the power to promote overseas only by passage of special legislation, the Tourism (Overseas Promotion) (Scotland) Act 1984 and then only with approval of the Secretary of State for Scotland after

Table 5.8   Scottish Tourist Board budget (1987–8 and 1988–9)

		1988–9		1987–8	
		£	%	£	%
Income					
HM Government Grant-in-aid		6 807 000	55.5	6 036 000	55.3
Tourist projects (Section 4 grants)		3 137 000	25.5	3 208 000	29.4
Income from activities		2 338 000	19	1 677 000	15.3
	Total	12 282 000	100	10 921 000	100
Expenditure					
Staff costs		1 953 000	16.0	1 809 000	16.3
Advertising		3 194 000	26.1	2 924 000	26.3
Other operating charges		3 033 000	24.8	2 396 000	21.6
Area tourist boards		888 000	7.1	859 000	7.7
Tourist projects		3 177 000	26.0	3 113 000	28
	Total	12 225 000	100	11 101 000	100

Source: STB (1989)

consultation with the BTA.

Under the terms of the 1984 Act, the STB supplements the activity of the BTA overseas. While NTOs may discourage sub-state organizations from promoting overseas – on the grounds of efficiency and that too many images in the market-place may confuse potential travellers – statutory separation of the right to undertake such activity is not common. More often, regional organizations are simply limited by the resources at their disposal.

The issue of overseas promotion had first been vigorously pursued as part of the devolution debate of the 1970s. The STB was to be given specific powers to promote overseas under the proposed Scotland and Wales Bill. The Scottish argument (STB, 1977, p.9) was that 'in the overall management of Scotland's tourism resources, overseas and domestic markets could not be separated as they are at present between two separate organizations' (ie the BTA and the STB). The Scots continued to press their case after the failure of the Bill, appointing a director of overseas tourism in 1981 and arguing (STB, 1982, p.2):

It is not our wish to establish an overseas organization parallel to the British Tourist Authority but it is our intention to press for considerably more freedom to differentiate and to promote Scotland as a destination in its own right.

Although the 1984 Act gave the STB the right to promote Scotland overseas, only modest amounts were made available to fund such activity: £200 000 in 1984, £500 000 in 1989. These limited resources have been directed at the travel trade in Scotland's major markets, particularly North America (Table 5.5). No advertising is undertaken overseas. A major strategy has been the AMNET/SCOTS project which seeks to establish an American network of Specialist Counsellors on Travel to Scotland (SCOTS) through hosting educational visits for specialist travel agents, conducting seminars and road shows in the USA and developing packages appropriate to the US market. In partnership with Scottish Airports, the STB began leading Scottish sales teams on Gateway Scotland missions to the USA and

Canada in 1985 and 1986, another specific response to a perceived Scottish need. An initial sales mission to Japan was undertaken in 1988. The STB also participates regularly in a range of European trade fairs and exhibitions, co-ordinating, often in association with the BTA, the Scottish presence at these events. Scotland-only brochures are also prepared for distribution overseas, again often through BTA offices as the STB maintains none of its own offices abroad.

Given the STB's budget constraints, the BTA representation abroad, and the integration of the Scottish and British markets, the BTA continues to be the major agency promoting Scotland overseas. Reasonably close links and relations appear to be maintained between the marketing staff of the STB and the BTA. STB input is provided into the BTA marketing plan and the STB plan takes account of what the BTA is doing. STB staff attend country marketing meetings with the BTA and BTA overseas office representatives are hosted on familiarization trips within Scotland. Direct contact between the STB and the BTA appears to be increasing with the Scottish Office becoming involved only when differences arise.

The STB continues to be active in the British market which still provides by far the largest source of visitors and tourist expenditure (Table 5.1). Here the STB participates with area tourist boards and trade partners in a variety of exhibitions and trade fairs, produces a wide range of brochures and holiday guides, fosters business travel and, in contrast to overseas, engages in advertising campaigns. The STB notes in its *Business Plan* (STB, 1986a, p.7):

collective marketing and local enterprise require leverage. For instance, our experience is that the Board must provide a minimum of 25 per cent of the gross costs of any national advertising campaign for it to meet our own objectives as well as those of the partner(s) providing the balance of the funding.

Development is the second major function of the STB. Most of the emphasis here has been on administering selective capital assistance under

Section 4 of the 1969 Act from funds provided by the Scottish Office. Tourist project assistance totalled £29 million in the period 1971 to 1986; Strathclyde (£6.2 million), Tayside (£5.4 million), Grampian (£4.4 million) and Lothian (£3.9 million) received the largest amounts (STB, 1986b). In the late 1980s around £3 million per year was budgeted for Section 4 assistance. Up until 1986 much of the assistance went on accommodation (Table 5.9), particularly on small grants (under £8 000). The STB's role was largely reactive, responding to the applications made. Since then it has become more proactive, setting priorities, targeting funds and streamlining procedures (applications under £8 000 are generally no longer considered). High priorities listed in the 1986 *Business Plan* are those projects which result in different or unusual visitor attractions and projects which improve the quality of accommodation, particularly in rural areas. The greater emphasis on attractions aimed at bringing more visitors into Scotland and increasing their stay has brought some new challenges in terms of project assessment as many are one-off projects less amenable to uniform criteria than hotels. Area development priorities were also being established.

The sums involved are not very large in terms of total investment in accommodation, attractions and other sectors but the grants nevertheless appear to play an important pump priming function and be effective in job creation. The STB (1986b) reports that the £6.7 million financial assistance it provided in 1984 and 1985, together with matching funds of £27 million from the private sector and other public agencies, created 701 full-time job equivalents at an average of £9 541 of STB funds per job.

The growing proactive role of the STB is also seen in the establishment of a Product Development Section in 1988 to augment the financial assistance programme. Its remit is 'to formulate development policy for the Board and to initiate projects or programmes that could not be achieved simply by reacting to outside proposals' (STB, 1989c, p.10). The object here is to identify and stimulate, but not necessarily finance, appropriate tourist development projects. To this end, the STB has undertaken or commissioned, often with co-sponsors, major product development

Table 5.9   Distribution of Section 4 assistance grants from the Scottish Tourist Board (1984–5 and 1985–6)

Type of project	1984–5		1985–6	
	Number	STB assistance £	Number	STB assistance £
Hotels	47	1 230 000	71	1 700 000
Caravan sites	5	70 000	10	230 000
Self-catering	7	230 000	7	120 000
Museums and visitor centres	9	340 000	19	540 000
TICs and signposting	7	80 000	13	90 000
Historic houses	1	10 000	7	130 000
Sporting	7	60 000	12	480 000
Restaurants	5	80 000	10	210 000
Other	4	230 000	9	260 000
Total	92	2 330 000	158	3 760 000
Average size of grant		£25 326		£23 747

Source: STB (1986b)

studies or reviews, for example of Edinburgh tourism, heritage attractions, salmon fishing, Scottish Airports and the implications of the Channel Tunnel. Information and advice on product enhancement and development opportunities is channelled to existing or potential operators through the production of development guidance booklets (eg on swimming pools for tourist businesses and heritage attractions), the organization of development seminars for area tourist boards and working with bodies such as the National Farmers Union or major developers such as Center Parcs.

The STB's marketing and development functions have long been supported by an active research programme involving major special purpose commissioned studies, as in product development above, and ongoing statistical series and surveys of tourist demand (eg Tables 5.6 and 5.7). Data on overseas visitors are obtained from the UK International Passenger Survey but in 1984 the STB withdrew its support for the combined British Home Tourism Survey and initiated its own survey of domestic visitors, the National Survey of

Tourism in Scotland. The STB has also been active in monitoring and evaluating its various operations and activities. Results of all these studies and surveys are disseminated widely in a useful series of fact sheets.

The STB also has a separate Visitor Services Division which aims at enhancing the quality of the Scottish product and experience. It operates voluntary accommodation classification and grading schemes, runs a central information department which handles enquiries and complaints and has responsibility for signposting. Two major travel centres – one in London, the other in Edinburgh – complement the STB's marketing effort, encouraging visitors to include Scotland in their trip or to stay longer when there. Scotland's Tourist Information Centre (TIC) network is however operated by the area tourist boards, liaison with which is also the responsibility of this division.

Press and public relations are the responsibility of another division, one which seeks to develop the general image of Scotland as well as highlight specific issues, for example direct flights to Scotland.

The Highlands and Islands Development Board

The HIDB was a broadly based regional development agency set up under a special Act in 1965 (ie before the STB) with a remit

- to assist the people of the Highlands and Islands to improve their economic and social conditions,
- to enable the Highlands and Islands to play a more effective part in economic and social development of the nation.

The HIDB consisted of a chairman and six members, was responsible to the Scottish Office, had its headquarters in Inverness, employed a staff of 250 and had a 1987–8 budget of £37.6 million.

Around a quarter of the HIDB's budget was spent on tourism (about £9 million), a sum not far short of that of the STB (£11.1 million in 1987–8). While not a tourist organization as such, the HIDB nevertheless played a significant role in Scottish tourism, effectively exercising many of the STB's functions in the region for which it was responsible. The board's longstanding involvement in tourism is not surprising given the HIDB's remit, the significance of the sector to the regional economy noted earlier (Duffield and Long, 1981) and the Highlands and Islands' share of Scottish tourism (Figure 5.1). For many years tourism was a separate division within the HIDB, as were other sectors such as fisheries, industrial and business development and land development. Internal restructuring in 1985 saw the major tourism functions become the responsibility of broader directorates for project development and marketing development.

The largest share of the HIDB spending went to development. Over £5 million of financial assistance to tourism was made available in 1987–8 through grants, loans and equity under Section 8 of the 1965 Act. Such assistance consistently exceeded comparable STB expenditure during the 1980s. For the decade 1979–88, tourism accounted for one-third of all HIDB grants and 17 per cent of its loans and equity but only 23 per cent of employment created and 12 per cent of jobs maintained. Hotels and other accommodation received 60 per cent of all tourism grants.

As with the STB, the HIDB's role in this process was largely reactive; within the limits of the funds available, grants were approved if applications met the basic criteria. However, in the late 1980s a more proactive stance was adopted with steps being taken to develop a more comprehensive strategy which would form the basis for future development and funding assistance. A major review highlighted the importance of the main centres – Inverness, Aviemore, Fort William and Oban – and the necessity for smaller centres to be developed on realistic scales. A need was also identified for local area development strategies which were to be prepared during 1989 based on local input and initiatives from the local authorities and, in particular, the ATBs. The board's role here was seen in these terms (HIDB, 1988, p.5):

> The Board alone, for the HIDB area, is in a position to draw together all the strands of the strategy which can command the respect of all the other parties in the Highlands and Islands. . . . Yet at the same time it cannot be a 'top-down' strategy only. There are so many variations in local conditions and needs, within our area, with a large element of 'bottom-up' thinking needed also if the strategy is to be relevant as a framework for action.

Shortage of in-house staff resources – there are only three people in the tourism division of the project development directorate – may also have influenced this approach.

Pilot development programmes were also being established in 1988 and 1989 in Orkney, Argyll and Easter Ross. In Orkney, for example, the aim was to put in a more intensive effort utilizing existing funds through the appointment of a tourist development officer jointly funded by the island council, the ATB and the HIDB.

With major projects, such as ski-field

development near Fort William, the HIDB acted as a catalyst and co-ordinator, pulling together local authorities and developers, co-funding feasibility studies, providing technical assistance and presenting the case to the Scottish Office for financial assistance.

Marketing was an essential complement to these development activities. While the HIDB did not have a specific remit to promote tourism, it could and chose to do so both within the UK and overseas. The HIDB saw itself as having a leadership role and developing a strong regional image (HIDB, 1984, p.17).

> While individual businesses and area tourist boards each have a role to play in marketing the Highlands and Islands, the board are uniquely placed to undertake the type of leadership campaign which is essential if the area is to be established in the minds of the masses of potential visitors as an attractive and accessible holiday destination.

The HIDB's main marketing objectives (HIDB, 1989, p.19) were

- to increase the amount and geographical spread of visitor spending,
- to extend the visitor season,
- to create job opportunities,
- to work with the STB and ATBs in promoting the Highlands and Islands as a holiday destination.

Overseas promotion was limited by funding and most such activity was undertaken jointly with the STB and BTA. With the domestic market, on the other hand, the HIDB ran its own campaigns emphasizing in particular those elements where it has strong and distinctive niches, such as hunting, fishing and skiing. A separate advanced booking system for the Highlands and Islands, Hi-Line, was operated out of Dingwall. The HIDB also had a joint marketing ventures scheme which offered financial assistance to operators and the organizers of festivals and events.

Restructuring in April 1991 saw the HIDB replaced by a new network comprised of Highlands and Islands Enterprise at the core and ten Local

Enterprise Companies (LECs). As well as its broad range of economic and social development work, HIE remains the lead public sector agency for the development and promotion of tourism in the Highlands and Islands, concentrating its energies into marketing the region within the UK, visitor servicing, assistance to tourism businesses (Section 4 assistance has been replaced by a new scheme), piloting ideas and projects, environmental improvement, training and research. The LECs have a role in some of these activities (e.g. training and pilot projects) while visitor servicing continues to be the responsibility of the ATBs. HIE is also represented on the board of the STB.

The budgeted expenditure figures for the HIE network for 1991/92 are as follows:

Financial assistance for business	£6 700 000
Central marketing	2 050 000
Support for ATBs	1 850 000
Projects and pilots	500 000
Market research	130 000
Training (excluding general schemes)	110 000
Total	£11 340 000

The total figure represents 18% of HIE's total operational budget for 1991/92.

HIE's strategic approach to tourism highlights seven priorities:

- extending the tourist season and raising occupancy levels,
- increasing length-of-stay and visitor dispersal,
- improving the quality of the tourist product,
- developing skills,
- enhancing the effectiveness of tourism marketing efforts,
- integrating tourism development and environmental concerns,
- strengthening the links between tourism and other sectors.

Area tourist boards

Scotland has a well developed network of thirty-two

5.3 Area tourist boards in Scotland
(Source: After STB)

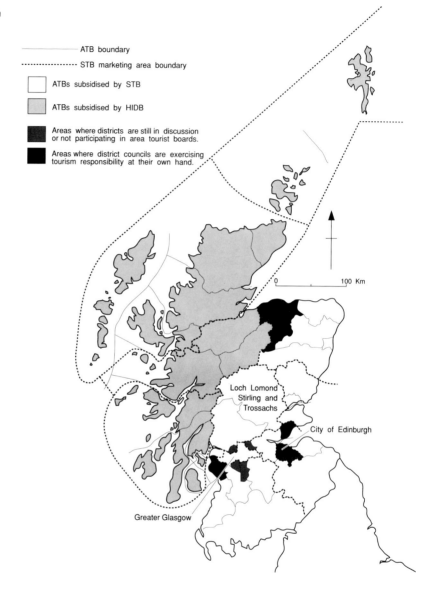

————————— ATB boundary

·················· STB marketing area boundary

▢ ATBs subsidised by STB

▨ ATBs subsidised by HIDB

■ Areas where districts are still in discussion or not participating in area tourist boards.

■ Areas where district councils are exercising tourism responsibility at their own hand.

100 Km

Loch Lomond Stirling and Trossachs

City of Edinburgh

Greater Glasgow

local tourist organizations known as area tourist boards (ATBs). These are voluntary associations which primarily bring together local authorities and tourist industry members and are grant-aided by either the STB or the HIDB. The ATB network covers most of Scotland although certain district councils, notably Edinburgh, have retained responsibility for tourism in their own hand and a number of less tourist-oriented districts have opted not to participate (Figure 5.3). Many of the ATBs bring together two or more district councils. Some, particularly the major metropolitan centres or larger rural districts, correspond to a single district council, while in the case of Argyll and Bute the council's district is split among three ATBs. The ATBs had a total budget of almost £8 million in

1988–9, an average of nearly £250 000 each. For the network as a whole, the local authorities contributed 40 per cent of the funding, the remaining income being derived almost equally from the membership, the STB or HIDB and other sources such as retail sales (Table 5.10). In 1987 the ATBs had a total of 14 000 members, many of them small accommodation proprietors.

Significant variations occur in the size and composition of the ATB budgets which on average are greater in the central and southern regions covered by the STB than in the more sparsely populated Highlands and Islands where the HIDB has responsibility. The average grants of the STB and HIDB are comparable but in the central and southern regions, particularly in the major urban

Table 5.10   Sources of income of Scottish area tourist boards (1988/9)

	Local authority £	STB/HIDB £	Membership £	Other £	Total £
Aviemore & Spey Valley	36 750	51 445	94 854	61 462	244 511
Caithness	24 440	36 509	16 809	12 309	90 067
Dunoon & Cowal	19 151	46 617	38 953	99 504	204 255
Fort William & Lochaber	28 500	48 080	119 993	106 223	302 795
Inverness, Loch Ness & Nairn	38 550	47 807	128 500	104 300	319 157
Isle of Arran	6 800	43 500	29 438	8 720	88 458
Isle of Bute	19 151	41 425	16 632	8 050	85 258
Isle of Sky & S.W. Ross	12 127	40 000	58 723	31 380	142 230
Mid Argyll, Kintyre & Islay	23 290	55 643	36 095	7 998	123 026
ban, Mull & District	23 172	38 538	94 854	61 462	218 026
Orkney	106 800	58 968	49 962	40 496	256 226
Outer Hebrides	17 672	47 112	33 059	17 200	115 043
Ross and Cromarty	57 750	47 800	63 065	81 080	249 695
Shetland	191 000	44 300	37 000	18 000	290 300
Sutherland	14 040	39 980	23 460	33 079	110 559
All HIDB areas: Total	619 193	687 724	841 397	691 263	2 839 577
mean	41 279	45 848	56 093	46 084	189 305
%	21.8	24.2	29.6	24.3	100
Angus	94 000	38 200	13 520	6 800	152 250
Ayrshire & Burns County	104 560	53 500	30 960	20 160	208 910
Ayrshire Valleys	40 000	35 108	2 396	12 017	89 521
Banff and Buchan	107 420	31 700	9 295	3 505	151 920
City of Aberdeen	273 000	59 100	30 650	51 000	413 750
City of Dundee	205 540	41 620	38 050	22 600	307 810
Clyde Valley	53 300	35 495	22 300	30 000	141 095
Dumfries & Galloway	124 180	68 500	101 600	87 270	381 550
East Lothian	154 240	43 210	17 410	13 250	228 110
Forth Valley	47 660	35 495	10 159	13 520	106 824
Gordon District	68 000	30 200	7 700	8 385	114 285
Greater Glasgow	659 900	65 500	89 500	177 000	991 900

Table 5.10   Sources of income of Scottish area tourist boards (1988/9) (continued)

		Local authority £	STB/HIDB £	Membership £	Other £	Total £
Kincardine & Deeside		60 000	31 700	35 986	26 914	154 600
Loch Lomond, Stirling & Trossachs		154 950	66 500	123 928	182 734	528 122
Perthshire		234 650	66 500	143 188	124 478	568 816
St Andrews & North East Fife		85 000	54 187	42 953	23 800	205 940
Scottish Borders		96 739	69 500	111 482	49 642	327 183
All STB areas:	Total	2 563 129	826 015	830 807	852 894	5 072 845
	mean	150 772	48 589	48 871	50 170	298 402
	%	50.5	16.3	16.4	16.8	100
Scotland	Total	3 182 322	1 513 739	1 672 204	1 544 157	7 912 422
	mean	99 447	47 304	52 256	48 255	247 263
	%	40.2	19.1	21.1	19.5	100

Source: After STB (1989c)

areas, local authority contributions are higher while the Highland and Island ATBs raise more income from their members.

The present ATB structure has its origins in local government reorganization and HIDB initiatives (STB, 1980, 1983, 1984b; Heeley, 1986b). In the period that followed the local government reform of 1973, responsibility for tourism was shared concurrently by both the regional and district councils. Some private sector associations were also developing. The STB in its annual report for 1979–80 (STB, 1980, p.8) called for greater co-ordination between the different bodies:

We must agree on roles for the various agencies involved and match the professionalism and vigour of the promoters of overseas holidays if we are to compete with them successfully in the home market. For these reasons the Board has welcomed the appointment of the Stodart Committee to look into the question of duplicated functions – of which tourism is one – in Scottish local government.

The outcome of the Stodart Report (1981) was the Local Government and Planning (Scotland) Act 1982 which limited responsibility for tourism to the district and island councils, removing regional council power in this field. Stodart had also recommended the local authorities become involved with the trade through area tourist organizations. Within the Highlands and Islands the HIDB had already established sixteen ATBs in the 1970s. This model was quickly adopted for the remainder of Scotland where the government provided additional funding to the STB to facilitate their establishment.

The Scottish Confederation of Tourism (SCOT) was created in 1983 to co-ordinate the ATB network and provide a forum to discuss issues of mutual interest. SCOT brings together twice a year representatives of each of the ATBs, the HIDB and the STB. In 1988 and 1989 topics covered included forestry policy, classification and grading and reports from SCOT's specialist sub-committees on salmon and sea-angling, rating and transport. Discussions were also held with the minister on the future funding of Scottish tourism.

The ATBs have played an important role in

visitor servicing, developing the network of TICs which provide local information and a booking service through the BABA (Book a Bed Ahead) system. ATBs also market their areas through producing local brochures, accommodation guides and other publications, many of which are distributed by the STB and HIDB, and advertising, usually in joint campaigns. They also do press and public relations work, host 'fam' trips and release staff to participate in trade fairs and exhibitions, where they provide an important complement to STB or HIDB personnel. ATBs also become involved in development. The more active will take development initiatives within their area, lobbying the local authorities on tourism issues and stimulating the trade. The STB and HIDB frequently seek the advice of ATB officers regarding grant applications from within their areas and, increasingly, the ATBs are playing a part in the formulation of area development strategies as noted above. While marketing and development staff may be in contact with the ATBs, general co-ordination with them is maintained by area liaison officers.

The structure and activities of ATBs will now be illustrated further by closer examination of the Greater Glasgow and the Loch Lomond, Stirling and Trossachs Tourist Boards, two of the largest and more progressive ATBs (Table 5.11). Both these ATBs, which were established in 1983, emphasize the public–private sector 'partnership'. The Greater Glasgow Tourist Board and Convention Bureau is quite explicit in the preamble to its annual report (GGTBCB, 1988):

> Tourism must recognize the role of the public sector in the provision of tourist attractions, amenities and facilities and that of the private sector in servicing visitor requirements.
> [The board] is a partnership between the constituent local authorities and trade members from all sectors of the industry formed specifically to present a 'corporate' view of the destination to the National and International markets.

This partnership is reflected in the structure of the executive committee, which is drawn from equal trade and local authority representation, plus one STB representative. The bulk of the funding though comes from the constituent local authorities, particularly Glasgow District Council. Trade membership in 1988 stood at 563, with the annual report noting, 'measured against the potential there is still scope for considerable expansion'.

Glasgow for long was not seen as an integral part of the Scottish holiday product – its image did not correspond with that of 'heather, haggis and tartan' and the city attracted mainly business travellers and those visiting friends and relatives. The board's strategy has been to reposition Glasgow from 'a commercial destination where visitors came because they had to . . . to an urban resort establishing a strong reputation in both the leisure, tourism and meetings markets' (GGTBCB, 1988, p.7). This thrust, drawing on the city's urban and cultural amenities, has capitalized on the 'short break' trend in the domestic market. Its introduction owes much to the appointment of a chief executive who had previous experience of urban tourism in the USA.

Developing the leisure market initially involved a lot of press and public relations activity to improve awareness and a soft sell campaign to create a positive and credible image of Glasgow as a holiday destination, an image strengthened by the Garden Festival in 1988 and its designation as Cultural Capital of Europe during 1990. Emphasis is now shifting to a harder sell. The board has also been active in the overseas market, hosting writers, participating in trade fairs and working with major tour operators to get them to include Glasgow on their British itineraries. Creation of the Convention Bureau has enabled Glasgow to be marketed more aggressively and effectively in this field. Such promotional activity has complemented the development of new plant, such as hotels and the Scottish Exhibition and Conference Centre, as well as the general urban revitalization which has characterized Glasgow in the 1980s.

The Loch Lomond, Stirling and Trossachs Tourist Board presents itself as 'a partnership organization linking the District Councils of Clackmannan, Dunbarton and Stirling, the Scottish

Tourist Board and local traders' (LLSTTB, 1988, p.1). Its objectives are

- to give special attention to the needs of all parts of the area in relation to the promotion and development of tourism,
- to administer and operate TICs within the area and to provide information about the area,
- to maintain contact with other bodies directing the local and national tourism effort and represent members' interests,
- to recognize and encourage local tourist organizations.

The board has its headquarters in Stirling where it has a staff of seven, plus over thirty TIC staff. This ATB has developed a strong membership base (over 900 members in 1988, half of them serviced accommodation operators), ranking third in Scotland on membership contributions and first in terms of 'other' income, primarily retail sales (Table 5.11). Easily accessible from Glasgow and Edinburgh, the region offers traditional Scottish attractions: lake and hill country scenery, 'typical' small towns (eg Callander), historical features (eg Stirling Castle) and local festivals and events.

The local authority–trade partnership, established by the creation of the ATB in 1983, marks a significant step forward in the promotion of tourism in the region. Prior to that time the Central Regional Council had two tourist officers, other local authorities had some separate involvement, the trade had formed a Central Scotland Tourist Association (it had one staff member but few other resources) and a number of small local associations, grouping trade members, ran TICs on a voluntary basis. Creation of the ATB has harnessed these different efforts (except those of the regional council which withdrew from tourism) into a more effective and co-ordinated organization, though traces of the earlier situation remain. The TICs, for example, have been put on a much more professional basis under the ATB, leaving the six local associations to direct their energies largely into organizing tourist entertainment and events (eg ceilidhs, concerts and festivals). They also have a local improvement function. The ATB is also very

member-oriented, having regular meetings with the associations and producing interesting newsletters to keep members up-to-date on promotional and development opportunities. Most marketing, whether advertising or trade fair participation, is done jointly with other ATBs or the STB. Recent effort has also been directed at improving signposting throughout the region, an important consideration for the sightseeing market. Fostering development is a further important function, with ATB staff working closely with the private sector, the district and regional councils and the Scottish Development Agency, for example in the joint Leven Valley initiative. Having local authority members on the board is seen as a definite advantage when planning and other tourist development issues are being pursued. While the ATB draws on and disseminates STB research, it has also co-sponsored specific local or regional studies.

These two examples illustrate well some of the diversity which is to be found among the ATBs. While each performs similar functions in promoting tourism in its area, the emphasis given and approach adopted reflect local conditions. Glasgow's marketing effort reflects a very specific response to the city's needs while the more wide-ranging, membership oriented activities of the Loch Lomond, Trossachs and Stirling ATB result from a different set of conditions and antecedents.

Interorganizational interaction

A complex network of organizations with responsibility for tourism developed in Scotland during the 1970s and 1980s. The development of this network has been characterized by certain stresses and strains as the various organizations have sought, in Benson's (1975) terms, to establish their respective domains regarding functions, authority and resources. As these issues have been worked through on one scale, interorganizational conflict has often emerged at another.

As discussed earlier, the main issue during the late 1970s and early 1980s was the STB's struggle to establish its right to promote Scotland abroad, overseas promotion being limited by the 1969 Act to the BTA. Passage of special legislation in 1984, argued on the grounds of Scotland's special case and the need to combine domestic and overseas marketing, gave the STB the authority to undertake such promotion but the corresponding resources allocated for it to do so were rather modest. As a result, the official marketing of Scotland abroad continues to depend heavily on the BTA with whom the STB now appears to have developed a good working relationship.

Within Scotland, the STB has shared the development and promotion of tourism with the HIDB which had assumed these responsibilities in the Highlands and Islands before the STB had been created and subsequently has sought to retain them as part of its broad regional development remit. The interaction between these two Scottish agencies has been characterized by both co-ordination and competition. Some co-ordination, for example, has been provided by the presence of an HIDB representative on the STB board. The STB, following the recommendations of the Stodart Report, set up its ATB network along the lines of that established in the north, at the same time recruiting as its chief executive the HIDB tourism director. However, in 1983 the STB also made a play to take over the marketing functions of the HIDB during an inquiry into that body's operations (Heeley, 1985, p.57):

> In essence, the STB case was that a 'simplified' and more cost-effective approach could be achieved by stripping the HIDB of its marketing responsibilities and transferring them to the STB. This would leave HIDB to continue its involvement in tourism but only as a development authority administering schemes of financial assistance to capital projects. . . . However, the real effect would be to emasculate HIDB as a tourism authority.

The arguments of duplication, centralization and special case put forward by the two parties are not dissimilar to those advanced at a higher level regarding the BTA–STB relationship. The HIDB retained its marketing functions and with some acceptance of their respective domains the relationships between the two bodies subsequently appear to have improved. An integrated national media campaign was undertaken by the STB, HIDB and the ATBs for the first time in 1987–8.

Local organizations, the ATBs, have been fostered by the HIDB and then by the STB. Their establishment was seen as a means of removing duplication of effort at the local level. Visitor servicing, particularly the operation of the TICs, has been viewed as an appropriate and uncontested ATB function. The ATBs also provide a 'focal point for contact with the trade', an important function in an industry characterized by a large number of small operators, many of them in rural areas. Marketing and other information has been disseminated by the STB and HIDB outwards to the trade via the ATBs and in the late 1980s local input into development strategies was increasingly being sought via the ATBs. The establishment of the Scottish Confederation of Tourism provided a forum for the horizontal co-ordination of ATB interests.

Relations between the STB and ATBs, however, became severely strained in 1988 and 1989 over STB proposals to promote Scotland as five major regions. The STB had found it difficult to advertise and distribute information on the more than thirty areas represented by the ATBs and other local authorities. Research commissioned in the English market bore out the STB belief that Scotland was not perceived by the potential holidaymaker in such small areas, with five major regions being identified as a more logical basis for marketing purposes. Such an approach, however, meant some loss of local identity which was resented by many ATBs who would not have been seen to be representing the interests of their membership if their local areas were not presented directly. Intensive lobbying followed from some ATBs, particularly those who felt their area's interests would be lost in a larger region. One Glasgow staff member expressed the view that 'The STB had got hooked on geography not product'. Many in Ayrshire felt their rural touring product was not compatible with the urban image fostered by Glasgow. Glasgow was subsequently separated out, which in turn led to separate status for Edinburgh, even though those in the Lothian region were keen to retain their links with the city. Further north, the Orkneys and Shetlands were felt to appeal to a different market than that of the rest of the Highlands and Islands. In the end the original five regions became seven, then nine, then eleven (Figure 5.3). These marketing regions will be used in holiday guides where appropriate, in advertising and at exhibitions. An interim compromise adopted over the questions of areas and regions was the inclusion of 'tick boxes' by which members of the public could request additional information on selected areas.

The STB's streamlining of Section 4 applications by considering grants only above £8 000 was also not viewed favourably by some ATBs. The Loch Lomond, Stirling and Trossachs ATB called for the introduction of a 'low bureaucracy' scheme of assistance for small-scale projects. The issue here would again appear to be

one of the STB taking a more general and larger scale view, this time of development priorities, with the ATB representing its members' interests at the local level. The Stirling District Council responded to the STB policy by an experimental grants scheme aimed at assisting smaller operators to upgrade and extend their tourist accommodation.

More generally, there was a feeling among some ATBs that the STB was distancing itself from the local organizations though this attitude runs counter to the increased local input being solicited in the formulation of development strategies. These various issues represent a phase of adjustment during which the relationships between the STB and the ATBs are worked through in the same manner that it took a number of years for the different domains of the BTA, STB and HIDB to be established. It is likely that further changes may occur before the process is complete, or at least there is a period of stability, a process that may see amalgamations and possible grant-aiding on a performance basis.

6

The Netherlands

The Netherlands provides a second example of tourism in a unitary state and one which provides further illustration of the influence of political structures and other environmental factors on tourist organizations. These factors are briefly outlined, the nature of tourism in the Netherlands is discussed and organizations, policies and planning are reviewed. Attention is then directed at the national tourist organization, the Netherlands Board of Tourism, and the nationwide network of local and provincial tourist organizations, the VVVs. Other organizations involved in tourism and recreation are then considered before conclusions are drawn.

Environmental factors

The Netherlands is a small densely populated country (1989 population 14.8 million, area 33 933 sq km, density 436 persons per sq km), forming part of the large urban industrial heart of north-west Europe. Much of the population and economic activity is concentrated in the three western provinces of North and South Holland and Utrecht, particularly in the large urban agglomeration known as the Randstad, comprised of Amsterdam, Rotterdam, the Hague and Utrecht and adjoining areas. There is also a well-developed urban network throughout the remainder of the country, but the northern provinces in particular are less densely populated. The Dutch economy is well developed and has a strong international orientation.

The Netherlands is a very flat, low-lying country with a long history of land reclamation and extensive polder construction. Uplands are absent but some rolling hill country is to be found in Limburg. The undulating heathlands, woods and sandy dunes of the Veluwe (in Gelderland) constitute an open and attractive area for outdoor recreation. Water is a dominant feature of the Dutch landscape: the North Sea coast, the many lakes, especially in Friesland, the large European rivers which traverse the lower central part of the country (the Rhine and the Meuse) and an abundance of canals.

The Netherlands is a unitary state with a constitutional monarchy. Central legislative power is held by the bicameral States-General, the first Chamber of which is indirectly elected by members of the twelve Provincial Councils, the Second Chamber directly by universal adult suffrage. The central executive power rests with the Crown (the monarch and the ministers), but is essentially exercised by the Council of Ministers led by the prime minister. Each of the twelve provinces is administered by an appointed commissioner and an elected representative assembly, the Provincial States. Its executive consists of six members and the royal commissioner. The Provincial States may issue ordinances concerning the province's welfare and raise taxes but provincial ordinances and budgets must be approved by the Crown. The unit of local government is the municipality (*gemeente*) which is governed by a municipal council.

The Netherlands has a rich tradition in the field of physical and regional planning, arising out of a long experience of land management schemes and

Table 6.1 Evolution of long holidays in the Netherlands (1981–90)

		1981	1982	1983	1984	1985	1986	1987	1988	1989	1990
Travel propensity	%	65.8	65.8	63.9	64.1	63.7	64.5	66.9	69.5	71.8	69.9
Total holidays	millions	13.0	13.2	12.4	12.8	12.8	13.3	14.8	15.4	16.6	16.3
domestic	millions	5.9	6.2	6.0	6.2	6.2	6.0	6.8	6.5	7.0	7.3
international	millions	7.1	7.0	6.4	6.6	6.6	7.3	8.0	8.9	9.5	9.0
% international		54	53	52	51	52	55	54	58	57	55

Source: After NRIT (1989, 1991)

the need to cope with the many pressures which develop in a small, densely populated country.

Tourism in the Netherlands

Tourism in the Netherlands is influenced by the size and location of the country, its dense population and its standard of living. Small size and limited variation in relief have restricted the range of recreational resources while high population densities have put pressure on those that are available. Levels of economic development have contributed to high travel propensities, particularly for international tourism.

Domestic bednights constitute over 80 per cent of all tourist bednights spent in the Netherlands. Table 6.1 shows that throughout the 1980s about two-thirds of the Dutch population took a long vacation (of four nights or more), with more than half of these being spent outside the Netherlands. For much of the decade the total number of domestic holidays taken was relatively stable. International outbound travel was checked in the mid-1980s but showed substantial growth by the end of the decade. In 1988 the Netherlands ranked sixth worldwide in terms of expenditure on international tourism but only sixteenth in terms of receipts. A growing imbalance between receipts and expenditure is shown in Table 6.2, although some reversal in this trend appeared to be setting in as the 1980s ended.

Table 6.2 also depicts a pattern of erratic growth in foreign arrivals and bednights for the decade

1977–86. Some growth occurred in the early 1980s (1983 excepted) but by 1986 some levelling off was apparent. Germany, Great Britain, the USA and Belgium/Luxembourg constituted the four leading markets in 1986 (Table 6.3). Germans accounted for half of all the foreign bednights.

Significant regional variations occur in the distribution of domestic and international bednights (Figure 6.1). Domestic tourism is the most dispersed, as many holidaymakers leave the crowded urban areas of the western provinces. Gelderland, with the Veluwe, is the most popular province with the Dutch. The coastal provinces are also important, along with North Brabant and Limburg in the south.

In contrast, almost half the international bednights are recorded in North and South Holland, with Amsterdam alone accounting for 17 per cent of the total. This concentration reflects not only the business component, but also the general attractiveness of Amsterdam with its canals, architecture, wealth of museums and art galleries and the nearby tulip fields. Schiphol airport is also the major point of entry for long-haul travellers into the Netherlands. The coasts of North and South Holland, together with that of Zeeland, also attract foreign visitors but the other provinces, with the exception of Gelderland and Friesland, are of only minor importance. The mix of international markets also varies from province to province. Germans accounted for 35 per cent of all arrivals in 1986 but over half in Friesland (76 per cent), Drenthe (52 per cent), Flevoland (65 per cent),

Table 6.2   Evolution of international tourism in the Netherlands (1977–90)

	Foreign arrivals in registered accommodation[1]		Foreign bednights in registered accommodation[2]		International tourism receipts (millions of guilders)	International tourism expenditure (millions of guilders)
	No.	%	No.	%		
1977	3 866 300		11 548 200		2 724	6 016
1978	3 600 000	−6.7	9 851 200	−14.6	2 708	7 360
1979	3 830 700	6.4	11 254 800	14.1	2 720	7 996
1980	3 849 400	0.5	11 327 200	0.6	3 305	9 273
1981	3 975 800	3.3	11 783 200	4.0	4 106	8 920
1982	4 203 700	5.7	12 763 500	8.3	4 835	9 612
1983	4 151 100	−1.2	12 362 300	−3.1	4 495	9 857
1984	4 629 300	11.5	13 905 500	12.5	5 438	10 528
1985	4 701 500	1.6	13 916 400	0.1	5 514	11 446
1986	4 536 800	−3.5	13 953 100	0.3	5 437	12 008
1987					5 471	13 009
1988					5 680	13 315
1989					6 471	13 739
1990					6 576	13 342

Notes: [1] hotels, camping sites, guest houses, youth hotels
[2] hotels, camping sites, guest houses, youth hotels, youth hostels
Sources: NBT (1988b); NRIT (1991)

Gelderland (54 per cent), and Zeeland (67 per cent). Proximity to the urban concentrations of the Ruhr and availability of water resources are major factors explaining this distribution. British, American and other foreign markets are especially important in the major cities of North and South Holland. Other provinces may also draw heavily on particular markets; Swedes are second ranked in Groningen and Belgians in Zeeland.

International tourism to Amsterdam and the western provinces often forms part of a larger circuit of Western Europe. The average length of stay in the major cities is only a couple of days, whereas averages of five to six days are recorded in Zeeland and Friesland, particularly for those camping or staying in bungalows.

Dutch domestic tourism is characterized by the prominence of self-catering (NRIT, 1989). In the late 1980s around 40 per cent of long holidays were spent in chalets and bungalows and a similar proportion in various forms of camping (in fixed and touring caravans and tents). Hotels accounted for about 6 per cent of long holidays and boats, 5 per cent. Recorded bednights for foreign visitors are shared relatively evenly between hotels and guest houses on the one hand and camping and bungalows on the other. Variations occur from province to province; camping and bungalow accommodation is especially important for foreigners in Zeeland, North Holland (excluding major cities), Friesland and Gelderland while hotels dominate the major cities.

Much tourism in the Netherlands is characterized by independent travel and a large number of small caravan park and chalet village operators. Exceptions to this include Center Parcs,

Table 6.3   Distribution of foreign tourism in the Netherlands by country of origin (1986)

	Foreign arrivals in registered accommodation[1]		Foreign bednights in registered accommodation[2]	
	No.	%	No.	%
FR Germany	1 586 000	35.0	6 932 000	49.7
Great Britain/Ireland	673 000	14.8	1 589 000	11.4
Belgium/Luxembourg	272 000	6.0	1 077 000	7.7
France	299 000	6.6	584 000	4.2
Switzerland	84 000	1.9	185 000	1.3
Italy	147 000	3.2	335 000	2.4
Spain/Portugal	104 000	2.3	231 000	1.7
Denmark	83 000	1.8	182 000	1.3
Sweden	119 000	2.6	233 000	1.7
Norway	61 000	1.3	122 000	0.9
Other Europe	141 000	3.1	323 000	2.3
USA	416 000	9.2	848 000	6.1
Canada	97 000	2.1	180 000	1.3
Other	354 000	7.8	1 133 000	8.0
	4 537 000	97.8	13 953 000	100

Notes: [1] hotels, camping sites, guest houses, youth hotels
       [2] hotels, camping sites, guest houses, youth hotels, youth hostels
Source: After NBT (1988b)

the Dutch holiday village operators, and international tourism in the western provinces where the integration into the international tourist circuit has brought a greater involvement of large hotels, airlines and tour operators.

Total spending on tourism in the Netherlands in 1987 amounted to an estimated 30 billion guilders, about 12 per cent of national private consumption (NBT, 1988a). Domestic tourism generated about 83 per cent of this sum. An estimated 240 000 full-time job equivalents were created by tourism, about 6 per cent of total employment. In 1985, receipts from domestic tourism, including day trips, was 25 billion guilders or about 6 per cent of GNP (OECD, 1987). Total receipts from international tourism represented about 2 per cent of total exports of goods and services.

Organizations, policies and planning

As in Germany, tourism has never occupied a major position within the Dutch Ministry of Economic Affairs, the branch of central government with responsibility for tourism. Tourism comes under the ministry's Directorate General for Services, Small and Medium Businesses and Consumer Policy. The tourism division is primarily responsible for national tourism policy and had a staff of six in 1989. Much input into the division is provided by consultants while NTO functions are exercised by the Netherlands Board of Tourism (Nederlands Bureau voor Toerisme: NBT) which is jointly financed by the

6.1 Regional distribution of tourism in the Netherlands (Data source: NBT)

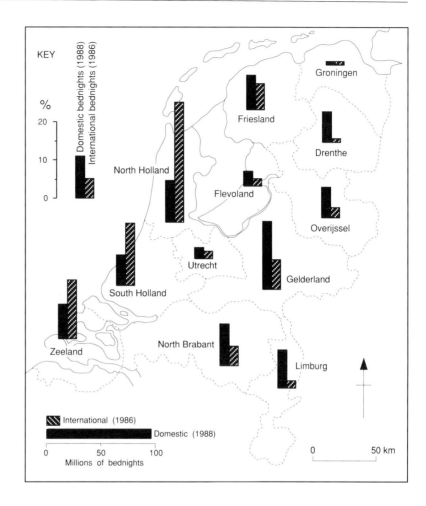

Ministry of Economic Affairs and the private sector (Figure 6.2). There is also a well established network of local, regional and provincial tourist organizations (Vereniging voor Vreemdelingenverkeer: VVVs) which come together under an umbrella organization, the General Netherlands Association of Tourist Information Offices (Algemene Nederlandse Vereniging van VVVs: ANVV). Recreation, an important allied activity in the Netherlands, is now the responsibility of the Ministry of Agriculture, Nature Conservation and Fisheries, having until the late 1970s been part of the Ministry of Culture.

Until comparatively recently the Dutch government took a fairly *laissez-faire* attitude towards tourism. Ashworth and Bergsma (1987,

pp.153–4) speak of 'a long period of relative neglect by governments during which the tourist industry in the Netherlands was severely weakened by the decline in the domestic market'. Broos and Ziegler (1984, p.13) observe:

> up to the mid-70s, Dutch policies related to tourism and recreation planning were in fact social policies directed at the physical distribution and accommodation of growing numbers of recreators. The economic prospects were hardly recognized by anyone outside the private sector. Many local governments even opposed tourism developments in their areas. . . . Also, antipathetic feelings towards the Germans . . . did not particularly help the country to turn

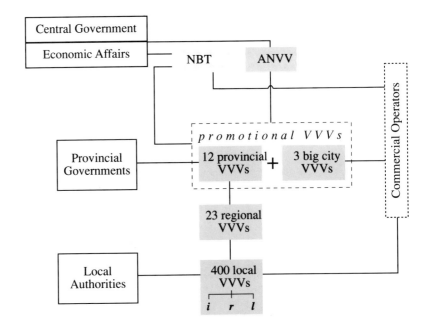

6.2 Network of tourist organizations in the Netherlands

incoming tourism into a healthy economic sector. As a consequence, the Dutch tourism product as it existed in the 70s was no longer able to increase the number of foreign visitors, nor could it retain Dutch holiday-makers, who escaped en masse to Mediterranean destinations.

Concern about the growing gap in international tourism receipts and expenditure (Table 6.2) resulted in the first major tourism policy paper in 1979 (Cornelissen, 1986). The 1979 Tourist Policy Paper focused on three main points:

• better quality and price control in the tourism product (infrastructure, accommodation),
• improved service provisions to enhance presentation of the product,
• stronger promotion of tourism.

Nevertheless, the underlying philosophy was that 'central government should normally limit itself to stimulating and creating favourable conditions for the development of private enterprises' (OECD, 1987, p.36).

Over the next five years some growth was experienced but the travel deficit widened (Table 6.2). Policy Paper II, 1985–9, was issued in 1985 to consolidate these gains. Less attention was now paid to the deficit as such, rather the emphasis was put on the general economic importance of tourism, obtaining the optimum growth in incoming tourism and stimulating the domestic market, for example for secondary holidays. The three policy priorities identified in the 1985 paper (OECD, 1989) were

• stepping up tourist promotion efforts by increasing the budget through the involvement of the tourist industry and better institutional integration,
• improving the tourist product by financial aid to public infrastructure of projects in so-called 'spearhead' regions,
• integrating tourism policy with other related policy fields, eg outdoor recreation, culture and sport.

Approximately 330 million guilders were budgeted over the five-year period to implement these policies, almost half going on promotion, 41 per cent on enhancing the tourist product and the remainder for convention canvassing, research and the improvement of tourist services.

Financial assistance for product development has gone in large part to provincial 'spearhead' projects, some of which were originally identified in the provincial tourism and recreation development plans (*Toeristisch Recreatieve Ontwikkelings Plannen*: TROPs) which were prepared in the early 1980s (Broos and Ziegler, 1984; Boonman, 1986). The TROPs originated in 1980 with a master plan for tourism in Limburg, a plan which had been prepared with assistance from the Ministry of Economic Affairs in response to a downturn in that region's industry and economy. Other provinces experiencing economic problems, such as Drenthe and Groningen, then sought assistance for the preparation of similar plans. Eventually grants were accorded by the Ministry of Economic Affairs, and later Agriculture, to all provinces to prepare a TROP, most of which were carried out for the provincial authorities by two consulting firms. Although planning was well entrenched in the Netherlands, the TROPs marked the first serious attention given to tourism at the provincial level. Up until then the emphasis had essentially been on recreational planning to conserve the landscape and to ensure adequate recreational provision for the residents of densely settled urban areas. With the TROPs came the first attempt to involve commercial operators and to consider economic, rather than just social and environmental issues.

The resultant TROPs were the subject of much debate, a major criticism being that they were based on insufficient or outdated market information. Moreover, being prepared province by province, there was a tendency to overestimate total demand in the Netherlands and to ignore the effects of projects in neighbouring provinces (Boonman, 1986). They did not become statutory plans but rather served as a policy framework for provincial and local governments whose awareness of the potential and the economic significance of tourism had been heightened and who now started to take tourism more seriously. Provincial governments, for example, had not had anyone responsible for tourism previously. There is some suggestion that the Ministry of Economic Affairs had always seen the TROPs as a means of awakening interest in

tourism in the provinces but this could simply be *post-hoc* justification for the plans which appear to have evolved initially without much general sense of direction. Assistance for product development outlined in the Second Tourism Policy Paper has been allocated through the joint five yearly Open-air Recreation and Tourism Programmes of the Ministries of Agriculture and Economic Affairs. Much of this has gone on infrastructural assistance, for example on improving areas for recreational boating. In 1986 eight projects were subsidized to a total of 13.3 million guilders from 52 project applications seeking 90 million guilders in assistance (OECD, 1987).

The Netherlands Board of Tourism

The NBT was set up in 1968 by the Ministry of Economic Affairs and the ANVV with the primary task of promoting tourism to and within the Netherlands. Its establishment resulted from a conscious decision to split off the promotion of tourism at a national level from the other activities of the ANVV. Although a national organization, the NBT was not imposed from above, rather it represents an outgrowth of activities originally initiated at the local level. The first tourist office or VVV in the Netherlands was established in Valkenburg in Limburg in 1885. Others followed on the coast and in towns where tourism was important. A national body, the ANVV, was formed as early as 1915 to further the interests of the local organizations. Gradually, the marketing and promotional functions of the ANVV increased but its ability to deal with these activities effectively suffered from the decision-making delays inherent in a system which required the agreement of more than 400 local offices. A separate national promotional body – the NBT – was therefore seen as desirable, with the VVVs remaining responsible for visitor servicing and local and regional promotion while the ANVV concentrated on furthering the interests of the VVVs and national co-ordination (Figure 6.2).

Headquartered in Leidschendam (near the

Hague), the NBT is an autonomous body, governed by a board, with a staff of about one hundred plus more than fifty personnel in sixteen offices abroad. The promotion and marketing of international and domestic tourism is supported by other functions, namely providing information for the consumer, press and travel industry at home and abroad; product development, planning and research and services provided by the Netherlands Service Center for Tourism (data bank, organization of study trips etc). The product development department, for example, handled advance preparations for the 'Holland Museum Land' promotion of 1988 but the NBT does not become involved in actual physical development, either directly or through allocating development grants.

The goals set by the NBT (1985) for 1985–9 were to

• improve the holiday traffic balance-sheet and increase employment,

• improve the profits of the tourist trade,

• advise the tourist trade and the government,

• offer promotional services,

• encourage co-operation in the promotional domain,

• improve the quality of the tourist product,

• inform the consumer and the travel industry.

The NBT is jointly funded by the Ministry of Economic Affairs and by the tourism industry. During the 1980s it was distinguished by a decrease in the public–private sector funding ratio at a time when its overall budget was increasing (Table 6.4). Some increase in private sector funding, in both relative and absolute terms occurred in the early 1980s but the significant changes come after 1985 as a consequence of the second tourism policy paper which linked additional public funding to proportional increases in the private sector's contribution, with a 50 : 50 target being set for 1989. In the event, the ministry's subsidy that year was 52 per cent. Additional funding was to go on marketing and promotion, with organizational costs (personnel, overheads, etc) to drop to one-third of the annual budget.

The NBT's marketing policy thus has the double goal of stimulating demand and attracting revenue from non-ministry sources. The increases shown in Table 6.4 testify to the NBT's success in developing programmes and campaigns which have attracted the support of the VVVs and the tourist industry. Three major forms of co-operative marketing which enable the participation of large and small partners are pursued by the NBT (NBT, 1985):

• Platform formula: the NBT develops promotional activities in which trade and industry can participate (eg trade fairs), the platform activities form the basis of market cultivation and provide the necessary continuity. The NBT finances roughly 50 per cent of the costs of these activities.

• Special projects, whereby big campaigns are developed and carried out together with a few

Table 6.4   Evolution of the NBT's budget (1980–9)

	1980	1981	1982	1983	1984	1985	1986	1987	1988	1989
					(millions of Dfl)					
Ministry of Economic Affairs subsidy	20.8	21.2	22.3	21.2	21.6	27.0	28.3	31.3	32.2	34.2
Other income	7.7	8.3	9.0	9.7	10.8	15.0	21.9	26.2	29.6	31.7
Total budget	28.5	29.5	31.3	30.9	32.4	42.0	50.2	57.5	61.8	65.9
Subsidy %	73	72	70	69	66	64	56	54	52	52

Source: After NBT (1988b)

participants, for example KLM, hotel chains and tour operators. The NBT finances up to a maximum of 30 per cent.

- Sector and regional promotion consists of a collective promotion plan for several years. The NBT provides a certain amount annually which must be supplemented by the sectors and regions; this is designed to stimulate co-operation between tourist businesses and the VVVs. The NBT finances up to 30 per cent of the promotional costs per project.

This mix of strategies is needed to match the NBT's marketing objectives with the interests – and thus the funding – of the different private sector and regional partners. The carriers, major hotels and inbound tour operators are especially interested in supporting intercontinental promotion, something which is primarily manifested in a higher demand in the western provinces (Figure 6.1). Other regions with less distinctive resources and smaller operators tend to look more to the neighbouring markets, particularly to Germany. The domestic market is also important for spreading the impact of tourism throughout the Netherlands and one that the NBT has fostered by encouraging the Dutch to spend their holidays, particularly their second holidays, in their own country with the slogan 'Have a nice stay in your own country' (*Lekker weg in eigen land*).

The final marketing mix in any year reflects a variety of influences including market trends, the strength of the proposals from the different foreign offices and the interests of the different partners. Although allocating the budget among the various markets is not a straightforward task, the NBT is generally in a good position to balance up competing claims and projects through its greater overall market intelligence.

Originally the NBT dealt with many individual VVVs. Since 1986 that relationship has been streamlined and formalized so that the NBT now undertakes co-operative marketing agreements on a contractual basis with fifteen so-called 'promotional VVVs' – the twelve provincial VVVs plus those of Amsterdam, Rotterdam and the Hague (Figure 6.2). The purpose of the contract is to co-ordinate

the national marketing policy of the NBT with the regional policies of the promotional VVVs, to undertake common activities and to recruit participants for the NBT's activities. The regional policies and activity plans of the promotional VVVs are drawn up in association with the local VVVs and tourist industry in each province. The promotional VVVs thus form a bridge between local and national interests and provide for some 'bottom-up' input into the marketing process.

VVVs

Historically and functionally it is useful to consider the hierarchy of VVVs depicted in Figure 6.2 from the local level up. As noted above, local tourist organizations developed in the Netherlands at the end of the nineteenth century essentially to service visitors to their areas by encouraging the development of appropriate facilities and providing local information. Advertising to attract further visitors followed. Over time, further functions have been added and today, under the umbrella of the national association, the ANVV, some 430 tourist offices operate throughout the country.

Local VVVs

The tourist offices run by the local organizations are classified according to the range of information they provide into three classes: national (*i*), regional (*r*), and local (*l*). Thus in the seventy *i* offices, information is provided on tourism throughout the whole of the Netherlands, whereas the many local offices offer material only on their own area (Plate 6.1). The *i* offices also have a much more extensive accommodation reservations system (many of them are linked into a national computerized network), they may make theatre and other entertainment bookings and act as travel agents, selling holiday packages, usually of other VVVs. Since 1965 the VVVs have acted as outlets for the sale of gift vouchers. In varying degrees the VVVs also advertise and promote their own area.

What distinguishes these Dutch tourist offices

6.1 The Arnhem VVV: one of a network of tourist information offices throughout the Netherlands

from those in many other countries is the extent to which the functions they offer serve a local clientele as well as visitors to the area, for example the theatre bookings, gift vouchers and sales of holiday packages. In Breda (pop. 121 000), for instance, about 45 per cent of the 150 000 customers served annually are estimated to be from the city itself.

Commissions from reservations and sales often add significantly to the VVVs' income. In general, subsidies are made by local authorities to the VVVs for personnel and overhead costs, typically about one-third of their budget, with the remainder being generated by commercial activities and members' contributions. Funding remains a problem in many areas.

Provincial VVVs

While the local VVVs may produce brochures and do some advertising, their primary role is visitor (and resident) servicing through the information offices. Accepting that effective promotional marketing needs to be done at a larger scale, the local VVVs have essentially passed this function to the provincial VVVs, who, as noted earlier, now form the sole point of contact with the NBT. The provincial VVVs also co-ordinate the work of the local tourist offices and provide a link to the ANVV.

A tier of regional (*Streek*) VVVs (not to be confused with regional information offices) exists in some provinces between the local and provincial VVVs (Figure 6.2). The two largest provinces – Gelderland and North Brabant – have six regional VVVs each while two others where tourism is

important – North Holland and Zeeland – have respectively four and five. The brochures of these regional VVVs may broadly correspond to distinct tourist regions, as in the Gelderland where three such areas are commonly recognized: the Veluwe, the Achterhoek and the Gelderland river areas. These form the basis of the regional VVVs, with the city regions of Arnhem and Nijmegen being separated out from the Veluwe and the river area respectively, and the Veluwe being further divided between two VVVs. The regional VVVs have lower level marketing and promotion functions.

Nine of the twelve provincial VVVs are foundations governed by a board, the composition of which varies from province to province. In 1987, the executive committee of North Brabant, for example, consisted of the six chairmen of the regional VVVs, two representatives of the Chamber of Commerce, a representative of the North Brabant provincial government, an auditor and a chairman. The remaining three provinces – Drenthe, Overijssel and South Holland – are associations of local tourist offices. Foundations are thought to provide a structure which provides greater freedom to act and to make decisions more quickly. In either case, the provincial VVVs represent a coming together of the lower level VVVs, as illustrated by the prominence of the regional chairmen in Gelderland, rather than a structure for delegating downwards to the local level. The provincial VVVs are heavily subsidized by the provincial governments and raise other revenue from commercial activities, for example selling advertising space (Table 6.5). The activities

Table 6.5 Budgets of the North Brabant and Rotterdam VVVs

	Provincial VVV North Brabant 1987		Rotterdam VVV 1986	
	Fl.	%	Fl.	%
Income				
Subsidies	464 475	56.4	2 212 362	71.9
Income from promotion and other activities	298 503	36.3	388 057	12.6
Members' contributions	–	–	256 227	8.3
Other	60 108	7.3	220 584	7.2
	823 086	100	3 077 230	100
Expenditure				
Personnel	245 294	30.7	1 659 387	54.0
Promotion	460 868	57.7	650 419	21.2
Overheads and other costs	93 082	11.6	764 049	24.8
	799 244	100	3 073 855	100

Sources: Provinciale VVV Noord-Brabant (1988); VVV Rotterdam (1987).

of the provincial VVVs of Gelderland and North Brabant will now be examined in more detail.

The linking and co-ordinating functions of the Gelderland VVV are well depicted in its own structure diagram (Figure 6.3). Internally, the VVV was divided in 1986 into two major and distinct departments below the level of the director. The general co-ordination of information provision, visitor servicing and other local VVV activities is the responsibility of one department, while marketing and promotion are undertaken by a second, the Gelders Bureau voor Toerisme (GBT). In each case, the provincial office co-ordinates the activities of the regional VVVs and provides the linkage upwards in the system, respectively with the ANVV and the NBT. The VVV also depicts itself as a bridge between demand on the one hand – domestic and foreign tourists – and supply – the tourist industry – on the other.

The North Brabant provincial VVV performs similar functions, though without the dichotomous structure of the Gelderland (it has only three staff).

In the case of North Brabant, the regional VVVs provide the formal and functional contact with the industry; the provincial VVV deals only with the regional VVVs. The provincial VVV, for example, will co-ordinate the compilation and distribution of a catalogue of self-catering holiday packages, with the regional VVVs approaching individual operators in their areas to become part of the programme (Plate 6.2).

The activities of the provincial VVVs are laid out in an annual activity plan drawn up in association with the regional VVVs and in the light of the NBT's annual plan. The Gelderland Activity Plan for 1989 (GBT, 1989, p.5) stresses the synergistic nature of this activity and its resulting benefits in the metaphor 1 + 1 = 3. Co-operative efforts are also emphasized in the introduction to the North Brabant annual report. The bringing together of regional interests and a provincial overview is not, however, necessarily straightforward and some tensions would appear to exist between the two levels, at least in North Brabant.

6.3 Structural diagram of the
Gelderland Provincial VVV
(Source: After Gelderland
Provincial VVV)

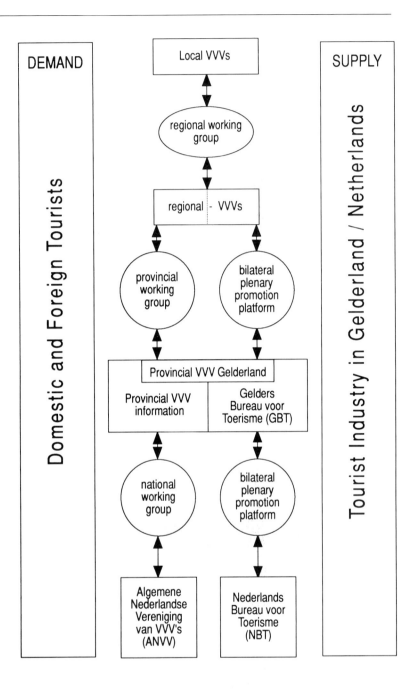

The activity plans for the Gelderland (GBT, 1989) and North Brabant (Provinciale VVV Noord-Brabant, 1988) set out a comparable range of promotional and marketing activities including: publication and distribution of brochures, catalogues, travel guides and manuals, advertising (often in NBT publications or campaigns) and participation in travel shows within the Netherlands and abroad, especially neighbouring Germany where the Gelderland VVV in particular is active

6.2 Catalogues of self-catering holidays compiled and distributed by the North Brabant and Gelderland VVVs illustrate a distinctive role of some Dutch regional tourist organizations

6.3 The activity plan of the Gelderland VVV sets out a range of promotional activities, including the publication of travel trade manuals and participation in 'the other Holland' campaign

(Plate 6.3). Both provinces also participated in 'The Other Holland' campaign with Drenthe, Overijssel, Flevoland, a campaign designed to draw attention to parts of the country other than the western provinces. North Brabant also produced a South Netherlands regional brochure in 1986 with the VVVs of Limburg and Zeeland. The participation of the regional VVVs in many of these activities is evident. The North Brabant VVV also notes in its 1987 annual report the introduction of a computerized reservations system and the co-ordination of training and short courses for information office staff.

A distinguishing feature of the provincial VVVs is the tour operator role they have assumed in packaging self-catering accommodation, cycling holidays and other activity programmes. Such activity is especially important given the overall prominence of this form of accommodation in the Netherlands, the small scale of bungalow park and camping ground operators and the competition from outbound tour operators.

'Big City' VVVs

The three 'big city' VVVs – those of Amsterdam, Rotterdam and the Hague – enjoy a similar status to the provincial VVVs, insofar as they undertake their own promotional activities and interact directly with the NBT as promotional VVVs. Their special status reflects their sheer size and the importance and distinctive nature of their urban tourism as well as their desire to act independently from the provinces of North and South Holland. In their structure, however, they differ significantly, being more compact and coherent both geographically and functionally and operating only on one level, that of the municipality.

Amsterdam is by far the leading destination in the Netherlands. Its tourist industry can be summarized by the following figures for 1987 (Groenendijk, 1988):

- 1.5 million overnight visitors; average length of stay two nights,
- 10.5 million day-visitors, of which 10 million are Dutch,

- total tourist expenditure of around 1.5 billion guilders, of which 850 million from international tourists,
- 25 000 tourism related jobs,
- accommodation capacity: 23 500 beds,
- leading attractions: canal cruise (1 800 000 visitors), Rijksmuseum (1 million), Artis (zoo – 1 million), diamond polishers (850 000).

The Amsterdam VVV is a corporation with a Board of Directors consisting of thirteen members: three nominated by the City of Amsterdam, three by the Chamber of Commerce and seven elected by the membership. In the late 1980s there were about 900 members from many different sectors of the tourist industry, including a number of large hotels, inbound tour operators and carriers. Members join for different reasons; the more upmarket hotels to participate in promotional campaigns, the smaller more modest ones to benefit from the reservations system. The annual budget in 1989 was some 8 million guilders, revenue being derived from members' contributions, subsidies from the city and the Chamber of Commerce and income from sales, advertising revenue and reservation commissions.

The Amsterdam VVV has a staff of about ninety during the high season, of whom over half are employed in the two city information offices and in a seasonal motorway kiosk. In its information activities the Amsterdam VVV shares a similar function to the other local VVVs, the scale of the activity being of course much greater. Amsterdam also has marketing (seven people), press (five), public relations (five), research (one), central documentation (four) and membership (one) departments.

Almost 3 million guilders were budgeted by the VVV for marketing Amsterdam in 1989. The basic strategy set out in the 1989 tourist marketing plan (VVV Amsterdam, 1988, p.9) is 'to make target groups aware that Amsterdam is an excellent choice for both business and recreational tourism throughout the whole year'. The target groups vary for the different markets but include tour operators, individual tourists, travel agents, travel managers, congress and incentive tourism organizers. In contrast to Gelderland, for example, the

Amsterdam VVV does not itself put packages together but works with inbound operators to see that the city is included in European itineraries. Again reflecting Amsterdam's strong image, gateway function and its appeal to tourists from diverse origins, the marketing plan sets out a variety of activities – advertising, participation in travel fairs, sales missions, educationals – on a much larger scale and in a greater range of European and other markets, particularly North America, than the provincial VVVs. This activity is supported by an extensive publications programme. Much of Amsterdam's promotion is frequently carried out in partnership with the NBT and KLM, the Dutch airline, as well as with Rotterdam and the Hague.

As a modern city and the world's largest port, Rotterdam to some extent complements Amsterdam though it lacks the latter's strong image and has a less well established tourist traffic (fewer than 200 000 international arrivals in 1986). Tourism and recreation have been important aspects of the city's urban revitalization projects, notably in Rotterdam Waterstad, a masterplan for redevelopment from the inner-city to the Meuse waterfront.

The Rotterdam VVV sees itself as having a bridging role (*brugfunctie*) between the many elements of the public and private sectors involved in tourism (VVV Rotterdam, 1987). Since 1987 it has been an independent foundation, governed by a board of directors on which the city now has only an advisory role. Nevertheless, the VVV is still substantially financed by the city purse though this share has been decreasing (Table 6.5).

The Rotterdam VVV has a staff of forty, of whom half are employed in the information offices. The promotion and marketing department is particularly active in the markets of north-west Europe but is much less involved elsewhere than Amsterdam. Much of its promotion is in association with the NBT under the platform formula. In 1976 the VVV took over the role of promoting conventions from the municipal promotions bureau and has a small section which promotes conventions and also acts as professional convention organizers. The public relations department has also recently extended its activities

to supporting events such as large concerts and festivals.

The ANVV

The Algemene Nederlandse Vereniging van VVVs is the national umbrella organization of the VVVs which has as its main tasks co-ordinating and furthering the interests of its 430 members. The ANVV has its headquarters in Amersfoort, a staff of six and derives three-quarters of its income from a Ministry of Economic Affairs subsidy and the remainder from membership fees. While the members take part in decision-making through the annual general meeting, much of the co-ordination is carried out by way of regular meetings between the national office and the provincial VVVs, who in turn act as a link with the local and regional organizations.

A major responsibility of the national office is to ensure that the VVVs, particularly with respect to the information offices, operate on a common basis and present a uniform service throughout the country. In this the ANVV appears to have been successful, with research showing that the public perceives the VVV offices belonging to one organization rather than to more than 400. The introduction of computerized reservation systems and standardization of booking fees, for example, are facilitated by national co-ordination. All VVVs must have the approval of the ANVV to become part of the national system, with ANVV policy being to have only one VVV, but possibly several information offices, per municipality. Local government restructuring has subsequently led to the amalgamation of some local VVVs. New tourist offices are also being created; these must conform to the ANVV's standards with assistance on their establishment being provided. The ANVV also offers general advice to the local member organizations in terms of administration, operations and finance.

At Amersfoort the ANVV also provides a range of training courses from basic sales and customer servicing, to more specialized courses on public relations and management. It also has wider interests in tourism training and education programmes. The welfare of VVV staff is also a concern of the ANVV, with agreement on uniform conditions of employment being reached in 1989. Having their own pension fund has facilitated mobility of staff within the system and opened up better career paths.

These different measures are all designed to improve the level of professionalism and quality of service offered. Difficulties do arise, however, given the mix of information offices in the Netherlands. The national *i* offices, for example, are generally run on a more professional basis and may integrate new ideas more quickly than the local *l* offices which may be staffed primarily by amateurs and operate seasonally but which nevertheless give strength to the network by increasing its geographical spread.

Lobbying is not yet a well established function of the ANVV but it is one which is being developed as it is recognized that tourism does not have a high profile in the Netherlands and greater efforts must be made to promote the work of the VVVs and the importance of tourism. The ANVV thus does not play the same role as the Deutsche Fremdenverkehrsverband in Germany, being primarily concerned with more basic, but nevertheless essential aspects of the operation and in-house activities of its members. These functions would seem well separated from the national promotional activities of the NBT.

Other organizations

A number of other organizations in addition to the NBT and the VVVs play a role in tourism in the Netherlands or in the related field of recreation. These will be reviewed briefly then special regional organizations will be considered.

The sector organizations, as in other countries, promote the interests of particular sectors of the tourist industry. Some of these, such as Horeca Nederland which represents the hotel and catering sector, have their counterparts elsewhere, in this case hotel associations. In other instances they have a more Dutch flavour, such as HISWA (Nederlandse Vereniging van Ondernemigen in de Bedrifjstak Waterrecreatie), which draws together the numerous water-based recreation operators and Recron (Vereniging Recreatie Ondernemers Nederland) which represents operators of camping grounds, bungalow parks, group accommodation and activities such as attraction parks. Recron, for example, had some 1 100 members nationwide and a staff of 14 in 1989. Recron basically fosters the interests of its members, both through lobbying on general issues which affect them (eg laws on camping) and, increasingly, education, for example day courses on taxation and hospitality. Individual members also seek advice from Recron, if necessary from its own consulting service. Recron was engaged in discussions during the preparation of the TROPs, and, with the NBT and other organizations, has been exploring the effects of the Single European Market in 1992. Labour issues are dealt with under the aegis of the Bedrijfschap Horeca which brings together the entrepreneurs of Recron and related organizations.

Some sixty organizations and groups with an interest in outdoor recreation, including Recron, the ANVV, the NBT and the Ministries of Economic Affairs and Agriculture, are brought together in the Stichting Recreatie (Dutch Foundation for Recreation). The Stichting Recreatie is financed by grants from the Ministry of Agriculture and has as its main objectives

- looking after the interests of people who wish to enjoy outdoor recreation,
- striving for the best possible environment for outdoor recreation, in the countryside as well as in urban localities.

The Stichting Recreatie pursues these aims by providing input into relevant policy-making, stimulating research, disseminating documentation and undertaking national campaigns influencing recreational behaviour.

Much of the responsibility for provision of outdoor recreation amenities occurs at the local level. Because of the costs involved, overlapping recreational hinterlands and the spatially interrelated nature of resources and activities (eg cycling and recreational boating), municipalities commonly form a joint community recreation body, a *recreatiegemeenschap*, to prepare, implement and manage recreational development plans and projects. Planned developments are subsidized by the central government (75 per cent), the province (15 per cent) and the municipalities (10 per cent) while operations and management are shared on a 50 : 50 basis by the province and the municipalities. The largest (area-wise) of these joint bodies is the Recreatiegemeenschap Veluwe, which covers twenty-three municipalities and some 200 000 hectares of the Veluwe. Here the emphasis has been on protecting the green heart of the region, limiting development there to such facilities as cycle paths, and locating major projects on the outer edge, notably marinas and other water-based facilities on redeveloped gravel-extraction pits, as at Rhederlaag.

At this local level comparatively little interaction appears to have occurred until recently between the *recreatiegemeenschappen* and the VVVs. The former were largely recreation-resource oriented while the latter engaged primarily in servicing visitors from beyond their local area. Many of the small commercial operators were often not heavily involved in either case. During the 1980s some changes were experienced in this regard as the *recreatiegemeenschappen* sought additional demand as their projects passed from the development phase to an operational one and the local authorities subsequently bore more of the costs. Commercial concessionaires started to be brought in to operate facilities and generate revenue and information and promotion were improved. The boundaries between recreation and tourism in the Netherlands, once quite distinct, have become increasingly blurred and greater interorganizational interaction is occurring. The Maasoevers project provides an interesting, though as yet not widespread, example of this process.

The Maasoevers (Meusebanks) Foundation represents an original organizational initiative established in 1984 to develop and promote in a coherent fashion a 100 kilometre stretch of the river Meuse (Maas) between Mook and Woudrichem (Figure 6.4). Here the river constitutes the focus of the new organization, not merely a boundary between administrative regions and their resultant organizations, notably of Gelderland and North Brabant. The organization is thus product based, encompassing not only the river itself but also adjoining pools created by sand excavation, small historic towns and castles on its banks, camping grounds, yacht harbours. All of these provide a wide spectrum of recreation and tourist activity: boating, wind surfing, fishing, swimming, cycling, walking, sightseeing, and so on.

The foundation brought together five inter-municipal bodies (three *recreatiegemeenschappen* and two with more diverse functions) and four regional VVVs from both sides of the river, that is from Gelderland and North Brabant. The initiative was essentially a local one, driven by a couple of local body personnel, who realized both the potential of the Meuse and the need for concerted action by various parties if the project was to succeed. Moreover, there was a feeling locally that the river had been neglected by the provinces which were more inward looking, with the Veluwe, for example, being the recognized tourist and recreational resource of the Gelderland. With some downturn in local demand in the early 1980s and some decline in central government funding for recreation came the realization that activities had to be more commercialized and that the region had to look further afield, notably to Germany and especially the Ruhr.

Becoming more commercial and tourism-oriented meant increasing the scale of activities and complementing development with promotion. Major recreational developments, as at De Gouden Ham, have been complemented by other foundation projects, such as nine small itinerant ports designed, along with the restoration of historic towns such as Heusden, to encourage boating and sightseeing the length of the Maasoevers domain (Plate 6.4). Likewise, planning and co-ordination of cycle paths has extended possibilities for this popular activity throughout the region. While originally not part of either the Gelderland or North Brabant TROPs, Maasoevers

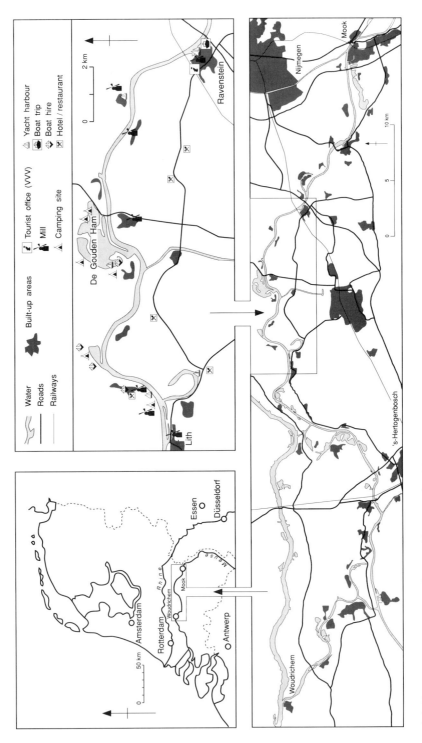

6.4 Maasoevers: location and features (Source: After Maasoevers Foundation)

6.4 The development of small itinerant ports has been an important element in the Meusebanks Foundation's strategy for encouraging tourist activity along the Meuse

projects have subsequently received 'spearhead' designation and received central government funding. 'Maasoevers' publications, guides and promotion have increased the profile of the river far beyond the capacity of the small local operators or even the regional VVVs. Local recreationists still generate the greatest demand but an increasing number of day-trippers are being drawn from other parts of the Netherlands and Germany and overnight stays are increasing to the benefit of the local accommodation and restaurant industry. Originally established for a period of five years, the life of the Maasoevers Foundation was to be extended in mid-1989, with greater private sector involvement being envisaged.

Closer co-operation between the public and private sectors was formulated from the outset in the establishment of the Parklands Public Private Partnership (PPP) in central North Brabant in 1989, the first such tourism PPP in the Netherlands. While the Parklands product – four major amusement parks – was different from that of Maasoevers, the underlying strategy was similar – increase the size of operations to extend the market

beyond that of recreational day-trippers, thereby benefiting not only the park operators but also regional accommodation and other sectors of the tourist industry. The goal is to double the annual number of visitors from 4 million to 8 million and to generate 6 million overnight stays. Plans to develop a European Disneyland near Paris may have contributed to this approach. Establishment of the Parklands PPP appears also to reflect some discontent with the promotional efforts of the regional VVV.

The partnership brings together the provincial government and local authorities, the amusement park operators, the accommodation sector, transport companies, Eindhoven airport and the Tilburg and 's-Hertogenbosch Chambers of Commerce. The foundation was established for a period of five years and a budget of 6.6 million guilders, including a 2.6 million subsidy from the Ministry of Economic Affairs. Parklands has been designated as a 'spearhead' project, the North Brabant TROP identifying the need for co-operative efforts in this field. One of the staff of four was one of the driving forces behind the

Maasoevers project. The PPP's three major tasks are promotion, private sector development (eg of the parks themselves and the accommodation) and public sector development (eg physical infrastructure, landscaping). Co-operative efforts include the possibility of linking the various parks by monorail, the use of 'smart cards' for transport and park entrances, and joint marketing and promotion (eg working with tour operators and developing products for special niches such as families and young visitors).

Conclusions

In the VVVs and the NBT the Netherlands has a dense and well established network of official tourist organizations from the local to the national level characterized by a large degree of domain consensus. The NBT and the ANVV have clearly defined functions while the promotional VVVs contract with the NBT to represent the promotion and marketing interests of the lower level VVVs in a relationship which features a significant grass roots input into the network's activities. This interaction, however, occurs within a reasonably narrow field. The VVVs and the NBT have concentrated essentially on visitor servicing, and promotion, but

have been much less conspicuous in terms of planning and development. Until recently, these latter functions have been associated more with outdoor recreation than tourism, as illustrated by the functions of the *recreatiegemeenschappen*. Moreover, there appears to be little integration between the two major policy elements of the Second Tourism Policy Paper, namely increasing promotion and product enhancement. There is, on the other hand, a growing trend towards increasing the private sector input into tourist organizations, as in the NBT's budget and the restructuring of the Rotterdam VVV. The Maasoevers and Parklands foundations reflect ways in which these different functions and trends have been brought together under new organizational structures which are product oriented, less constrained by existing administrative boundaries, but nevertheless still recipients of central government funding. Both these organizations provide a much closer integration of marketing and development, of recreation and tourism, of public and private participation. The emergence of these new structures suggests inadequacies in existing organizations. Their success may encourage similar developments elsewhere or lead to some restructuring of the existing VVV network, perhaps a broadening of their functions to be more development and industry oriented.

7

Republic of Ireland

The Republic of Ireland constitutes a further example of tourism in a small, centralized unitary state where the network of tourist organizations and their functions reflects the influence of broader environmental factors. The impact of centralization is felt here as in the Netherlands, perhaps even more so; smallness is again an important factor but Ireland's insular character and peripherality contrast strongly with the continentality of the Netherlands and its proximity to the urban, economic and demographic centre of Europe. Following a brief outline of the country and its tourist industry, this chapter focuses first on the changing interrelationships between the national tourist organization, Bord Fáilte, and the regional tourist organizations. Other tourist organizations are then considered before the interaction of these different bodies in a period of significant change in the late 1980s is analysed. The recent history of Irish tourist organizations is very much one of domain establishment.

Environmental factors

The Republic of Ireland is a small unitary state made up of twenty-six of the thirty-two counties of Ireland, the territory comprising the six counties of Northern Ireland in the north-east having opted to remain part of the United Kingdom on independence in 1922. Johnson (1987, p.285) observes:

> political independence should not be allowed to mask its very strong economic, social and demographic connections with the United Kingdom. The single most important factor influencing many aspects of the human geography of Ireland is the presence nearby of the larger island of Great Britain, while the existence of Northern Ireland as a political unit separate from the rest of Ireland also complicates the operation of various aspects of policy making in the Republic.

In terms of tourism Great Britain constitutes a significant intervening opportunity for the large continental European market, a factor exacerbated by both countries' island character with its consequent implications for accessibility.

Ireland's geographic peripherality was for long reinforced by its relative isolation from the economic development of much of Western Europe. It was not until the 1960s and 1970s that new policies of modernization and internationalization opened up the economy of Ireland and transformed its traditional rural-based society. As Brunt (1988, p.xiii) notes:

> Following the 1950s, Ireland traded a dependency on Britain for a dependency on international capital to bring about the social and economic transformation of the country. . . . The huge debt built up during the 1970s and 1980s to finance the development of a new social and physical infrastructure has, however, created a serious problem. The nation's obligations to international financial institutions have intensified and the government's freedom of action is restricted.

Ireland emerged from the recession of the early 1980s much more slowly and less vigorously than many other Western economies and today still lags towards the bottom of the list of European countries for many socio-economic indicators.

In 1989, Ireland had a population of 3.5 million. Although small, Ireland nevertheless exhibits significant internal diversity in landscape and levels of socio-economic development, the rural, less prosperous west contrasting with the more urbanized, industrialized and better-off east. Dublin, with a population of just under 1 million, continues to dominate the country. According to Brunt (1988, p.171):

> The overwhelming primacy of Dublin has remained untouched by the process of modernization. If anything, its dominance as a centre of control has been further emphasized by its new responsibilities as an international capital within the European Community. Failure to decentralize services and decision-making has not provided the few other major cities (and the country) with a sufficiently well-developed functional base to offer an effective balance to Dublin.

Dublin's primacy reflects in part the very centralized nature of Irish government, politics and decision-making. While county identities in Ireland may be strong, local authorities are not. Regional administration essentially takes the form of the deconcentration of field services as Paddison (1983, p.37) notes:

> With few exceptions . . . all government ministries deconcentrate the mundane operation of services such as the administration of social welfare and education to territorial units. Alongside these exist the field-service structure of semi-state bodies, for example those for the railways and tourist development.

Paddison also points out that in general 'field services generally lack the democratic control and degree of autonomy' of local government and that they act as 'a vehicle by which central government is able to penetrate the state, ensuring that policies decided nationally are implemented locally'. He

also shows that in Ireland there is a considerable mix of regional boundaries with few services replicating the standard regions. Commenting on the lack of territorial identity, Brunt (1988, pp.57–9) argues that 'With an extremely strong tradition of local and county identities set against a background of growing centralization at the national level, regional considerations remain under-emphasized within Ireland'. Brunt later points out (pp.96–7) that although Irish politics are essentially national in orientation, they are also characterized by 'localism' whereby 'Successful politicians are forced to create, protect and become identified with particular territories (bailiwicks) within constituencies'.

Tourism in Ireland

Ireland has a comparatively small but distinctive tourist industry, ranking second lowest ahead of Luxembourg in the European Community in terms of absolute foreign exchange revenue from international tourism (US$999 million in 1988). As an island with a lengthy coastline and ample beaches, Ireland saw a number of coastal resorts develop earlier in this century. However, its climate and location are such that Ireland will never experience the development of a mass 'sun-sand-sea' market such as has occurred in the Mediterranean and indeed has suffered from the development of package tourism to Spain and other similar destinations. Nor has Dublin the size and attraction of London or Paris. Rather,

> The appeal which should be communicated to visitors has two elements: the first reflects a basically emotional response to Ireland, evocative of its cultural and romantic heritage and distinctive way of life. The second is the scenery, atmosphere of tranquility and the friendliness of the Irish people. (Bord Fáilte, 1975).

Touring, sightseeing holidays are complemented by activity-based vacations such as those involving fishing, golfing and cruising on the Shannon or, for

Table 7.1 Distribution of tourism numbers and revenue in Ireland by major market (1988)	Visits/trips		Revenue	
	no.	%	(IR£m)	%
Out-of-state				
Britain	1 508 000	50.1	267	41.7
North America	419 000	13.9	165.5	25.9
Cont. Europe	408 000	13.6	123.7	19.3
France	111 000	3.7	28.8	4.5
FR Germany	113 000	3.8	33.4	5.2
Netherlands	38 000	1.3	9.1	1.4
Other Europe	90 000	3.0	37.6	5.9
Other Overseas	90 000	3.0	37.6	5.9
Northern Ireland	582 000	19.4	46.1	7.2
Total	3 000 700	100	639.9	100
Excursionists	7 348 000		15.1	
Domestic travellers[1]	4 164 000		311.1	

Note: [1] On home holidays and other non-business domestic trips.
Source: After Bord Fáilte (1989)

Americans in particular, tracing one's roots.

The visiting friends and relatives (VFR) market constitutes a significant share of the international tourist traffic to Ireland. In 1988 54 per cent of all holidaymakers were staying with friends and relatives; considerable variation occurred by origin (Britain, 74 per cent; North America 26 per cent; Mainland Europe, 23 per cent; Other, 53 per cent). Over 80 per cent of all holidaymakers were travelling independently, though this figure would diminish if the VFR segment were excluded.

Minor fluctuations have occurred from year to year but the overall composition of the out-of-state traffic to Ireland has been characterized by a marked stability for much of the 1970s and 1980s. Britain constitutes the largest market in terms of visitor numbers and, to a lesser extent, revenue generated as the expenditure of those visiting friends and relatives is generally lower than that of other holidaymakers (Table 7.1). Revenue from Northern Ireland visitors is significantly less than their market share in visitor numbers. Conversely, the North Americans and Europeans contribute

relatively more to revenue than to total numbers.

Out-of-state visitors generated about two-thirds of all tourism revenue in Ireland in 1988, by far the highest international : domestic ratio of the examples studied here. This can be attributed to a great extent to the small size of the domestic market within which there has been a growing tendency to take holidays abroad. At the same time, short holidays at home have also increased (Table 7.2).

The regional distribution of tourism revenue within Ireland has remained reasonably constant during the late 1970s and 1980s (Figure 7.1).[1] In 1988 just over half the total direct revenue from tourism was concentrated in two of Ireland's seven tourist regions – Dublin Eastern (29.5 per cent) and Cork/Kerry (22.5 per cent). The West (13 per cent) was the third most important region. Similar levels of revenue were generated in the four remaining regions (Midwest, 9.9 per cent; South East, 9.7 per cent; Donegal Leitrim and Sligo (DLS), 8.0 per cent; and the Midlands, 7.3 per cent). The pattern depicted in Figure 7.2 reflects

Table 7.2 Holiday taking by Irish residents (1985–8)

		1985	1986	1987	1988
Total holidays	no.	2 660 000	2 319 000	2 897 000	3 565 000
(excl. duty trips)	IR£m	512.8	542.2	617.4	730.2
Home long hols	no.	1 153 000	693 000	917 000	1 118 000
(4+ nights)	IR£m	138.2	86.8	107.9	124.4
Home short hols	no.	696 000	662 000	911 000	1 244 000
(1–3 nights)	IR£m	45.3	48.8	60.9	92.3
Holidays abroad	no.	811 000	964 000	1 069 000	1 203 000
	IR£m	329.3	406.6	448.7	513.5
Other domestic	no.	1 971 000	1 876 000	2 661 000	1 799 000
(Duty trips)	IR£m	85.7	81.0	122.0	94.4

Source: Bord Fáilte (1989)

the distribution of attractions and facilities, international gateways, levels of development and investment and market preferences. Significant regional differences occur in the composition of demand. Overseas tourists generated 62 per cent of the revenue for the country as a whole. This share was exceeded in Dublin Eastern (70 per cent), the Midlands (70 per cent), and Midwest (65 per cent). The South East drew 45 per cent of its revenue from the domestic market and DLS was the most reliant on Northern Ireland (19 per cent). While the regional distribution of different overseas visitors is reasonably uniform, certain spatial biases stand out in Figure 7.1: British visitors are significantly over-represented in the Midlands (famed for its angling), the Midwest has a disproportionately high share of North Americans due to the location of Shannon airport and European visitors are over-represented in Dublin Eastern but under-represented in the South East.

Tourism expenditure accounted for 6.2 per cent of GNP in 1988 (excluding multiplier effects) and 6.8 per cent of all exports. Tourism is estimated to have supported 69 000 job equivalents in 1988, of which 44 000 were supported by out-of-state visitor expenditure.

Perhaps more than in many other European states, the Irish tourist industry is characterized by the small scale of enterprises involved. Some Irish hotel chains exist (Doyle Group, 1 400 rooms; Ryan Hotels, 900 rooms; Great Southern Hotels, 700 rooms) and larger operators are to be found among the carriers (eg Aer Lingus, Ryanair and the CIE companies) but the majority of tourism businesses are small, family and owner managed businesses, employing on average five people with a high proportion of seasonal and part-time staff (CHL Consultants, 1987; McEniff, 1987; CERT, 1988). Most hotels are small (average size, 18.5 beds in 1988) and family run. A significant share of the accommodation capacity is provided in the bed and breakfast sector (farmhouse, town and country homes). There has been very limited penetration by international capital, especially when compared to foreign investment in manufacturing; this might be attributed in part to the low levels of profitability seen in the Irish tourist industry.

Major reviews in the mid-1980s pointed to a lack of performance by Irish tourism and in particular to a loss of market share in the major British and American markets (Stokes Kennedy Crowley et al, 1986; Price Waterhouse, 1987). Constant value earnings from tourism highlight the lack of growth in recent years with earnings in the

7.1 Regional distribution of
tourism revenue in Ireland
(1988)
(Data source: Bord Fáilte
1989)

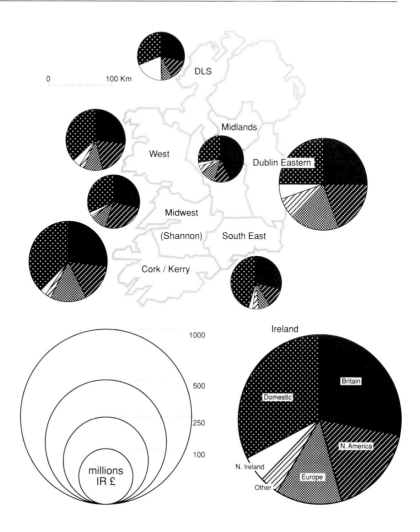

1980s generally being exceeded by those of the
growth years of the late 1960s (Figure 7.2). While
some of this stagnation can be attributed to external
conditions such as the troubles in Northern Ireland
and to more general factors such as high rates of
inflation in the decade from 1973, the Price
Waterhouse report also pointed to deficiencies in
product development, cost competitiveness
(especially in access transport from continental
Europe, internal transport and drink prices) and
weaknesses in overseas marketing. Some growth
was being experienced in the late 1980s, with
foreign exchange earnings from tourism in 1988 up
by 13 per cent in real terms over 1987.

Bord Fáilte and the regional tourist organizations

Ireland provides a very useful and interesting
example of the ongoing interaction between an
NTO, in this case Bord Fáilte (the Irish Tourist
Board), and regional tourist organizations within a
centralized state. The structure of Bord Fáilte and
the RTOs is examined briefly then their interaction
analysed in terms of a series of different functions
and activities.

In Ireland, the national tourist administration
since 1987 has been the Department of Tourism

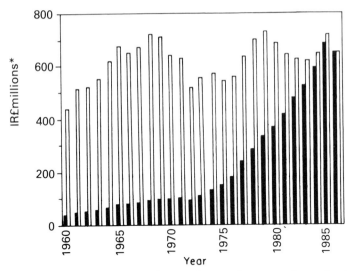

7.2 Evolution of out-of-state visitor revenue in Ireland (1960–86) (Data source: Bord Fáilte)

*includes carrier receipts and revenue from day trippers

■ Current terms
◻ Constant 1986 terms

and Transport (previously the Department of Tourism, Fisheries and Forestry) headed by a minister with full Cabinet status. The formulation of national policy for tourism is the responsibility of the department in consultation with Bord Fáilte, the latter being primarily responsible for its implementation. Government policy on tourism has varied over time but for much of the recent past has been embodied in the following statement (Bord Fáilte, 1987):

> The national objective is to optimise the economic and social benefits to Ireland gained by the promotion and development of tourism both to and within the country consistent with ensuring an acceptable economic rate of return on the resources employed and taking account of:
>
> • tourism's potential for job creation,
> • the quality of life and development of the community,
> • the enhancement and preservation of the nation's cultural heritage,

• the conservation of the physical resources of the country, and
• tourism's contribution to regional development.

This objective in its general form appears in Bord Fáilte's (1974) *Tourism Plan 1973–1976* where the emphasis is on net value added rather than rate of return. The regional development element first appears in the 1976–80 plan and job creation in the 1982–6 plan. In 1987 'it is accepted that the balance between the two aspects [economic and social benefits] will remain strongly in favour of the economic one over the next five years' (OECD, 1987, p.29).

Bord Fáilte, as it presently exists, was established in 1955 with the consolidation of two previous organizations (Gillmor, 1985), being charged under the Tourist Traffic Act 1939 with 'making further and better provision for the encouragement and development of the tourist traffic'. It is based in Dublin and has offices in Belfast, London, Paris, Amsterdam, Frankfurt,

Table 7.3   Bord Fáilte budget allocations (1986–8)

	1986 %	1987 %	1988 %
Marketing	59.6	63.9	80.8
Development	17.6[1]	13.8[1]	5.8
Administration	11.9	11.9	6.4
Superannuation	2.4	2.1	1.7
Regional tourism organizations	8.5	8.3	5.3
	100	100	100

Note: [1]   Including capital expenditure.
Source: Bord Fáilte annual reports

New York, Toronto and Sydney as well as representation in a number of other overseas cities. Bord Fáilte is a semi-state agency whose board consists of a chairman and eight members appointed by the minister.

Bord Fáilte engages in a range of operations similar to those undertaken by NTO's elsewhere, these include marketing, promotion, planning, development, research and regulation (eg inspection of hotels). The emphasis given to these activities has varied over time but in general their relative importance can be gauged from Table 7.3 which shows marketing accounted for around 60 per cent of Bord Fáilte's budget in 1986 and 1987, before being boosted to 80 per cent with the additional allocations in 1988. In constant terms, however, Bord Fáilte's operating budget declined significantly from 1979 to 1990, with its total budget in real terms in 1990 being only two-thirds of the 1979 level (Figure 7.3).

Bord Fáilte's subsidies to the regional tourism organizations (RTOs) constituted 5–8 per cent of its budget during the mid-1980s. The eight regional tourism organizations established by Bord Fáilte in 1964 were reduced to seven in 1984 when the Dublin and Eastern Regions were merged as a cost reduction measure and on 1 January 1988 the

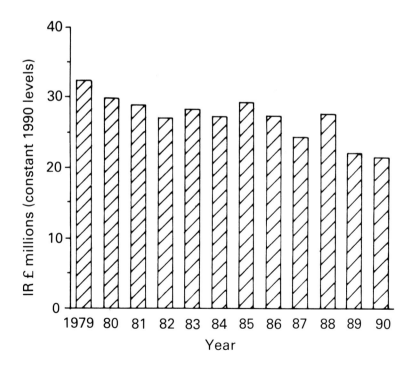

7.3 Evolution of Bord Fáilte's budget (1979–90) (Source: After ITC–Bord Fáilte 1990)

RTO functions of the Midwest Region were transferred to SFADCo, a multi-sectoral agency discussed in more detail below.

Several factors appear to have led to the creation of the RTOs. The regionalization of certain aspects of tourism administration might be seen as part of a more general concern with regional policies and regional development which emerged in the 1960s, not only in Ireland but also in other parts of Europe (Gillmor, 1985; Walsh, 1987). There appears too to have been some direct transfer to Ireland of the continental European experience with regional tourism. Regionalization was also a response to the growth in the tourist traffic in the 1960s and the advent of the more mobile motoring holidaymaker following the widening of car ownership and the introduction of the first car ferries to the Republic in 1965 (Stewart, 1985). Servicing the visitor was seen as a prime function of the new regional organizations which took over and expanded the booking and tourist information offices of the Irish Tourist Association (an umbrella organization set up earlier by local authorities and subsequently disbanded).

The general function of the RTOs was to stimulate increased local effort in the development of tourism through encouraging local authority and private sector investment in plant and infrastructure and 'organizing the tourist resources and services of the Regions so as to ensure that the control and development of tourism at local and regional level is carried out in harmony with the overall national programmes of Bord Fáilte and other related bodies' (Bord Fáilte, 1973, p.48).

The delimitation of the eight original regions did not necessarily correspond with other administrative boundaries but brought together groups of counties on the basis of area, population, tourism plant, local authority funding and the compatibility of counties with a view to avoiding overly strong or weak regions. However, as Figure 7.1 showed, in terms of revenue the distribution of tourism among the regions is far from uniform.

Within each region the RTO was set up as a public company limited by guarantee with no share capital. Such a structure was designed to enable the RTOs to own property, to carry out commercial

operations effectively and to employ personnel on a firm basis. RTO personnel at one stage numbered in excess of 150 but staffing cut-backs saw this reduced to about ninety nationwide by the late 1980s. The chief executive of each RTO is the regional tourism manager. Most RTOs have a sub-regional staffing structure wherein some staff are based in and responsible for specific counties or parts of their region, a structure which enhances local contact. The RTOs draw their membership from the local authorities in their region and from other ordinary members, both individuals and companies resident or active in the region. Each RTO is managed by a board of directors appointed by the local authorities and Bord Fáilte or elected by the ordinary members. The RTOs thus provide a forum for local input and initiative though the board structure has drawn criticism for being too large and unwieldy (the Dublin Eastern board had thirty-seven directors in 1987) and being dominated by local politicians.

In their structure, the RTOs do not strictly constitute a deconcentration of centralized services as suggested by Paddison (1983). However, the influence of Bord Fáilte over the RTOs must be recognized. First, by their articles of association the RTOs must 'act in accordance with the policies and directions of Bord Fáilte Eireann' (Cork/Kerry Regional Tourism Organization Ltd, 1964). Second, Bord Fáilte exercises a strong measure of control over the appointment of the regional tourism manager (who is, however, not a Bord Fáilte employee but responsible to the board of directors) and also members of the board (directors can be requested by Bord Fáilte to resign). Third, and perhaps most significantly, the RTOs have always depended heavily on Bord Fáilte for the bulk of their funding. The anticipated increase in local authority and tourist industry contributions following a formative period of Bord Fáilte assistance has been slow to materialize and revenue from commercial operations (sales of brochures, souvenirs, booking fees, rental space, etc) is a relatively recent development. RTO budgets have always been comparatively small, that for 1983 amounted to IR£2.5 million and was drawn from the following sources (Oireachtus Eireann, 1984):

Bord Fáilte	67%
Local authorities	15%
Other members	8%
Commercial accounts	10%

An interesting situation has thus always existed in terms of the relationships of the RTOs with the national body, Bord Fáilte. Aspects of the RTO structure provide a channel for local and regional participation and initiative in the expansion of Irish tourism and the harmonization of these activities with those of the national body, as expressed in the articles of association, is in many respects logical and positive. However, the lack of resources available to the RTOs coupled with the influence exercised by Bord Fáilte over them has meant that their role has always been a subordinate one. It is not surprising therefore that debate has occurred

from time to time over the functions and activities of the national and regional bodies.

Visitor servicing

Provision of information and booking facilities has been particularly significant in Ireland given the small-scale and non-industrialized nature of much tourism plant and operations there, the number of independent travellers and the amount of touring undertaken (Plate 7.1). The RTOs quickly built on the base of the existing Irish Tourist Association network and by 1970 more than 100 offices, many of them seasonal, were handling 1.6 million enquiries, booking almost 400 000 bednights and producing 4 million pieces of holiday literature annually. These services have improved over time with moves in the late 1980s towards

7.1 The office of the Donegal Leitrim and Sligo Regional Tourism Organization in Sligo: Irish RTOs have played an important visitor servicing role and provided a point of contact with local operators

computerization of booking and information. However, the volume of business has not increased significantly. In 1988, eighteen all-year-round and sixty-one seasonal information offices serviced 1.8 million callers and booked 265 000 bednights. The RTOs have been effective in co-ordinating local and regional efforts, often by local destination associations, to produce and distribute maps, brochures and other material. Servicing the visitor in these ways has generally been seen by Bord Fáilte as fulfilling an essentially practical function best carried out at a local and regional level and one not sought after by the national body.

Planning

Numerous plans for tourism have been produced in Ireland at different scales since the 1960s (Gillmor, 1985). Much of the early planning effort consisted of practical local plans undertaken by the now disbanded state planning agency, An Foras Forbartha; these included the Brittas Bay study which made important contributions to carrying capacity methodology (An Foras Forbartha, 1973). An Foras Forbartha, together with Bord Fáilte, also commissioned the National Coastline Study in 1973. Most subsequent planning for tourism, however, has been undertaken by Bord Fáilte. Their plans have predominantly been national in nature though a strong regional structure characterized their first development plan. Bord Fáilte also has statutory input into local authority plans where relevant.

The first national tourism plan covered the years 1973–6 and was prepared as part of a broader government policy introduced at this time to adopt a rolling programme approach to all publicly financed operations (Bord Fáilte, 1973). This plan, like subsequent ones, emphasized the market areas and specific product programmes (eg angling, cruising, equestrian activities and golf) but there was no explicit regional orientation. However, the question of where development should be carried out was addressed briefly in the strategy chapter where it was stated preference should be given 'other things being equal, to developments in the following order of priority by location':

- special development areas,
- location of greatest social need,
- rural areas,
- location where a spirit of self-help exists by way of local finance and community enterprise,
- other areas.

The regional and spatial component in Irish tourism planning is most apparent and explicit in the eight regional development plans which complemented the national Tourist Development Plan of 1976–80 (Plate 7.2). The RTOs played a significant role in the preparation of these regional plans, particularly in the detailed inventorying of local resources. Preparation of these plans involved a common approach incorporating a system of designated areas (designed to identify and conserve areas of scenic value), tourism planning zones (eighty-one for the country as a whole) and link zones. The rationale for the tourism planning zones is embodied in a statement explicitly recognizing the issues of scale and function (Bord Fáilte, 1978):

> The need for a zoning strategy arises from the diversity of tourism, the seemingly endless variety of goods and services that add up to the tourism product. Many of these goods and services are used not only by the visitor but by domestic holidaymakers, businessmen and the local population. Because of the local nature of tourism, national supply and demand aggregates would not be helpful in decision making. Zonal planning was, in effect, a move from macro to micro assessment.
>
> Zone-by-zone development plans identify where comprehensive sets of facilities for holidaymakers are needed. Strengths and shortcomings are analysed at local level. Priorities are defined. By having smaller units, the likely demand and supply patterns of each area can be worked out in detail. Available resources can be used more effectively and the scale and timing of investment is easier to calculate.

Little appears to have come from the 1976–80 Tourist Development Plan. Some broad elements are retained in the more general *Tourism Plan*

7.2 Irish RTOs played a major role in the preparation of regional tourism plans but little came of these as the emphasis switched to international marketing

1978–82 (Bord Fáilte 1978) but the development emphasis is absent from subsequent plans in which national marketing issues are stressed and where all regional orientation is abandoned. The failure to implement and pursue the development of tourism on a regional and zonal basis might be attributed to several factors. Enthusiasm for regional policy in the Republic in general had waned by the 1970s. Following the stagnation in tourism during the decade Bord Fáilte's emphasis on marketing over development increased. More particularly, the abandonment of the regional plans has been attributed to their very specificity, notably to government opposition to a project in the West which was subsequently shown to be consistent with the plan for that region. To avoid any similar embarrassment in the future, detailed planning such as that contained in the regional plans appears henceforth to have been discouraged. One former regional tourism manager also dismissed the plans as 'pious expectations of what we would like to see done'. There was little financial back up for the plans and no additional allocation of resources to the RTOs. The Tourist Development Plan (and others) was presented as being indicative in nature and little effort appears to have been directed towards actively identifying and encouraging other developers in the regions. With the cut-backs and the emphasis passing almost completely to national marketing plans, the role of the RTOs in the planning process basically dissolved.

Development

In line with other government spending, major reductions in public capital expenditure on tourism occurred during the 1980s, but in the previous two decades Bord Fáilte made a significant contribution to the expansion of tourism plant in Ireland through the provision of various grants for accommodation, attractions and infrastructure. During the period 1956–77, incentive payments and grants of £34 million were made towards the development of tourism under six fund headings as follows (National Economic and Social Council, 1978):

- accommodation (£13.5 million),
- interest grants (£8.6 million – almost wholly to the hotel sector),
- Major Resort Fund (£4 million),
- general development (£4 million),

Table 7.4   Regional distribution of accommodation grants and tourism revenue in Ireland

Region	% of accommodation grants (1971–8)	% of tourism revenue (1978)
Cork/Kerry	25.8	21.5
Dublin Eastern	20.3	27.7
West	14.0	12.0
DLS	13.9	10.8
South East	12.3	12.2
Midwest	9.3	9.2
Midlands	4.4	6.6

Source: Bord Fáilte annual reports

- special holiday accommodation – a 'relatively small fund' for encouraging farmhouse and town and country home development,
- Capital Development Fund – £4.75 million provided under the Tourist Traffic Act 1975.

Some regional variation occurred with the provision of the accommodation incentives, higher grants being accorded to hotels in the Special Development areas. Table 7.4 shows the regional distribution of accommodation grants during the period 1971–8 corresponded broadly to the spread of tourism revenue at the end of the period (Figure 7.1), with DLS and Cork/Kerry receiving a relatively larger share of the grants and Dublin Eastern proportionately less. The single largest grant, however, was made to a Dublin hotel, with County Dublin (15.9 per cent) ranking second only to County Kerry (16.2 per cent) in terms of total grants received. Through the Major Resort Programme Bord Fáilte contributed to the development of a series of resorts and resort areas, mainly on the coast, through property acquisition, infrastructural improvements and the provision or enhancement of public recreational facilities such as recreation centres, swimming pools and golf clubs. Provision was also made for the upgrading of cruising facilities on the Shannon.

Bord Fáilte's annual reports in the late 1960s

and early 1970s record with some enthusiasm the role of the RTOs in increasing supplementary accommodation (in farm houses) 'largely due to the personalised local approach of the Regional Organisations', the encouragement of local entertainment and assistance with the administration of the various grant schemes, particularly the Major Resort Programme. Nevertheless, an 'uneasy relationship' appears to have existed between the national and regional bodies in this latter regard. The RTOs never had any of their own grants to disburse and the counties, who were responsible for carrying out much of the actual development work, seem to have preferred dealing directly with Dublin as the purse strings were controlled from there. Bord Fáilte administered the hotel grants directly. There has also been some limited involvement by the RTOs themselves in the development and running of attractions, one of the more notable examples being Dublin Eastern's Malahide Castle operation (57 000 visitors in 1987) but such direct participation has been hindered by the RTOs' resource base.

Deane (National Economic and Social Council, 1978) argued a case against more RTO participation in funding development:

> Facilities are mainly provided through the private sector, and while a regional agency with sufficient funds to disburse might bring an addition to the supply of facilities it is unlikely it would do so in a way that would represent an efficient use of public funds or in a way that would lead to an improved tourist product. The reason for this is that local interests can exert an intense pressure on RTOs to undertake projects. These projects, while they might be of benefit to the local community, are not necessarily of any real benefit to tourism.

This might be seen as a particular problem in Ireland, a country which has a long history of local political patronage.

A subsequent report (Oireactus Eireann, 1984) by a parliamentary committee later recommended the opposite strategy, suggesting the RTOs should have a co-ordinating role for all tourist activities in a region including:

> The identification and discretionary grant aiding of specific amenity projects including all weather facilities from an 'amenities budget' for this purpose. . . . The National Tourism Authority could determine whether this would operate on a rigid percentage basis as does IDA grant aid or on a flexible basis within the overall confines of the financial allocation for this purpose.

No such allocation eventuated, however, and reductions occurred in Bord Fáilte capital expenditure.

Marketing and promotion

Early and continuing debate has occurred over the division of national and regional responsibilities for marketing and promotion (Stewart, 1985). With the exception of the domestic and, to some extent, the Northern Ireland markets, Bord Fáilte has always reserved to itself the responsibility for marketing Ireland as a tourist destination. The approach traditionally adopted has been to promote the image of Ireland as a whole abroad, with any segmentation occurring in terms of specific products or activities (golf, angling, cruising, riding) rather than any given region. It is a national image, sometimes directed at specific interest groups, which has been promoted, presumably because this is seen as the most effective method of marketing a small country in large and competitive markets such as the United Kingdom, the United States and Germany, with a very modest total budget. During the mid-1980s, Ireland's expenditure on travel and tourism advertising in the United States amounted to over US$3 million but accounted for just over 0.3 per cent of all such spending (ITIC – Bord Fáilte, 1990). Bord Fáilte policy appears to be that increases in the total traffic will benefit all regions and that the less frequented areas north of the Dublin–Galway line do best when overall visitor numbers are up.

The interest of local and regional groups lies not so much in the growth of total tourist numbers but

in the expansion of visitors to their particular area. As such an expansion is perceived to be directly related to marketing and promotional efforts, a desire exists to become more directly involved in marketing and promoting their own region abroad. This is the case both where there is regional differentiation in market preferences and in the tourist product (in which case the regional concern would be marketing their given strengths or spending money in the markets most disposed to visiting them) and where regions offer attractions and appeal to the same markets as others (in which case they would feel some additional effort would give them an edge over their competitors). Both sets of conditions are to be found within Ireland. As noted earlier, for instance, some regions depend more on the American or Northern Ireland markets while European visitors are more evenly dispersed (Figure 7.1). Angling is particularly important in the West and the Midlands while 'scenery, atmosphere of tranquility and friendliness of the Irish people', although not without regional differentiation, are perhaps of more general appeal.

What the regions do not have, however, are the resources for sustained marketing and promotional efforts abroad. Small campaigns might be mounted by Cork/Kerry in Wales or DLS in Northern Ireland but the RTOs do not have the capacity to undertake research in the major markets, to set up their own offices and operations abroad as Bord Fáilte has done nor to undertake substantial campaigns on their own. The RTOs rely heavily on interpreting trends in the number of callers to their tourist offices and on trying to regionalize national patterns identified in Bord Fáilte surveys. The RTOs' lack of resources results in part from the appropriation of this role by Bord Fáilte itself (compare the budgetary provisions for marketing and the RTOs in Table 7.3). The RTOs' general difficulties in obtaining local funding may also be exacerbated by the central body's role in marketing and promotion. Both these activities are commonly perceived by sub-national interests to have more immediate returns for them than the other RTO functions noted earlier. Organizations which cannot readily engage in them may thus attract less financial backing.

This is not to say, however, that Bord Fáilte has not called upon the RTOs at all, for indeed the regions are often requested to host visiting journalists and travel writers or provide people with expertise, for example in angling, to take part in campaigns abroad. Any broader participation by the regions is seen to lead to undue duplication of effort and dilution of effectiveness in the market-place and is not encouraged. Where total monies available for marketing and promotion are modest by international standards there are clearly strong arguments for Bord Fáilte's continued central involvement in this field even if such a policy does not meet all regional aspirations. Faced with this situation, some regional tourism managers have seen their challenge as being to produce quality products and packages which will more readily be picked up and promoted by the national body. Their ability to do this, however, is conditioned by the efficiency with which marketing intelligence is channelled by Bord Fáilte to the regions and by the resources which are made available there to provide products which meet market demand. The trends depicted in Figure 7.2 suggest the process could be improved. Both total revenue (in constant dollars) and the regional spread of visitor spending have remained relatively unchanged in the decade from 1976.

The need for greater co-ordination with private sector marketing efforts was being increasingly recognized in the late 1980s. Bord Fáilte expenditure was estimated to account for about a quarter of all spending on marketing Ireland to tourists in 1989, by far the greater sum coming from the private sector. However, it was also argued (ITIC – Bord Fáilte, 1990, p.6) that

> though the industry is the main spender, State spending is the *driver* in Irish tourism promotion. Its role is to provide the foundation on which the Industry spending can operate; it should set a direction that the Industry can follow.
>
> The more long-term planning there is for the State's spending, the greater will be the Industry's ability to support and integrate with it and so the more effective will be the overall spending on tourism promotion.

Delays in allocating state funds each year were seen to be a major obstacle to levering additional industry expenditure.

Other organizations

As in other countries, public sector involvement in Ireland is not limited solely to these specifically tourist-oriented organizations and other state and semi-state agencies also play a role. The Office of Public Works, for example, is responsible for national parks and monuments, Aer Rianta operates Dublin, Cork and Shannon airports and Aer Lingus, B & I and CIE are major carriers. Local authority activities, particularly the provision of infrastructure and district planning, also impinge on tourist development. Ireland also has a special state agency, CERT, responsible for the recruitment, education and training of staff in the hotel, catering and tourist industry. CERT was established in 1963 'to develop a highly skilled tourism workforce and to ensure high operational standards in the industry' (CERT, 1988). CERT had a budget of IR£6.4 million in 1989, with a significant grant (45 per cent) coming from the European Social Fund. In addition to running a wide range of training programmes, CERT also undertakes regular manpower surveys and consultancies. A number of private sector tourist industry associations and organizations have been formed to represent, promote and protect the common interests of their members. The most significant are national associations representing particular sectors of the industry, for example the Irish Hotels Federation and the Coach Tourism Council. These associations are brought together along with the major carriers and two semi-state agencies, Aer Rianta and SFADCo, as members of the Irish Tourist Industry Confederation (ITIC).

ITIC was established in 1984 as a trimmer and more effective umbrella organization for the Irish tourist industry, replacing the former National Tourism Council. It is a purely national organization, having no regional structure or members. Each of the twenty-one member organizations or companies is represented by its president or chief executive making ITIC a decisive body whose role is to act as a single voice for and on behalf of the tourist industry in Ireland. ITIC acts as a lobbying group, pursuing issues of common interest, such as a reduction in VAT rates, an area in which some success has been achieved. A recent position paper has been prepared on tourism and the environment and submissions have been made to the Minister for Tourism and Transport on key issues affecting the industry. Among the priority areas identified in the latter report are improved customer perception of Ireland, the strengthening of Ireland's image in the market-place, more competitive access fares and new product development. ITIC has also taken more direct action in this latter regard, commissioning in 1988 a major study of new product opportunities in the main markets. This concluded that 'The main barrier to growth is that Ireland, as presently positioned and perceived, is not especially attractive to potential visitors' (ITIC, 1989, p.3). New opportunities were identified in six areas: history and culture, activity holidays, mega-events, language learning, food and entertainment. A more strategic approach to developing and marketing these opportunities was needed. ITIC believes the RTOs as well as Bord Fáilte can play an important role in initiating the better organization of particular products in the regions and also feels that the local authorities could take a greater part in the provision of facilities.

The different sector organizations, for example those dealing with accommodation, cater for the more specific interests of their members, often acting as a lobbying group at a national level while also providing more practical services to individual members. The Irish Hotels Federation (IHF) was founded in May 1937 and in 1988 its membership comprised about 400 of the 694 registered hotels and 179 guest houses. The prime function of the federation is 'to promote and defend the common interests of its members'. This is done in various ways and at different levels. Nationally, the IHF seeks to increase greater public awareness of its members' interests, and lobbies the government and political parties, particularly on fiscal and

financial matters. The IHF also provides more specific services to individual members, furnishing, for instance, confidential reports on travel agencies and offering access to technical, legal and economic advice. More recently these activities have extended to marketing and the publication of a hotel guide to Ireland.

Irish Farm Holidays was formed in 1966 and by the late 1980s had about 350 members from among the 450 Irish farmhouses which take in guests on a regular basis. The Town and Country Homes Association was established in 1972 and its 870 members represent about half of all the operators of this type of accommodation. In addition to acting as lobbying groups, both these voluntary associations have provided essential services for their small, independent members. Both associations have produced handbooks listing all their members, they have been active in overseas marketing, and they act as intermediaries between the individual members and tour operators and travel agents, processing travel vouchers and organizing group visits when needed. The associations have also been concerned with upgrading guest facilities in their members' homes, seeing that sources of finance are available and providing appropriate training and advice, for example with regard to hygiene and dealing with visitors.

The aims and interests of these different groups are not necessarily the same and some points of conflict or disagreement may occur between them. The IHF sees the supplementary accommodation as providing unfair competition through the non-application of VAT to many farmhouse and town and country house operations (VAT applies only above a certain threshold which is not obtained by many of the smaller operators).

In general, the interests of these different organizations are thus primarily sectoral and their activities are either undertaken at a national scale or directed at providing services to individual members. Such an approach is not unexpected in a small country where a national grouping of predominantly small owner operators is needed to be effective in pursuing common benefits. The different associations can point to many areas where they have successfully furthered the interests of their members. Irish farmhouses, for instance, are a distinctive and well organized element of the tourist product in Ireland. Such an orientation tends to transcend regional questions. Consequently, although a regional structure may exist (the IHF has eleven branches) and regional issues may arise (eg questions of regional access relating to the Swansea–Cork ferry, environmental considerations arising out of gold-mining proposals in the West), regional activity has not been very strong or evident. The national organizations do not have the resources to deal with anything other than national or common issues (ITIC has a staff of one executive and a secretary) and regional branches scarcely have any resources at all.

The RTOs, of course, do draw members from different sectors of the tourist industry but, as has been noted above, they have not been as successful as originally anticipated in stimulating local participation, they too have limited resources and are also subject to the national policies and directions of Bord Fáilte, a situation which constrains certain activities such as lobbying the government. Moreover, any additional comprehensive regional body, for example regional branches of ITIC, would undoubtedly be unnecessarily duplicative given the size of Ireland. During the late 1980s the IHF was encouraging its members to become more involved in the RTOs. Changes to the RTOs may also see them emerge with a stronger regional role and voice though their mixed public/private structure will continue to present some difficulties. Many private operators will no doubt continue to look first to their national sector organisation rather than their RTO.

It might be argued also that achievement of national goals by ITIC and the different sectoral associations is more critical than regional matters in any part of the country, for example enhancing the Irish farmhouse as an attractive product rather than farmhouses in specific regions or improving the general fiscal regime of the tourist industry. One of the most notable successes in this regard has come with the government's adoption of the main features of a report commissioned by the IHF (Stokes Kennedy Crowley et al, 1986) which has

led to a more positive government stance on tourism in Ireland.

Recent changes

The objectives of the study commissioned by the IHF in 1986 were to examine the feasibility of doubling Irish tourism income, in real terms, over five years, to show what national economic benefits would result and identify the measures needed to achieve this doubling. Doubling of income was shown to be feasible over a six to seven year period, providing an intensive plan for growth was implemented incorporating greater government recognition and support for tourism, substantially increased promotion, more competitive access transport and an improvement in value for money of the Irish tourist product.

The government's new tourism policy outlined in its Programme for National Recovery of October 1987 (Stationery Office, 1987, p.24), closely parallels this earlier report:

> The Department of Tourism and Transport has been established to ensure a new co-ordinated strategy to develop the tourist industry. The objective is to create an extra 25,000 jobs and to attract an additional £500 million of foreign revenue. To achieve this, we will need to double, over 5 years, the number of foreign visitors through radical changes in airline policies. We will need to become more inward-tourist oriented by lower access fares, by the development of inward air charter traffic in place of outward charter traffic, by better marketing including more targeted marketing and by the aggressive promotion of the incentives for investment in the tourist industry including business tourism under the Business Expansion Scheme.

Achievement of these targets will provide considerable challenges for Bord Fáilte. Doubling of visitor numbers over the period will require a 15 per cent annual growth rate for each of the five years, an ambitious goal in the light of Ireland's performance over the previous decade. A National Tourism Forum, of over 100 industry representatives, was convened by the government early in 1988 to obtain the industry's input on appropriate measures and initiatives to be taken.

Bord Fáilte's central task is now simply stated as being 'to attract more visitors to Ireland and to increase revenue yield from them'. They have responded to the challenge by producing a new four-part strategy:

- product strategy, offering a more attractive range of holiday and activity options,
- competitiveness strategy, providing a better-value product, in terms of both price and quality,
- promotion strategy, increasing sales to existing market segments,
- distribution strategy, ensuring that the Irish product is available to the potential customer in travel agencies and other outlets, and in a form that attracts the customer to buy.

Implementation of this strategy has provoked some restructuring of the roles and relationships of the RTOs and Bord Fáilte for it has been recognized that each must play an effective part if the new targets are to be met (Bord Fáilte, 1988). The redefined tasks for the RTOs within their areas are

- to provide leadership and co-ordination for the industry,
- to service the visitor and to develop the servicing role so that it contributes to the holiday experience of visitors,
- to secure the development of products and facilities to meet demand,
- to improve and monitor standards as the agent of Bord Fáilte,
- to assist and participate in the marketing process,
- to engage in commercial projects and facilities which enhance the product or holiday experience.

In some instances these represent an extension of existing functions (eg the monitoring of standards has been extended from the self-catering units to include Irish Homes, more emphasis is being given

to commercial activities, in large part to increase self-funding). In other cases some changes have occurred, as in the area of visitor servicing where Bord Fáilte contributions will henceforth be made only to a defined network of tourist information offices at points of entry and key tourism centres. Other existing functions have been reinforced, for example the RTOs' role in product development where they will participate in identifying opportunities and in the implementation and supervision of projects (see below). The RTOs' role in the marketing process appears to be largely directed to motivating the private sector to 'get involved in marketing' and to support and co-ordinate their efforts to do so, as well as continuing existing functions (publishing promotional material, developing domestic tourism and providing marketing support services, eg hosting familiarization tours). It is noted that 'There will be opportunities for RTOs to participate in the market place as part of planned marketing campaigns' but that 'Tight resources in line with new results orientated and targeted programmes will exclude waste and ineffective effort' (Bord Fáilte, 1988, p.30).

A new two-tier corporate structure for the RTOs was being advocated by Bord Fáilte, involving a Regional Council representing 'all valid tourism interests' which would review the RTOs' work on a quarterly basis and a nine-member Management committee which would meet more frequently to direct the ongoing work of the organization on behalf of the council. It is hoped that tourism industry interests could be incorporated more effectively into this new structure. The RTOs would continue to operate at a regional level and would not be integrated into Bord Fáilte.

Funding changes were also planned. The existing 'block grant' funding of the RTOs by Bord Fáilte was to be abandoned with contributions being made henceforth for specific support services, operations and purposes (eg operating the national tourist information network, Irish Homes inspections). A declining grant-in-aid is also to be made available to cover a transitional period through to 1993 by which time the RTOs are expected to have substantially increased their income from greater local authority contributions, expanded business membership and growth in commercial income (eg merchandising, investment in new projects).

This change in funding will provide a spur for enhanced performance by the regions and underlines the new emphasis in Bord Fáilte's relations with the RTO boards and executive of moving from 'control to results'. Regionalization of the national tourism targets further underlines this emphasis on performance and also illustrates the way in which the RTOs are being brought more closely into the product development process.

The regional tourism managers now have targets set for the amount of revenue to be generated and jobs created in their region. Disaggregation of the national targets to a regional level was initially undertaken on the basis of the stable trends in the regional spread of bednights and revenue recorded throughout the previous decade. Employment multipliers were then used to derive and monitor job creation in the regions. The initial regional targets will subsequently be reassessed in the light of product development.

In contrast to the situation surrounding the 1976–80 Tourist Development Plan, significant resources are becoming available to stimulate private sector investment in tourism. Rather fortuitously, the new tourism strategy broadly covers the period in which structural funds allocated from the European Community (EC) to Ireland and other peripheral EC regions are being almost doubled in the period leading up to the implementation of the Single Market in 1992. Previously Ireland had been reluctant to use European Regional Development Fund (ERDF) grants for tourist development with only one tourism project representing 0.04 per cent of all grants made in Ireland, being supported in the period 1975–84 (Pearce, 1988). Not only are more ERDF monies becoming available but also tourism is now being recognized in Ireland as an appropriate recipient for this assistance. EC grants worth £25 million were allocated to tourism projects from the structural funds in 1990. The government's Business Expansion Scheme was also expanded to

include tourism. This scheme provided tax relief for investors in unquoted companies engaged in specified aspects of tourism subject, among other factors, to Bord Fáilte approval of a three-year development and marketing plan by the company 'designed to increase foreign tourist traffic and revenue' (Bord Fáilte, nd). In the scheme's first operational year Bord Fáilte issued certificates of approval to thirty-three applicants whose projects represented a total investment of £45 million, of which £18.5 million was raised through the scheme. However, cut-backs to the scheme in the 1991 budget saw tourist accommodation projects henceforth excluded from it.

The increase in EC structural funds has been accompanied by a change in the procedures for their allocation. There has been a move away from funding individual projects to supporting multi-sectoral regional programmes based on newly created regional divisions. Central control and co-ordination of these programmes is retained by the Department of Finance, with some responsibility being given to relevant agencies (eg Bord Fáilte for tourism) and regional consultative committees being set up. Although the new regions did not correspond to the boundaries of the RTOs (nor indeed to other existing administrative divisions), the existence of the RTOs perhaps meant that tourism was able to respond more readily than other sectors such as agriculture and manufacturing which did not have any comparable regional framework.

The boundaries of the RTOs were subsequently redrawn to fall in line with those of the funding regions (Figure 7.4). In particular, Dublin has been separated out from the Eastern region which was combined with the former Midlands in a new Midlands East region. An enlarged Northwest region was created from the remainder of Midlands and the former Donegal, Leitrim and Sligo, while the Shannon region, now administered by SFADCo, was also enlarged.

The regional tourism managers played a key part in this funding process, being directed by Bord Fáilte to approach the industry in the regions to encourage the submission of potential tourist development projects in line with their new tourism

7.4 Regional tourist organization boundaries and airports
in Ireland (1991)
(Source: After Bord Fáilte)

strategy. Lists of appropriate projects were then
forwarded to Dublin where an initial vetting of the
multitude of projects put forward occurred in terms
of the following criteria:

- eligibility under the EC guidelines,
- contribution to the tourism targets outlined above,
- capacity to draw down funds in 1989 (there is no
  rollover of ERDF grants).

A modified list of vetted projects was then prepared
for insertion in the regional programmes following
further consultation between Bord Fáilte staff and
the RTMs.

Recognition of the need for more co-ordinated
and strategic marketing efforts to back up new
product development resulted in the preparation of
a joint three year state–industry marketing plan for
1991–3 by ITIC and Bord Fáilte (1990). This
emphasizes the need for additional marketing
expenditure by both the public and private sectors
and outlines the roles of each in the major markets.

An alternative model – Shannon development

Recent changes in the Midwest or Shannon region
provide an alternative model of tourism
organization at the regional level. On 1 January
1988 the functions and assets of the Midwest RTO
were transferred to the Shannon Free Airport
Development Company (SFADCo), along with
those which had previously been held in the region
by the Industrial Development Agency. These
moves strengthened SFADCo's role as a semi-state
multi-sectoral regional development agency, moves
which were later complemented by extending
SFADCo's responsibilities geographically to an
enlarged Shannon region under the programme for
EC funding.

SFADCo had originally been set up in 1959 to
help reduce the effects of overflying Shannon
airport following the introduction of jet aircraft on
transatlantic routes (Callanan, 1984). To this end
SFADCo developed an aggressive and innovative

7.3 Rent-an-Irish-Cottage scheme: developing new tourist product in the Shannon region has been an important role for SFADCo

approach to industrial development, through the creation of a large industrial free zone, and the stimulation of terminal tourist traffic. While the latter was aided by the introduction of a compulsory Shannon stopover on all transatlantic flights to Ireland, SFADCo have been very active in attracting new air services, working with tour operators and developing new tourist products including medieval castle banquets and the Rent-an-Irish-Cottage scheme (Plate 7.3). Duty-free shopping was also introduced to the world at Shannon airport in 1947. The emphasis has been on the American market (Figure 7.1) but more recently attempts have been made to expand European charters through the airport. North American visitors entering Ireland through Shannon spend twice as long in the country as other Americans.

A review of SFADCo's activities in 1984 concluded that their investment in promoting Shannon airport and developing the tourist infrastructure in the Midwest region 'has yielded a good national return' (Committee on Public Expenditure, 1984). The same review also pointed to some overlap of functions between SFADCo and other national agencies such as the IDA, Aer

Rianta and Bord Fáilte, in the latter case especially with regard to promotion. Some of these issues have been resolved not by the transfer of functions to the national agencies but by the strengthening of SFADCo. Shannon Development, as it is now known, is seen by some as a major innovative experiment in regional development; others see it as the furthering of an 'institution of favour' in a region which has always had strong political support since the founding of the republic (Schaffer, 1979; Callanan, 1984).

Shannon Development in 1989 had an asset base of £150 million, an annual operating budget of £40 million, a permanent staff of 250 and was managed by a board of directors appointed by the government. The company is divided into six functional areas including traffic and tourism, industry, and regional development. Given the incorporation of tourism into this broader agency, the previous RTO board and membership structure became redundant or inappropriate and was replaced by two new avenues for tourist industry input and participation. First, a small twenty-six member consultative forum was formed to provide a two-way exchange between the company and the trade. Second, the Shannon Tourism Partnership was established to draw in a broader regional participation, including local authorities. Instead of membership rights (as under the RTO), the 'partners' are provided with a range of advisory and other services enabling them to develop their tourist businesses better. Launched in the summer of 1988 it attracted about 750 partners (compare 500–600 members for the RTO) and raised about £100 000. However, as administrative costs are already covered, the sum raised goes directly into activities such as marketing.

One of the newly established services provided by Shannon Development is a tourism innovation centre which provides assistance and guidance in developing new tourist products from concept through to profitable operation and in general attempts to stimulate better management and develop entrepreneurial skills. The centre is also well advanced in the identification of potential new products and the preparation of a regional tourism plan. As a multi-sectoral agency Shannon Development not only is able to provide this specialist input but also has a much broader backup through its large staff which includes accountants, engineers, architects and landscape designers. Shannon Development is also able to provide venture capital and low interest loans. The company is a major partner in the new £8.5 million marina development at Kilrush, a project which has also attracted £2 million from the EC and £5 million in private investment. Only one of the six marina project team members is from the tourism division.

The presence of a major international gateway is clearly an overwhelming asset to the region and the capacity to have marketing staff overseas has also been instrumental in the success which SFADCo has had in attracting visitors through Shannon airport. When SFADCo's concern was solely with stimulating airport traffic the west of Ireland in general was promoted. Now with its extended remit to develop tourism within its own region, more effort might be expected to be directed at retaining visitors in the Midwest at the expense perhaps of some loss of tourist business to Cork/Kerry and the West regions.

This change came at a time when a new challenge was coming to Shannon airport from other smaller regional airports, notably Connaught International Airport near Knock (Figure 7.4). Knock constitutes an interesting example of regional initiative, an international airport built largely through the determined efforts of the late Monsignor Horan who sought to facilitate pilgrimages to the Marian shrine at Knock and managed to extract the resources to do so from the government and from parish and public appeals. Officially opened in December 1986, the airport handled 120 000 passengers in 1988, most of them travelling on the budget scheduled services of Ryanair who appear to be concentrating on the United Kingdom market. While much of this traffic has been stimulated by the recent heavy emigration from the area (and subsequently return visits to relatives and friends) an incipient tourist business is developing. Such moves, while welcomed by tourism interests in the West and DLS, have been greeted much less enthusiastically by those in the Shannon region who see part of their long established privileges being eroded. Further deregulation of air services with the completion of the Single Market within Europe may also affect Shannon. Airports in Galway and Sligo were opened in the late 1980s to enable Aer Lingus to develop feeder services to Dublin to compete with Ryanair in the western Ireland market, with regional airports at Waterford and Kerry also being developed. Nationally, the introduction of Ryanair services has had a major impact on the lowering of access fares across the Irish Sea which in turn contributed to the upturn in total arrivals in 1988 (up 13 per cent). Regional impacts are also starting to be felt.

Conclusion

The dominant position assumed by Bord Fáilte *vis-à-vis* the RTOs reflects the centralized nature of Irish administration in general. The analysis of the changing interaction between the national body and the regional organizations suggests a cyclical element may be emerging. In the decade following their establishment, the RTOs seem to have been viewed very positively by Bord Fáilte, with the regions playing a significant role in visitor servicing, planning and development. Nevertheless certain tensions did arise, particularly in the area of marketing, as the RTOs sought to extend their domain while Bord Fáilte reasserted its authority. As more attention was given by the national body to marketing in the late 1970s and 1980s and as planning and development assumed lesser importance so the RTOs saw their positions and functions diminish. For a time the national body almost appears to have turned its back on the regions. Part of this might be attributed to changing national circumstances, part to threats seen by middle management in Dublin to the growing ambitions of the RTOs (Stewart, 1985). By the late 1980s, however, the RTOs were being integrated more fully into the implementation of Bord Fáilte's new strategy for doubling tourism as development functions were again emphasized and responsibility for meeting targets regionalized. This cyclical swing in the centralization and devolution and functions and responsibilities is not peculiar to Ireland and tourism (Yuill, Allen and Hull, 1980) but may be more evident there due to the earlier establishment of the RTOs compared, for example, to Scotland.

The recent changes in Irish tourism represent an interesting combination of regional, national and even international factors. Government policy in the late 1980s appears to have been adopted in large part from a report commissioned by a national sector organization, the Irish Hotel Federation. To meet the substantial challenges involved in the targets set, Bord Fáilte had to mobilize more effectively all of its available forces, giving more responsibilities to the RTOs and working more closely with commercial operators through ITIC. In particular, the RTOs were heavily involved in the preparation of project applications to the ERDF, an international institution whose grants will be instrumental in developing new tourist products. The regionalization of targets might be seen as further integrating the regions into the achievement of national goals. This strategy appears to have been successful; at the end of year three both the targets of doubling tourism revenue and creating 25 000 new jobs 'were on course for achievement' (personal communication: R.C. O'Connor, CERT, 30/11/1990).

Note

1. The 1988 figures used here are those from the newly published CSO series which are not strictly comparable with regional figures for earlier years.

8

New Zealand

New Zealand, the last of the national case studies, provides a further example of the development of tourism within a centralized state. New Zealand has a very distinctive national tourist organization due to its early establishment (in 1901), its full departmental status throughout much of its long history, an active role in a wide range of operations and a period of major restructuring during the 1980s. Once the broad environmental factors and the nature of tourism in New Zealand have been outlined the historical evolution of the department of tourism is examined. Attention is then focused on the restructuring of the department which has occurred since 1984 and the emergence over this same period of a network of regional tourist organizations. Finally, issues of interorganizational interaction are considered.

Environmental factors

New Zealand is a relatively small country (268 000 sq km), comprised of two main islands – the North and South Islands – located in the southwest Pacific. First inhabited by the Maori, a Polynesian people who arrived about 1 000 years ago, the country was colonized and settled by the British during the nineteenth century. Although the country's population has doubled since the end of the Second World War, its current population (3.4 million in 1991) remains the smallest of the countries studied here. Today over three-quarters of the population live in the North Island. Auckland (884 000, 1991) is the country's largest urban area, followed by Wellington (325 000), the capital, and Christchurch (306 000).

After an initial period of development based on extensive pastoralism and gold mining, the country's economy came to depend quickly and heavily on the export of pastoral products – wool, meat, butter and cheese – to the British market. Manufacturing, initially for import substitution and then for export, began to expand in the 1950s. Further diversification in the economy and export markets was prompted by Britain's negotiations during the 1960s for membership of the European Community. Britain's eventual entry in 1973, the consequent reduction in assured markets for traditional exports and significant increases in imports occasioned by the energy crisis of the 1970s placed great strains on the country's economy and paved the way for subsequent restructuring.

Although production in New Zealand has largely been based on privately owned enterprises, central government has long been heavily involved, both directly and indirectly, in the country's economic affairs (Easton and Thomson, 1982). Central government played a major role in the land settlement of the young country and even today remains a significant land owner and resource manager. Public sector investment provided much of the infrastructure to open up the country and government departments assumed major responsibilities in such fields as communications, energy, forestry, health and education. A strong tradition of government regulation developed during the 1930s as a response to fluctuations in the world markets for a narrow range of exports and as a consequence of the emergence of the welfare state, a tradition which persisted through to the early 1980s. Easton and Thomson (1982, p.68) noted:

> The government's concern about the way resources are allocated, how certain activities have to be regulated for the stability of the economy, and the way income and wealth is distributed implies a deep involvement with all aspects of economic life in New Zealand. The power behind this involvement comes from Parliament, operating through government departments and government owned trading enterprises.

Strong central government has been complemented by territorial local authorities which provide services and amenities at the local scale and are responsible for land use planning. Only a very weak intermediate tier of government has existed at the regional scale. In addition to the Regional Authorities of Auckland (est. 1963) and Wellington (1980), twenty united councils were established in the period 1977 to 1983 with mandatory responsibility for regional planning and regional civil defence as well as other discretionary functions (eg regional reserves or roading).

It is against this background of central government intervention in New Zealand that the activities of the Tourist Department must be viewed. Likewise, more recent changes within the department need to be seen in the context of the radical economic and administrative restructuring which began in the early 1980s and which characterized the six year, two term period of the fourth Labour government which came to power in July 1984.

Known popularly as 'Rogernomics', Labour's new policies emphasized more competition, market deregulation, state asset sales, reduced government intervention, greater accountability and significant public sector restructuring (Bollard and Buckle, 1987). Liberalization, privatization and corporatization were the hallmarks of this new phase, summarized by Fielding and Johnston (forthcoming) thus:

> Change has occurred in all governmental activities: the national airline and Telecom have been sold; competition is encouraged on domestic air routes; the exchange rate has been allowed to float with the foreign exchange market; restrictions on imports have been reduced and eliminated on many commodities; state forests are for sale; railways, postal services and electricity production have been converted into state-owned enterprizes; school administration has been decentralized; and local governments reduced from more than 600 to 94 authorities and restructured into 14 regional councils. The entire fabric of government has been torn apart, restructured, and challenged to operate efficiently. New Zealand, once regarded as an experiment in welfare socialism, now professes economic liberalism.

Tourism in New Zealand

Tourism in New Zealand has been greatly influenced by the country's geography, both in terms of its internal diversity and its location with respect to the major world markets. New Zealand's varied climate, relief and landscape constitute bountiful natural resources for tourism. The country's long coastline, many rivers and lakes provide abundant opportunities for water sports, ski-fields have been developed in the Southern Alps and on the volcanoes of the North Island and the glaciers, geysers, fiords and other scenic splendours have long attracted sightseers. Moreover, only localized pressure on these resources has been felt due to the country's small population and low population densities. Cultural attractions on the other hand are more limited; Maori culture is of interest to many visitors but the

Table 8.1   The economic contribution of tourism in New Zealand (1988 and 1989)

		Domestic		International		Total	
		No.	%	No.	%	No.	% of national total
Total trips (domestic)	1988	10 818 000		855 492			
or visitors (int.)	1989	10 257 000		867 533			
% change 88/89			−5.5	1.4			
Person nights	1988	45 409 000	73.3	16 558 688	26.7	61 967 688	
	1989	42 704 000	72.7	16 024 757	27.3		
% change 88/89			−6.0	−3.2			
Total expenditure	1988	$2 345m	59.3	$1 612	40.7	$3 957m	
	1989	$2 215m	59.2	$1 525m	40.8	$3 740m	
change 88/89			−5.5	−5.4			
Total employment	1988	42 357	49.9	42 453	50.1	84 810	5.5
(direct and indirect)	1989	41 311	52.1	37 992	47.9	79 303	
change 88/89			−2.4	−10.5			
GDP	1988	$1 222m	53.1	$1 079m	46.9	$2 301m	3.9
Government revenue	1988	$423m	60.8	$273m	39.2	$696m	3.0

Source: Pearce (1990b)

relatively short history of European settlement has meant the country lacks the historical resources of many 'old world' destinations while the small population base and city size have constrained the development of urban attractions and entertainment.

On a more global scale the development of international tourism has been handicapped by New Zealand's distance from the major world tourist markets – Sydney is three hours' flying time from Auckland. Significant growth in the international tourist traffic to New Zealand did not occur until the introduction of jet aircraft in the 1960s (1960, 36 557 overseas arrivals; 1970, 154 991; 1980, 445 195; 1990, 933 431). Arrivals are concentrated in the three international gateways: Auckland (two-thirds of all arrivals), Christchurch and Wellington. The typical pattern is for international holiday visitors to enter the country through one of these points then to take a

one to two weeks' sightseeing tour of the country, often by coach but increasingly by plane, rental car and campervan (Forer and Pearce, 1984; Pearce 1987a, 1990b). During the 1980s more active market segments also developed, attracted, for example, by the growing opportunities for tramping and adventure tourism.

Domestic tourism has traditionally been larger than international tourism but the latter assumed increasing importance throughout the 1980s as the number of overseas visitors grew and, in the latter part of the decade, the home market stagnated. As Table 8.1 indicates, the relative contribution of domestic and international tourism varies depending on the measure used. In 1988 the domestic component generated almost three-quarters of all person nights, 60 per cent of expenditure and government revenue from tourism, and about half of tourism-related employment and GDP. Much of this variation is due to differences in patterns of demand, with a large proportion of domestic person nights being spent in private homes and with much travel being by private transport. Differing inputs into the domestic and international sectors also account for differences in their respective contributions to employment, GDP and government revenue (NZTP, 1989a). Generally, small but constant increases on each of these measures have been recorded in the estimates which have become available since 1984. In addition, international tourism makes a significant contribution to New Zealand's balance of payments, particularly in terms of diversification. In 1988 international tourism is estimated to have earned the country NZ$2 266 million if Air New Zealand's 654 million dollars of airfares are included. This sum represented 13.82 per cent of New Zealand's total exports in 1988, compared with 7.14 per cent in 1984.

The downturn in domestic person nights shown in Table 8.1 represented a fourth successive year of decline (earlier estimates of the size of the domestic market are not available). In contrast, significant growth occurred in international arrivals to New Zealand during the 1980s (Pearce, 1990b). The boom period of 1985–8 when annual growth rates ranged from 12.1 to 15.4 per cent is sandwiched between years of much smaller increases at the beginning and end of the decade (Figure 8.1). The different international markets have contributed unevenly to this growth with significant changes

occurring in the visitor mix throughout. The Australian share dropped from almost a half of all arrivals in 1980 to under one-third in 1989, but recovered to hold 35 per cent in 1990. Major growth segments have been the Japanese market (3.9 per cent to 10.8 per cent) and, for much of the decade, the American market which peaked at 21.4 per cent in 1987 but subsequently declined dramatically to its pre-1980 share. The British share has remained relatively constant throughout with some growth also being experienced in some of the smaller Asian and European segments.

The change in the visitor mix has been as critical as the evolution in total numbers. For much of the decade a relative increase in the higher spending, shorter stay Japanese and American segments and a proportionate decline in longer stay, lower spending Australians have seen growth progressively concentrated in the metropolitan areas while more peripheral regions have experienced little increase as the visitor circuit has contracted to key nodes (Tables 8.2 and 8.3).

Figure 8.2 depicts the spatial distribution of domestic and international tourism throughout New Zealand and further illustrates Auckland's dominance. Whereas most regions depend heavily on the home market, bednights in Auckland are spread almost evenly between domestic and overseas visitors. The three metropolitan regions – Auckland, Wellington and Canterbury – accounted for over half of all international bednights in

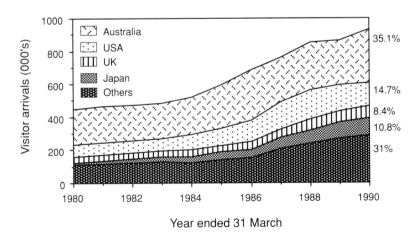

8.1 Evolution of visitor arrivals in New Zealand (1980–90) (Source: Pearce 1990b)

Table 8.2   Distribution of international tourism in New Zealand by country of residence (1989)

| | Arrivals[1] | Total person Nights[2] | Total expenditure[2] | Expenditure per person per day[2] |
	%	%	%	
Australia	31.0	25.2	23.3	$87.89
USA	18.5	14.3	20.3	$134.79
Japan	11.0	4.2	16.8	$384.03
UK	8.3	15.5	9.4	$57.54
Canada	4.2	4.8	4.8	$94.05
West Germany	2.4	3.8	3.4	$84.53
Other	24.6	32.2	22.0	$63.93
All countries	100	100	100	$95.15

Notes: [1]   All arrivals.
[2]   Visitors aged 15 years and over.
Source: Pearce (1990b)

Table 8.3   Evolution of visits to selected locations in New Zealand, all overseas visitors (1981 and 1988)

	Change in number of visits 1981–8[1]	% change 1981–8
Auckland	462 776	150.9
Christchurch	186 449	73.3
Queenstown	111 903	70.4
Rotorua	93 994	43.8
Wellington	65 241	36.8
Bay of Islands	56 757	91.0
Te Anau	36 059	37.4
Taupo/Wairakei	28 182	45.9
Dunedin	22 500	24.4
Tauranga	19 186	86.8
Picton	18 516	46.5
Franz Josef	14 644	28.6
Wanaka	13 935	43.5
Mt Cook	13 157	28.6
Nelson	12 927	21.5
Lake Tekapo	10 029	45.6

Note: [1]   Years ended 31 March
Source: Pearce (1990b)

1988–9, with Bay of Plenty (Rotorua) and Clutha Central Otago (Queenstown) also attracting a significant share. The metropolitan centres' share of international holidaymakers' bednights is slightly less pronounced but still very important. Marked regional biases occur (Figure 8.3). The concentration of the Japanese demand stands in sharp contrast to the more dispersed pattern of Australian, British and German vacationers. Auckland and Canterbury accounted for 60 per cent of Japanese holidaymaker person nights while Clutha Central Otago and Bay of Plenty made up a further 22 per cent. In comparison, these four regions accounted for only 51 per cent of Australian person nights. The three metropolitan regions are also the major sources of domestic visitors, with coastal regions close to Auckland – Northland, Thames Valley and Bay of Plenty – being particularly popular holiday destinations. In general, domestic holidaymaking is regionalized: residents of most areas find a range of resources and facilities relatively close to home. This pattern contrasts sharply with the circuit travel of the overseas tourist.

As in several of the other examples, the tourist industry in New Zealand is characterized by a large

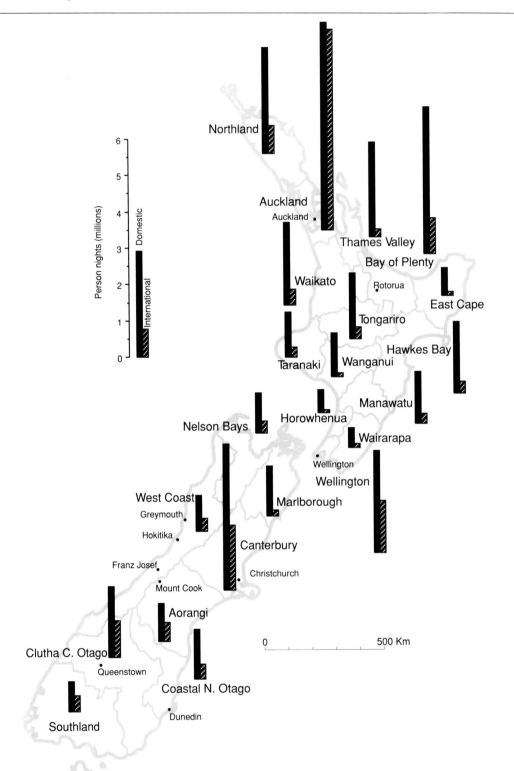

8.2 Regional distribution of domestic and international tourism in New Zealand (1988–9)
(Data source: NZTP)

8.3 Regional distribution of international person nights in New Zealand (1988–9) (Source: Pearce 1990b)

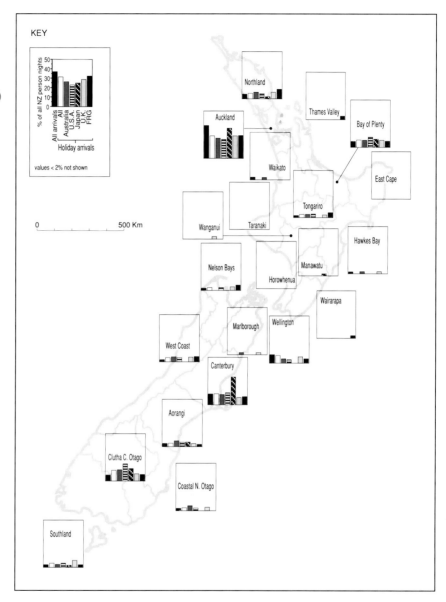

number of small operators. Small owner-operated motels, for example, are a distinctive feature of the accommodation sector (Pearce, 1987b) and many of the attractions are also small-scale ventures (eg jet-boating, white-water rafting, local sightseeing tours). During the mid-1980s a period of larger scale hotel development occurred in the major cities and resorts accompanied by increasing

foreign investment. Large operations have also developed in the inbound tour operators sector, with coach tours being traditionally popular among overseas visitors although the 1980s saw a move to more independent travel. Air New Zealand, the national carrier, has been a major player given the importance of air travel. The state has also played a key role through Crown ownership or management of land in scenic areas. About half of all overseas visitors to New Zealand, for example, visit at least one national park (Pearce and Booth, 1987; Pearce and Richez, 1987). The government was for long also actively involved in the hotel sector and with running coach tours as well as with more traditional airline and railways operations.

New Zealand Tourism Department

Evolution

The New Zealand Tourism Department traces its origins to the Department of Tourist and Health Resorts which was established on 1 February 1901, making it one of the earliest, perhaps even the first, NTO in the world. During its ninety year history the department has evolved in name, status and function (Tourist and Publicity Department, 1964, 1976; Moran, 1979). In the context of this study attention is drawn in particular to tourism's departmental status, the range of functions undertaken and the geographic spread of offices and activities throughout the country.

The new tourist department was an outgrowth of the short-lived tourist traffic division of the Railways Department which had been established in January 1901 as 'part of the scheme for utilizing the railways to a greater extent than is now done in popularizing the sanatoriums'. This represented an explicit bringing together of two related activities in which the government of the young country had become involved. The new tourist department assumed responsibility for the development and administration of fifteen scenic and thermal resort areas which the government had established as part of its policy of opening up the country for settlement or had acquired by default, as with the Hermitage at Mount Cook where the private developers had gone into liquidation in 1894 (Pearce, 1980; Pearce and Richez, 1987).

In addition to directly managing and developing resort areas, the tourist department started serving the visitor and ended up running a comprehensive tour operating division. 'Tourist Inquiry Bureaux'

were opened in Auckland, Rotorua, Wellington, Christchurch, Dunedin and Invercargill in 1902; a comprehensive booking system was instituted in 1911, rail tickets and accommodation coupons were sold in the 1920s, loose leaf itineraries were introduced in the 1930s, group travel for both international and domestic tourists was encouraged during the 1940s, Tiki Tours (New Zealand-wide coach tours) began in 1947. Over time, the Government Tourist Bureaux (GTBs) came to offer full scale travel agency and tour operations.

Overseas representation, both for sales and promotion, has also long been a function of the Tourist Department. Overseas offices established in Sydney (Plate 8.1) and Melbourne in 1911 were followed by those in London (1929), San Francisco (1950), New York (1956), Brisbane (1962), Los Angeles (1964), Tokyo (1973) and Frankfurt (1974). Marketing and promotion, particularly overseas, became increasingly important from the 1950s and in 1965 expenditure on these functions exceeded spending on facilities and amenities for the first time (Moran, 1979).

A new Development and Research Division was added in 1970 to provide input into planning, research support and an advisory service on development.

The broadening role of the department is also reflected in the new Tourist and Publicity Act 1963 which defined the department's principal functions as

- to encourage and develop the New Zealand tourist industry and tourist traffic to, within, and beyond New Zealand,
- to establish, maintain, develop and operate publicity, information, and public relations services and to charge for these services where appropriate,
- to establish, maintain and operate a travel service for reward,
- to act as an agent for any person or organization where the minister considers it necessary or expedient for the operation of the travel service,
- to administer the Tourist and Health Resorts Control Act 1908 and to carry out the functions of the former department.

8.1 Front counter staff handling customer enquiries at the New Zealand Tourism Department's Sydney office (Courtesy of New Zealand Tourism Department)

With the expanding emphasis on marketing, the tourist department in New Zealand moved more into line with the activities of other Western NTOs. Nevertheless it remained distinctive in terms of the wide range of commercial operations undertaken such as Tiki Tours, the travel agency operations of the GTBs, and, until their transfer to the government Tourist Hotel Corporation (THC) in 1957, the management of a chain of tourist hotels. Seen in the broader New Zealand context – a young, sparsely populated country, with limited private sector capital and a tradition of public sector intervention – these activities are perhaps less remarkable. The attractive Southern Alps region, for example, did not have the same human resource base for developing tourism as did the longer settled European Alps. Nor was there during the first half of this century any other agency or company able to cater comprehensively for the circuit travel of international visitors.

The early establishment and wide-ranging activities of the Tourist Department should not, however, be taken to imply New Zealand governments have always had a strong, consistent proactive tourism policy. While generalizations are difficult over such a long period, official policies towards tourism in New Zealand often appear to have been *ad hoc* and incremental (Hayward, 1989). Until recently tourist numbers have been relatively small and the economic importance of tourism limited. The tourism portfolio never ranked very highly.

The establishment of the Department of Tourist and Health Resorts in 1901 owed much to the drive and ability of the first general manager and minister but it was not until the Tourist and Health Resorts Control Act 1906 that the department was formally constituted *ex post facto* (Dollimore, 1971). Likewise the Tourist and Publicity Act 1963 conferred authority which had previously been lacking to enter into negotiations and complete contracts affecting its functions (Tourist and Publicity Department, 1976).

Continuing debate occurred over the roles of the public and private sectors in tourism. In general the emphasis was on operating hotels in key scenic areas where private operators had failed, for example at Mount Cook and Tongariro, although under the third Labour government (1972–74), there was a move to extend THC operations into the resort areas of Rotorua and Queenstown. The general manager expressed the view in 1926 that 'The Tourist Department was never intended to be a directly profit-earning institution, but was established with a view to the development of the tourist resorts, and as a help to the railways, customs, hotels and other businesses' (Tourist and Publicity Department, 1976, p.8).

Tourism gained more attention as numbers grew slowly during the 1950s but as Lloyd (1964) points out government policies were often contradictory and lacked a clear sense of direction. Hotel development in the postwar period had been constrained by price controls, something that the 1962 Tourist Accommodation Development Scheme was introduced to remedy. As overseas arrivals expanded with improved air services the foreign exchange earnings capacity of tourism became increasingly recognized. In 1967 the Cabinet post of tourism was raised to a full portfolio because of 'the importance to the country's economy of tourist receipts and the increasing role of tourism as a vital earner of

overseas exchange' (Tourist and Publicity Department, 1976, p.13). Likewise the fundamental purpose of government support to the THC was 'to assist in earning overseas funds'. The 1969 National Development Conference set 'export targets' for tourism along with other sectors of the economy (NDC, 1969). The 1978 Tourism Advisory Conference also emphasized overseas visitor arrivals, setting a growth target of 8 per cent per annum over the decade 1978–9/1987–8 while at the same time recognizing tourism contributed to regional development and employment (TAC, 1978). Accordingly the conference called for greater marketing efforts, a sentiment which was echoed in a wide-ranging report published early in 1984 (NZ Tourism Council and Tourist and Publicity Dept, 1984). Mings's (1980) comprehensive review of attitudes towards international tourism over the period 1969–78 showed general support for the industry and further highlighted the perceived foreign exchange earning capacity of tourism, among not only politicians but also the public at large. This widespread support, however, did not extend to generous funding of the country's NTO.

Years of change: 1984–90

During the six years of the fourth Labour government the Tourist and Publicity Department underwent a period of unprecedented change. Restructuring saw the department reorganized, renamed, trimmed and given a more sharply focused marketing function. When Labour came to power in July 1984 the department had a combined staff of 530, of whom 300 were in the tourism division. When Labour's second term came to an end in October 1990 the department had been divested of all its publicity functions and had a total staff of 180. NZTP Travel offices (formerly the GTBs) were disposed of in August 1990 as the government moved out of commercial tourist operations; the THC hotels were also sold off and Air New Zealand privatized. Overseas offices were closed in Perth, Adelaide, Melbourne, Brisbane, Osaka, San Francisco and New York, as was the regional office in Dunedin. Various incentive

Table 8.4   Evolution of budgets of New Zealand Tourism Department (1986–91)

| Divisions | Year ended 31 March[1] | | | | | | | |
| | 1986 | | 1987 | | 1988 | | 1989 | |
	$m	%	$m	%	$m	%	$m	%
Travel marketing	16.230	49.4	21.314	52.8	33.498	53.6	33.986	51.7
Development and advisory	7.984	24.3	3.611	9.0	7.809	12.5	9.645	14.7
Commercial operations/								
travel	4.906	15.0	8.266	20.5	11.709	18.9	13.501	20.6
Administrative	1.326	4.0	2.855	7.0	4.003	6.4	3.855	5.9
Finance	0.804	2.5	1.010	2.5	1.112	1.8	0.455	0.7
EDP/TRAITS	1.296	4.0	2.238	5.5	2.638	4.2	2.256	3.4
Policy and research	0.272	0.8	1.085	2.7	1.610	2.6	1.991	3.0
Total	32.818	100	40.379	100	62.379	100	65.89	100

Note: [1]   Former NZ Tourist and Publicity Department, excluding publicity division.

| Outputs | | Year ended 31 March 1991 | | |
		$m	%	% excl. 6
1	Policy advice and ministerial services	1.623	3.7	4.22
2	Marketing of New Zealand as a travel			
	destination in overseas countries	32.730	74.1	85.43
3	Tourism development	3.547	8.0	9.34
4	Administration of government assets	0.150	0.3	0.45
5	Administration of grants	0.240	0.5	0.66
6	Residual management services			
	departmental business units	5.870	13.3	
		44.160	100	100

Source: NZ Tourism Dept, annual reports

schemes were also terminated in line with broader policies that 'commercial ventures should stand or fall on their attractiveness to commercial investors' (NZTP, 1989d). Changes in budgetary allocations further highlight the effects of restructuring, notably the elimination of the travel division and the greatly increased expenditure – at least in relative terms – on marketing (Table 8.4).

While restructuring occurred almost continuously throughout this period the single largest change came in August 1990 when the department, divested of its business operations, was renamed the New Zealand Tourism Department and given a redefined mission:

to develop and market New Zealand as a tourism destination where this is beyond the interest of the private sector, and where this is a cost effective contribution to the Government's desired outcomes.

The specific outcomes desired by government to which tourism would contribute were: increased overseas earnings, growth in employment attributable to tourism and soundly based and sustainable development of New Zealand as a tourism destination. The government's role was not to subsidize industry but 'to add to and not displace what industry could do for itself' (NZTD, 1990, p.14).

The increased emphasis on overseas marketing reflects the continuation of a trend which had begun much earlier, but one which was given additional impetus by the large Tourism 2000 conference convened by the minister in May 1989 (NZTP, 1989b, 1989c). The Taskforce 2000 recommended *inter alia* the adoption of a target of 3 million foreign visitors per year by the year 2000 and the establishment of a New Zealand Tourism Board, a joint private–public sector directed and funded body responsible for the marketing and development of 'Destination New Zealand' which would have an initial target budget of $100 million. The call was for a better targeted and co-ordinated marketing effort by the public and private sectors combined, a recognition of the need for greater co-operation to market New Zealand effectively in large and distant markets. While the idea of a board was not immediately adopted, the minister announced the formation of two new organizations in April 1990 to work 'in partnership' with the restructured Tourism Department, the Tourism Forum and the Tourism Strategic Marketing Group. The Tourism Forum replaced the former advisory Tourism Council and was seen as 'The consultative mechanism between the public and the private sector on major issues affecting tourism in New Zealand'. The Forum is a sixty member body comprised largely of members of sector and regional tourism organizations. It met with the minister three times in 1990. In contrast the Tourism Strategic Marketing Group (TSMG) was to be (Wilde, 1990, p.7)

> a small and specialized group of companies with the simple objective of doing good business for themselves and New Zealand by working as a team.

This marketing group will facilitate co-operation amongst the big investors in the marketing of New Zealand so we can get the most clout from our limited resources and compete successfully against bigger and wealthier tourist destinations.

It is our hope and expectation that the group will develop the vision and confidence to share their knowledge and talent for the common good. When they do so we will have the core of a global strategy for the marketing of New Zealand as a destination. To begin the process the Department will lay its marketing plans on the table.

The TSMG consisted of eight major players in addition to the Tourism Department: the privatized Air New Zealand and its wholly owned subsidiary the Mount Cook Group, two tour operators, American Express, Hertz, South Pacific Hotel Corp and the Helicopter Line.

In late 1990 the TSMG (1990) outlined its vision for the future in a strategic report, a vision of 'a highly focused, profit oriented, internationally competitive inbound tourism industry' generating $10 billion foreign exchange in the year 2000 from almost 3 million visitors per year. The emphasis was on increased growth from the major markets concentrated on the gateway destinations of Auckland and Christchurch and the major resorts of Rotorua and Queenstown. The strategy called for improved targeting and competitiveness, a supportive policy environment, sustainability of resources, more effective industry structures and better matching of supply with demand. The accent was exclusively on the inbound market; domestic tourism was all but ignored.

While there was much merit in the strategy, particularly improved co-ordination between public and private sector efforts, it clearly reflected the interests of the major players. Accelerated spatial concentration may be one response to market forces but it is not necessarily compatible with resource sustainability and the spreading of benefits to other regions and operators may be some time in coming.

Other divisions and activities of the Tourism Department primarily complement and support its marketing function. Development, broadly defined, is the largest of these in budgetary terms (Table 8.4) and is split between two divisions – industry development and planning. The industry development division is largely concerned with private sector and regional issues. The division, for example, is responsible for the department's five regional offices, for industry quality assurance programmes and Maori liaison. Initiatives undertaken in 1990 included the introduction of the KIWIHOST tourism awareness and hospitality skills programme and the establishment of a nationwide Visitor Information Network. The latter was designed in part to compensate for the loss of visitor information services occasioned by the closure of the NZTP travel offices. Under the new scheme, the department no longer operates its own information services, but makes grants to selected offices which meet specified criteria. These are often, but not exclusively, run by regional or local tourist organizations.

The role of the tourism planning division is not to implement a national tourism plan for the country has never had such a plan. Preparation of one was begun in the early 1980s but what finally emerged was a watered down 'Issues and Policies' discussion report (Hayman, 1983; NZ Tourism Council and Tourist and Publicity Department, 1984). The tourism planning division is primarily concerned with infrastructural matters and frequently works with local authorities and other government agencies such as the Department of Conservation and Transit New Zealand to help ensure adequate provision is made for tourism in district planning schemes, national park management plans, roading programmes and so on. The division, for example, had a major liaison role in the recent redevelopment project for Milford Sound, a popular but congested destination within Fiordland National Park and provided a $250 000 grant to fund investigation and design work. The project also received a $2.8 million tourism facilities development grant for this project in 1990–1. If 'sustainable development' is to be more than a trendy catchphrase and if demand is to increase at anywhere near the rates projected, questions of infrastructural provision and carrying

capacities of scenic areas will become increasingly critical in the future.

Other divisions in 1990 were those responsible for policy and ministerial services, corporate planning and evaluation, public affairs (including the visiting agents and publicists programme), information management (encompassing the research section and a NZ Host Database), support services and residual management functions (handling the wind-up of the business units).

Regional activities

From its very early years the Tourist Department had a strong regional presence through the administration of reserves, the development of resort hotels and the operation of the GTBs, though this diminished over time as, for example, the hotels passed to the THC. Until the 1980s, however, comparatively little interaction occurred in the regions with operators, local government or the various localized and rather weak promotional associations which had grown up.

Early in 1983 the department established a Tourism Advisory Service 'in response to an increasing demand from the industry and from different regions throughout New Zealand for advice, assistance and information about all aspects of tourism' (Tourist and Publicity Dept, 1983, p.16). Such a service had been called for the previous year in the National Tourist Association sponsored Henshall Report (Henshall, 1982). The objectives of the service were 'to assist regional and local authorities and tourist operators to develop and promote tourism within their regions' (Tourist and Publicity Dept, 1984, p.45). Nine regional liaison officers (RLOs) were appointed and based in Auckland, Wellington, Rotorua, Christchurch, Queenstown and Dunedin. The RLOs initially had a fairly broadly defined role to provide advice and assistance in terms of marketing, development (eg explaining the various incentives available and vetting projects) and information (eg disseminating an increasing amount of regional research data). Considerable activity in the industry at this time occasioned by the growth in overseas arrivals (Figure 8.1) generated much demand for these services. The RLOs also played a major role in the establishment of a network of regional tourist organizations.

The *Issues and Policies* report of March 1984 (NZ Tourism Council and Tourist and Publicity Dept, 1984, p.103) called for the adoption of 'formally agreed tourism regions . . . so that integrated tourism marketing and development can proceed on a regional level' and noted that the RLO activities were now based on united council boundaries. A month later, the industry body, the National Tourist Association, restructured itself as the New Zealand Tourist Industry Federation (TIF). TIF's membership consisted of major operators, sector organizations and branches, some of which served individual communities or localized areas. As part of the new changes, TIF moved to restructure its branches into regional members whose boundaries were also to be aligned with those of the united councils. The adoption of the twenty-two united councils' boundaries appears in part to have been undertaken to enhance local government funding for the regional tourist organizations and to facilitate tourism input into regional planning. The choice of these boundaries might also have provided some pragmatic justification for enlarging and amalgamating the smaller branches. In the event few regions other than Canterbury provided much input into regional plans and not all TIF regional members corresponded to a single united council (eg Central Otago had representatives from Queenstown and Wanaka).

The RLOs played an important role in setting up many of the new regional organizations by liaising with individuals, groups and local authorities and trying to get them to work together co-operatively at a larger scale. Such external input and guidance was critical given the large distances concerned in cases such as the West Coast and the varied strength of local communities. This behind-the-scenes work was complemented by financial incentives. In May 1985 the new Labour Minister of Tourism announced that grants of $5 000 would be made available for the preparation of a regional marketing plan for each united council region with further funding being made available under the

Regional Promotion Assistance Scheme (RPAS) to subsidize promotional projects contained therein. After 1 August 1985 all applications for such assistance had to be lodged by a regional member of TIF and be approved by the department. The department also provided technical assistance by way of guidelines for the preparation of the regional marketing plans as well as through RLO advice. Marketing plans, of varying quality and emphasizing the domestic market, were subsequently prepared for each region. Late in 1987 the RPAS was extended to include subsidies for regional tourism organization staff salaries in a scheme which phased out over three years. The government also agreed to support a major three year domestic marketing campaign – the Great New Zealand Campaign – centred on domestic packages put together by the regions.

After this peak departmental support to the regions contracted as the effects of restructuring began to bite following the July 1988 budget. During 1989 the promotional subsidies section of the RPAS was cancelled and the department withdrew from the poorly performed Great New Zealand Campaign. New regional offices were set up separately in early 1990 to ensure continuity after the closure of the travel offices. The advisory service role of the RLOs and regional managers was dropped and their activities refocused on the department's more tightly defined outputs. In effect this has meant greater support for international marketing, particularly hosting visiting agents and publicists. The regional offices also provide head office with regular reports on developments and marketing opportunities in their regions (Plate 8.2).

The reduction in support to the regions resulting from the department's restructuring was to have been compensated in part by the government's broader restructuring policies. Under local government reforms in 1989 fourteen regional councils replaced the twenty-two united councils. Both TIF and the department, with varying degrees of success, encouraged the realignment of the regional tourist organizations with the new regional boundaries. The government proposed making the new regional councils take a more active role in tourism by giving each council statutory

8.2 A montage of travel articles on New Zealand: the return on hosting familiarization trips
(Courtesy of New Zealand Tourism Department)

responsibility for the preparation of an annual tourism plan outlining 'the co-ordination of the strategic planning, development, marketing, and funding of tourism within its district'. To support this the department carried out a Regional Tourism Action Campaign (RTAC) in 1990, a series of one-day workshops in the regions designed to increase community awareness, stimulate new ideas for regional tourism and address questions of funding and improved public–private partnerships. While RTAC generated much interest, the new regional council provisions were not passed before Labour lost power and the legislation was shelved. Moreover, the new regional councils, faced with additional responsibilities and ratepayer resistance

to rate increases, have been strapped for resources and generally been unable or unwilling to make substantial contributions to regional tourist organizations. Indeed, in 1991 their own existence looked threatened under National policies.

Regional organizations

Considerable variety is to be found among New Zealand's regional tourist organizations as well as in the local associations and other bodies which exist below this level. Moreover, the early 1990s were a period of much change and instability as a result of

Table 8.5   Projected funding for New Zealand regional tourist organizations (1991–2)

| | Regional tourist organizations | | | | | |
| | Without infor-mation offices | | With infor-mation offices | | All | |
	$	%	$	%	$	%
Local authority	40 800	18	219 200	52	138 120	42
Regional council	47 300	21	21 700	5	33 318	10
Private sector	88 600	40	71 000	17	79 011	24
Sales commission	800	–	40 200	10	22 318	7
Other	45 700	21	67 200	16	57 455	17
Total	223 200	100	419 300	100	330 222	100

Source: After Murray-North (1991a)

broader restructuring policies. Presentation of a comprehensive national overview is limited by this diversity and fluidity, together with the lack of a systematic data base. A major review of regional tourist organizations undertaken in early 1991 generated the first comparative data on the activities and funding of these organizations (Murray-North, 1991a).

This study showed the average regional tourist organization to have 4.3 staff (ranging from 1.5 to

14) and a projected 1991–2 budget of $330 000, though whether all of this would eventuate was doubtful given existing uncertainties in council funding. Major variations occur in the source of funding depending on whether information offices are provided or not: those with information offices tend to draw more of their funding from local authorities; regional councils contribute proportionately more to the others (Table 8.5). Figure 8.4 indicates that, in addition to

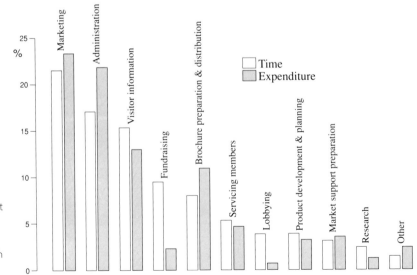

8.4 Average allocation of New Zealand regional tourist organization staff time and budget by function (Source: After Murray-North 1991a)

administration, marketing, provision of information services and brochure preparation and distribution were major activities, followed, in terms of time spent, by fundraising and servicing members. Lobbying, research and product development were minor activities.

This national overview provides a context within which the structure and functions of particular organizations can now be examined in more detail. These range from the two main gateway regions (Auckland and Canterbury), through those having major resorts (Rotorua and Queenstown), to three secondary destinations: Coastal North Otago (with Dunedin), Taranaki and the West Coast (Figure 8.2).

Auckland, New Zealand's major international gateway and the leading destination (Figure 8.2) has a wide range of urban tourism and gateway functions as well as other recreational attractions particularly those based on its harbour setting. Within the region a division of responsibility has emerged, with regional promotion being undertaken by Tourism Auckland while visitor servicing is carried out by three visitor centres supported by three different city councils.

Tourism Auckland is a non-profit organization established in 1987 by the Auckland Regional Authority and administered by an eleven member board consisting of industry and local government representatives (five from the Auckland Regional Council (ARC), one from Auckland City Council). In 1990 it had a staff of five and about ninety members, including some of the largest operators in the country. For 1990–1, Tourism Auckland had a cash income of under $400 000, of which over half was derived from an ARC grant, with the remainder generated from membership fees and activities (Tourism Auckland, 1990). Tourism Auckland's mission is

> To be the focal point for the promotion of tourism in Auckland which best serves the economic and social needs of our members and the people of the Auckland region.

Its primary goals are 'to be the official non-aligned focal point for the promotion of tourism in

Auckland' and 'to achieve and maintain higher than national average growth in visitor numbers to the Auckland region'. The 'focal point' emphasis suggests that the organization is still trying to establish its identity and role within the region. In its marketing and promotion efforts particular attention is put on conventions and events. Tourism Auckland also participates in trade shows in Sydney and Melbourne, has launched a regional promotions brochure and hosts 'fam' trips. Research is collated and distributed to members but little primary research is initiated.

Tourism Auckland also manages two self-funded information centres at Auckland airport. Other visitor servicing is left to the information centres supported by the city councils, members and associations: Auckland Visitor Centre, funded largely by the Auckland City Council, is the largest of these, having a staff of eight. Its aims are

- to optimize tourism revenue in the medium/long term for the benefit of the Auckland economy,
- to provide an efficient, impartial and quality based tourist and public information and reservation system within the restraints imposed by available finance.

No formal links exist between the visitor centres and Tourism Auckland although some liaison and joint activity does take place, for example visitor centre staff may assist Tourism Auckland at trade shows.

In contrast, the Canterbury Tourism Council (CTC) undertakes both visitor servicing and marketing, as well as other functions. This mix reflects the evolution of the organization, which began after the First World War as the Canterbury Progress League, was reconstituted in 1979 as the Canterbury Promotion Council (and became the regional member of TIF in 1984) and restructured as the CTC in 1990. Along the way tourism became the central focus as broader promotional activities were dropped, the public relations office became a modern visitor information centre and a marketing officer was appointed in 1986. In 1990 the CTC had a staff of nine, 500 members and a

8.3 Canterbury Tourism Council staff and members distribute material from their stand at the 1991 Melbourne Holiday and Travel Show
(Courtesy of the Canterbury Tourism Council)

budget of $680 000. Local authorities contributed 43 per cent of the revenue, members 11 per cent, with most of the remainder coming from self-generated revenue, particularly publications advertising.

The CTC has as its mission

> To develop Christchurch and Canterbury as a major tourism destination; to solicit and service conventions and other group business and to engage in visitor promotions which generate overnight stays, thereby enhancing and developing the economic fabric of the community.

Despite these broader goals, running the visitor information centre absorbs a significant amount of the CTC's resources with only $46 000 (7 per cent) being spent directly on 'marketing, promotion and research' in 1989–90 (publications costs excluded). In effect research activity has disappeared, and the promotions effort, in addition to the distribution of publications, is concentrated on a couple of trade shows in Australia and two or three others in New Zealand (Plate 8.3). Attempts are also being made to boost conventions. The merging of the chief executive's and marketing officer's positions in

1991 further constrained marketing activity. The CTC also hosts 'fam' trips, provides advice and support to members and runs a commercial punting operation which it took over primarily to enhance the city's image. With RLO support the CPC had established a broad-based Tourism Advisory Committee in 1985 to advise the united council on tourism matters but while some useful input was provided the council gave no financial support and the committee lapsed in 1989.

In contrast to some other large geographical regions, the CTC functions as a regional tourist organization. While the greater name recognition of Christchurch is used in international marketing rather than Canterbury, and while the Christchurch City Council is the largest contributor and the only information centre run is that in the city, the CTC does draw funding and members from throughout the North Canterbury region and in turn promotes and distributes information on places outside Christchurch. There appears to be a general acceptance and recognition of the links between Christchurch's urban and gateway functions and those of smaller, outlying resort towns such as Hanmer (hot springs), Methven (skiing) and Akaroa (historic French settlement). Nevertheless the city council has also embarked on its own promotions ventures from time to time and the restructuring and enlargement of the regional council boundaries in 1989 did not result in the amalgamation of the CTC with South Canterbury Promotions, the smaller body located in the former Aorangi district. The Canterbury Regional Council itself also initiated major research projects in 1991 to assess further directions for tourism development and to remove impediments to tourism growth (Murray-North, 1991b).

Organizational structures in the regions containing the country's two major resorts – Rotorua in the North Island and Queenstown (Pearce and Cant, 1981) in the South – differ significantly from that of Canterbury. In each case the most effective organization is a local resort-based, marketing-focused body with no information centre functions, substantial local authority funding and little interaction with the surrounding region.

Rotorua District Council appointed its own promotions and marketing co-ordinator in 1988, after the local public relations office had been disbanded in 1983 and a subsequent promotions society had not proved particularly effective. The co-ordinator's initial budget of $250 000 had increased to $800 000 in 1991, much of this being spent on a domestic television advertising campaign, newspaper supplements and the publication of a Rotorua visitors' brochure. Future plans include the establishment of a visitor monitoring system and greater activity in overseas markets. It should be recalled that up until mid-1990 the NZTP travel office in Rotorua provided a significant visitor servicing function. Although the council initially picked up its lease the subsequent operation of the centre remains doubtful.

At the regional level Rotorua, the major player, has effectively gone its own way. A Bay of Plenty Tourism Council was formed in 1987, bringing together local promotion associations in the area covered by the Bay of Plenty United Council. This, however, has played little more than a token co-ordinating role, having a projected budget of only $60 000 in 1988–9 and no full-time staff. With RPAS funding removed, its future looks doubtful.

The Queenstown Promotions Bureau (QPB) was established in 1984 from the former branch of

the NTA, with its main function being to promote Queenstown outside the region. A marketing director was appointed in 1989. QPB had a total budget of around $240 000 in 1990, of which over $200 000 came from the district council which began levying a special rate on local businesses in 1989 to fund promotion. Particular emphasis is put on marketing Queenstown at ski shows in Australia and New Zealand and fostering event tourism. One of the QPB's three staff was also designated part-time to co-ordinate the activities of the Central Otago Tourism Council Incorporated (COTCI). COTCI had been created in August 1988 as a regional body bringing together the QPB and the smaller local promotion associations of Wanaka, Alexandra and Cromwell, largely, it seems, to take advantage of RPAS funding. COTCI put together a regional brochure, helped foster the Otago Goldfields Heritage Highway and co-ordinated the region's presence at South Island shows. Again its future looked in doubt with the cut-back in departmental funding.

As in the larger Canterbury region, regional government restructuring in Otago has not resulted in an amalgamation of regional tourist organizations. QPB and COTCI continue to function separately from the Dunedin Tourist Promotion Association (DTPA) which serviced Dunedin and the former Coastal North Otago district. This reflects strong parochial differences, different tourist markets and structures and the effective functioning of the QPB and DTPA before the creation of the Otago Regional Council (Coughlan and Kearsley, 1991). The DPTA is an incorporated society and the regional member of TIF. However, it is strongly supported by the Economic Development Department of the Dunedin City Council which provides the bulk of its funding (70 per cent of $695 000 in 1991) as well as staff and administrative support; the executive, tourism marketing and promotions officers in the department carry out equivalent functions for the DPTA. The council in turn sees the DPTA as its tourism advisory board and its interface with the private sector. In addition Dunedin City Council has a Tourism Development Section, runs the visitor centre, provides a conference management service and operates 'Dunedin Unlimited Tours'. Responsibility for different activities is shared between the Dunedin City Council and the DPTA.

Taranaki is one of New Zealand's more modest tourist regions, depending heavily on domestic visitors, particularly those visiting friends and relatives (Figure 8.2). Nevertheless, Tourism Taranaki is one of the country's more dynamic regional tourist organizations and one which is particularly membership responsive. Tourism Taranaki was established in 1986 from the convergence of two sets of conditions. Concern from the united council over the wind-down in the region's energy projects and the rural downturn coincided with the Tourism Department's support for the preparation of regional marketing plans. Although several local public relations offices had existed since the 1970s, it was recognized that for the plan to be implemented successfully, a new region-wide body, incorporating support not only from the local authorities but also from the private sector was needed. Visitor servicing was left to the existing local associations and Tourism Taranaki was formed to undertake regional promotion, the society's main objective being (Tourism Taranaki, 1991)

> to promote and foster the development of tourism and the attainment of a satisfying tourist experience within the Taranaki region and to secure long term benefits from tourism for Taranaki by increasing the number of visitors to Taranaki, increasing their length of stay and by increasing their average expenditure.

Within the limits of its resources (one full-time and two part-time staff) Tourism Taranaki has sought to package and promote the region's resources and harness the energies of its members. A notable success has been the Rhododendron Festival, which involves opening almost 100 gardens to the public, an event which now attracts 10 000 visitors during the 10 days of the festival. Historic sights are also being packaged and promoted as a Heritage Trail. In addition, more traditional

activities such as producing and distributing publications and taking part in domestic promotions are carried out. Modest surveys are also undertaken with membership assistance. Particular attention has been paid to keeping the more than 300, mostly small, members informed and generating public awareness of tourism's role in the regional economy. Members are even asked to submit priorities for the society's budget and in this way contribute to determining Tourism Taranaki's activity programme (Figure 8.5) although final decisions are made by the director and board.

The West Coast, the last of the regional examples, has significant natural features (eg the Fox and Franz Josef Glaciers) and an interesting historical heritage dating from the gold rushes of the 1860s, but is relatively remote, difficult of access and experiences high rainfall. Consequently, it is very much a second-tier destination (Figure 8.2). Promoting the region has been rendered difficult by the sparseness of the population and the large distances involved – the region covers a similar distance as Auckland to Wellington but has a population of only 30 000. The West Coast Tourism Council (WCTC) was set up in 1984 with the help of the RLO but it was not until 1987 that a marketing officer, still the only staff appointment, was created. The WCTC does not operate a visitor centre (but three local associations do) and concentrates on marketing and promoting the region in a similar but generally more modest way to other regional organizations. Co-ordinating a stand at the Agricultural and Pastoral Show in Christchurch is a major annual event.

In the context of this study, interest in the West Coast stems not so much from the WCTC but the West Coast Tourism Development Group. This was a special purpose development group, set up by the Minister of Tourism (with representatives from the WCTC, the West Coast Regional Council and his own nominees) to implement the recommendations of the 1988 West Coast PATA Task Force. PATA, the Pacific Asia Travel Association, each year undertakes taskforce activities in member countries. When interest was expressed in coming to New Zealand, the West Coast, with assistance from their RLO, succeeded

ANNUAL ACTION PLAN - What do you think?

Each year Tourism Taranaki writes an Annual Action Plan which sets out what activities the Society will carry out in the following year.   The activities to be carried out are determined by what has been successful the previous year, the budget and what you the members think.   Final approval of the Plan is given by the Board of Directors.

This is your opportunity to tell us what you think we should do during the 1991/92 year.   The Plan to be produced will run for 12 months 1 July 1991 – 30 June 1992. Our budget for that period will be $175,000.   Below is a list of activities and costings. Please in order of priority list your preference, that is 1 for the most preferred option and 40 for the least preferred.   Remember you cannot spend more than $175,000.

List your preference	ADMINISTRATION	Cost
☐	Employment of staff to action Plan (includes salary of Chief Executive, Secretary and one off occasional assistance)	$60,000
☐	Employment of Promotions Officer	$25,000
☐	Administration – office rental, telephone, postage, stationery, photocopying, travel, insurance	$18,500
☐	Research, includes Visitor Surveys (included in above)	
	PRINTING	
	"Destination Taranaki" reprint –	
☐	English edition	$20,000
☐	Foreign Language edition (state which)......................	$10,000
	Brochures –	
☐	Reprint of five trail brochures	$12,000
☐	Dining Guide	$ 4,000
☐	Art and Craft Trail Guide	$ 4,000
☐	Heritage Trail brochure	$ 5,000
☐	Education folder – aimed at attracting school groups to the region	$ 1,500
☐	Rhododendron Festival brochure	$ 4,000
☐	Rhododendron Festival posters	$ 700
☐	Rhododendron Festival programme	$ 4,000
☐	Taranaki brochure (One colour tourist attraction guide)	$ 2,000
☐	Other brochures (name)	$ 4,000

8.5 Tourism Taranaki's questionnaire to members (Source: Tourism Taranaki 1991)

		Cost
☐	**ADVERTISING**	
☐	Tabloid insert to distribution in market areas	$ 6,000
	Magazine Advertising of:	
☐	(a) Rhododendron Festival; and/or	$ 6,000
☐	(b) Taranaki as a Holiday Destination	$ 6,000
☐	Television Advertising—with present advertisement	$ 6,000
☐	—with new advertisement	$10,000
☐	Radio Advertising Tonight Show	$ 3,000
☐	Newspaper Advertisement	$ 3,000
☐	Other advertising	

PROMOTION

☐	Shopping Mall promotions Specify number .... Place	$ 2,000 each
☐	Mystery Creek Field Days	$ 2,000
☐	Travel Trade Show—Auckland	$ 5,000
☐	—Wellington	$ 4,000
☐	Australian Travel Trade—Melbourne and Sydney	$ 8,000
☐	Hosting Travel Agents	$ 3,000
☐	Hosting Travel Journalists	$ 1,000
☐	Conference Bids	$ 1,000

OTHER ACTIVITIES

☐	KiwiHost Training Courses	$ 1,000
☐	Membership Meetings	$ 1,000
☐	Newsletters	$ 1,000

EVENT TOURISM

☐	Hawera Dairy Festival Stratford Shakespeare Festival Others (name)	$ 5,000
☐	Tourism Awareness Day	$ 1,000
☐	Tourism Awards	$ 1,000
☐	**FURTHER DEVELOPMENT** - Heritage Trails	$ 2,000

8.5 Tourism Taranaki's questionnaire to members (*continued*) in being the region chosen to have their development possibilities explored. Not only did the PATA report provide guidelines for future development but its international status also enabled the region to obtain financial support from the government to follow them through. While the sums involved are not great ($150 000), and only one fixed term appointment was made, the group have been able to undertake development and promotional activities not otherwise envisaged. Much emphasis has gone on developing the concept of a heritage highway, with gateway information centres, improved signage and landscaping studies being undertaken. Such activity ultimately results from a sequence of inter-organizational interaction involving an international body (PATA), the NTO (through head office and RLO support), and regional organizations of the WCTC, the regional council and the West Coast conservancy of the Department of Conservation).

National and regional issues and interactions

Until recently New Zealand did not have a systematically developed national/regional network of tourist organizations. From its earliest days, the central NTO – the Tourism Department in its various forms – had a strong regional presence and a deconcentration of functions without parallel in the other examples studied here. This, coupled with the absence of a strong regional tier of government and the overall size of the tourist industry, meant effective regional tourist organizations were very slow in emerging. The subsequent development of regional organizations in the mid-1980s was actively fostered by the department as well as the Tourist Industry Federation. The variety of regional organizations which resulted nevertheless testifies to the strength of strong local and regional characteristics. Then, in a process not dissimilar to that experienced in Ireland, initial strong central support for the regions waned as the national organization,

influenced by changing external conditions, focused its efforts more tightly on international marketing. The regional organizations enter the 1990s facing a difficult period of readjustment and it is questionable whether all are sufficiently well established to survive.

While the future of the regional organizations lies to some extent in their own responses, resources and initiatives, tourism in the regions, particularly international tourism, will continue to be determined in large part by developments at a larger scale. The regions themselves lack the resources to influence distant international markets, having at best limited campaigns in east coast Australia, and have never had any direct voice in the Tourism Department's international marketing activities. Rather, the regions are seen to have a role once overseas visitors have reached the country, with the Tourism 2000 Taskforce recommending (NZTP, 1989b, p.85)

> that New Zealand continue to be promoted by a central body with an objective of increasing the average length of stay of visitors from a variety of markets. It then becomes a regional responsibility to ensure that product and supporting infrastructure appropriate to the needs of those markets is put in place to encourage visitors to spend time in the regions.

Concentration versus dispersal scenarios were debated (McDermott Millar, 1988) as the regional consequences of the trends and patterns depicted in Figures 8.1 and 8.2 and Tables 8.2 and 8.3 began to be felt, notably much more rapid rates of growth in the gateways and major resorts than in other parts of the country. Nevertheless national rather than regional concerns continued to predominate. Although the department may organize 'fam' trips throughout the country and widely solicit input into some publications, a review of its marketing plans for the late 1980s indicated little or no emphasis was put on the regional spread of visitors (Pearce, 1990b). Indeed, the Tourism Strategic Marketing Group's proposed strategy accentuated growing differences between the key hubs – Auckland, Rotorua, Christchurch and Queenstown – and the 'regions' (TSMG, 1990).

Inter-regional interaction and co-operation has also been limited and attempts to develop larger regions have met with little or no success. Early in the 1980s 'tourism product regions' were proposed, for example 'coastal', 'volcanic' and 'alpine' New Zealand (Town and Country Planning Directorate, 1984). While there may have been some merit in this idea from a product development and marketing perspective the proposed regions cut across administrative boundaries. Moreover, the proposal came from the Town and Country Planning Directorate of the Ministry of Works and Development rather than the NZTP and did not survive the change of government in 1984. In 1987, NZTP with the Tourist Industry Federation's (TIF) agreement, proposed the use of six 'macro-regions' for overseas marketing purposes rather than the twenty-two existing TIF regions. Some publications appeared using the new 'macro-regions' but the idea was never widely endorsed by the regional tourist organizations themselves.

The South Island Promotion Association (SIPA) has existed since 1936 to promote New Zealand's southern regions. SIPA has experienced varying levels of support over the years, its activities sometimes being seen as duplicating existing efforts. However, it appeared to be rejuvenated in 1990, with an office being opened in Auckland not only to foster domestic tourism but also to tap international arrivals in the country's main gateway and encourage them to travel farther south. There has never been a North Island equivalent to SIPA. All the regional tourist organizations do come together in the Tourist Industry Federation but although TIF has been supportive of the regions they are only one group of its members, along with the major industry representatives and sector organizations. During 1991 as a consequence of the study of regional tourism options noted earlier (Murray-North, 1991a) efforts were being made to develop a strengthened network of regional tourist organizations and to formalize their relationship with a newly created New Zealand Tourism Board. This report and the formation of the network might

in part be seen as a regional response to the concentration trends discussed above and more particularly the marketing strategy being proposed by the Tourism Strategic Marketing Group.

New Zealand Tourism Board

Restructuring of the Tourism Department continued in 1991 under the new National government. In a move that echoed the earlier recommendations of the Tourism 2000 Conference, it was announced in July 1991 that a New Zealand Tourism Board would take over most of the department's activity, with an increased emphasis on international marketing. Legislation establishing the board was expected to be passed before the end of the year. The July budget made provision for an additional $10 million for a Joint Tourism Marketing Fund to encourage joint activity with the private sector. A small tourism policy unit within the Ministry of Commerce was also to be formed to advise the minister and government on policy issues relating to tourism, providing support services to the minister and managing government grants schemes relating to the tourism sector. Effectively New Zealand has now moved into line with several of the other countries discussed earlier – Germany, the Netherlands and Ireland – having both a small NTA (national travel administration) and a larger NTO managed by a board. The ministerially appointed board reflects the interests of the major private sector players, particularly the now disbanded Tourism Strategic Marketing Group. The chairman, for instance, is executive chairman of the Mount Cook Group and former chief executive of Air New Zealand; another board member is acting chief executive of that airline while a second is regional manager for Southern Pacific Hotel Corporation. Given such membership, closer links between the public and private sectors in international marketing seem certain. According to the new chairman, N. Geary (quoted in NZ Tourism Dept Newsletter, June/July 1991 pp.1–2):

what we are going to see is the Department's image being lifted, because it will be operating in a quite different environment. We will not have the same constraints because we'll be following the private sector model which is more flexible and market driven, with high levels of accountability.

What remains to be seen is how this new public–private sector partnership evolves, what accountability occurs and what policies and practices are established. While the more effective harnessing of public and private sector efforts to market New Zealand abroad is desirable, some disquiet has been expressed over the amount of control certain large players in the industry now seem to have over public funds. Further retrenching away from a broad base of activities seems likely as increased efforts are directed towards marketing. The way the new board reacts to the TSMG's Destination New Zealand strategy

and its dealings with the regions will also provide early indications of the board's policies.

Conclusions

The ninety years since the Department of Tourist and Health Resorts was first established in 1901 have thus seen considerable change in the structure and functions of tourist organizations in New Zealand. In general, the changes have seen New Zealand's NTO lose much of its distinctive character – departmental status, a range of development and operational activities and a regional deconcentration of functions – and move more into line with those NTOs having a board structure and an overwhelming emphasis on international marketing. The past decade has also demonstrated vividly the impact of broader environmental factors on tourist organizations.

9

Comparisons and Conclusions

The discussion of the nature and functions of tourist organizations with which this book began was necessarily general given the empirical material available, the lack of a conceptual base and the general absence of any prior systematic treatment of the topic. Drawing on the broader organizational literature and aspects of earlier work in tourism, Figure 1.1 was developed later in Chapter 1 as a theoretical framework for the interorganizational analysis of tourist organizations. Figure 1.1 constituted the framework around which the subsequent comparative case studies were structured, enabling a large amount of detail on a range of tourist organizations in six countries to be presented and analysed in a very similar if not wholly identical manner. Individually, each of these chapters offers insights into the operations of different networks of organizations. Collectively, they provide a comprehensive body of material from which to establish some general characteristics of tourist organizations, and their associated networks,

to draw some general conclusions regarding these and to identify avenues for future research in this emerging field. These are the purposes of this concluding chapter.

Tourist organizations

As the examples in Chapters 2 to 8 have shown, tourist organizations come in many shapes and sizes. Any attempt at synthesis must therefore address at the outset the question of how to describe and classify these organizations so as to bring some order to the field. Two key dimensions – scale and function – were identified in Figure 1.1 and have been used to structure the substantive chapters (2 to 8). The nature of the public–private partnership underlying organizations also emerged in the case studies as being a third critical dimension.

Table 9.1 depicts these three dimensions and ways in which they can be measured or described. Scale is not an absolute measure in the sense of the sheer size of the organization, but rather a measure of the geographical or administrative level represented by it, ranging from the national to the local. International organizations also exist but were not the focus of this book. Organizations can be classed as multifunctional or monofunctional depending on the range of functions they undertake and the nature of these, for example, marketing, planning or research. Of the different facets of the public–private partnership dimension, sources of funding are the most readily quantified. Organizations may draw all their funding from either the public or the private sector or depend on some mix of the two. Additional funding may also be self-generated. Tourist organizations may be structured in different ways reflecting varying degrees and types of public sector control and influence.

Scale

Spatial scale is perhaps the most explicit and straightforward dimension for distinguishing between tourist organizations. In each of the six countries, organizations operating at each scale –

Table 9.1   Dimensions of tourist organizations

Scale

National	Inter-regional	Regional	Sub-regional	Local

Function

Multifunctional				Monofunctional

Public–Private Partnership

Funding

100% public				100% private

Structure

degree of public sector control

Government department office, division	Semi-state agency	Corporation Foundation	Limited liability company

from the national to the local – can be clearly identified. Those at the national scale, for example the USTTA, Bord Fáilte or the Deutsche Zentrale für Tourismus (DZT), are concerned with the promotion and development of tourism for their respective countries – the USA, Ireland and Germany. At the other end of the scale, local organizations exist to promote the interests of particular communities or resorts, for instance the Amsterdam VVV, the Queenstown Promotions Bureau or the Kaanapali Beach Operators Association. Between these a range of intermediate regional organizations are to be found: the State Travel Offices (STOs) of the USA, the Irish Regional Tourist Organizations, Tourism Taranaki, and so on. Sub-regional organizations may also develop: the island chapters of the Hawaii Visitors Bureau, the *streek* VVVs in the Netherlands, the organizations within the larger German *Länder* (eg the FVV München-Oberbayern). Inter-regional alliances may also lead to larger organizations such as Travel South USA. Nevertheless some grey areas do exist. The English, Scottish and Wales

Tourist Boards, for instance, are known as country tourist boards but the NTO in the United Kingdom is in effect the British Tourist Authority (BTA) and the Scottish Tourist Board (STB) might be regarded as a special regional tourist organization.

Table 9.2 enables some basic comparisons between organizations in different countries and at different scales to be made. To facilitate comparisons, budgets from different countries are also expressed in United States dollars. Exchange rate fluctuations can limit comparisons from year to year, as in the case of the DZT. Use of the US dollar for comparative purposes may also not provide a complete picture of the effectiveness of a given budget, particularly as far as domestic operations are concerned. Nevertheless, some general patterns can still be determined.

Particularly when the countries' size is taken into account, Bord Fáilte's budget stands in marked contrast to that of the USTTA and the budgets of the NZTP and DZT are shown to be comparable when greater differences might have been expected.

Table 9.2   Tourist organizations: selected statistics

Organization	Year	Annual budget		Staff	Members
		National currency	US$[1]		
National					
USTTA	1991	US$14.6 m	$14.6 m	95	–
DZT	1988	DM41.4 m	$23.6 m	180	16
	1989	DM44.1 m	$23.3 m	180	16
NBT	1989	Dfl65.9 m	$30.8 m	150	–
Bord Fáilte	1988	I£25.5 m	$38.9 m		–
NZTP	1988–9	NZ$34 m	$22.3 m	180	–
NZTD	1990–1	NZ$41 m			
Regional					
US STOs	1988–9	av. US$6.3 m	av. $6.3 m	36	–
		range US$1.1–24.3 m	range $1.1–24.3 m		
Hawaii State Tourism Office	1988–9	US$16 m	$16 m	6	–
HVB	1988–9	US$13.6 m	$13.6 m	89	2745
LFV Bayern	1988	DM3 m	$1.7 m	8	23
STB	1988–9	£12.2 m	$21.7 m	120	–
HIDB	1987–8	£37.6 m	$61.6 m	250	–
		(about 25% on tourism)			
North					
Brabant VVV	1987	Dfl800 000	$395 000	3	n.a.
Irish RTOs	1983	av. I£281 000	$350 000	15	n.a.
NZ RTOs	1991	av. NZ$277 000	$158 000	4.3	200
		range NZ$47 000–880 000		1.5–14	
Local					
102 US Cities	1978	average US$0.53 m	$0.53 m	n.a.	n.a.
Atlanta CVB	1988	US$8.1 m	US$8.1 m	n.a.	n.a.
Fremden-verkehrsamt München	1989	DM23.2 m	US$12.25 m	140	–
Amsterdam VVV	1989	Dfl8 m	$3.7 m	90	900
Rotterdam VVV	1986	Dfl3 m	$1.2 m	40	n.a.
Scottish ATBs	1988–9	average £247 000	$440 000	n.a.	n.a.
		range £85 000–£992 000	$151 000–$1.76 m		
Greater Glasgow	1988–9	£992 000	$1.76 m		563
Loch Lomond, Stirling & Trossachs	1988–9	£528 000	$940 000		7900

Note: [1]   Exchange rates based on Table 1479, *Statistical Abstract of the United States*, 1990.
Sources: Chapters 2 to 8

In part this reflects different political systems. The federal NTOs are underpinned by a stronger network of state tourist organizations, particularly in the United States. The STOs in turn are also complemented in many cases by strong municipal tourist organizations. Munich's tourist office budget is half that of the DZT. In contrast, the Irish, Dutch and New Zealand regional bodies are much smaller and financially weaker in absolute terms, though not necessarily in relative ones if population and the amount of tourist activity were also taken into account. The special status of the STB also comes through in Table 9.2 as does the average budget of the Scottish ATBs.

Politics and policies also play a major role in determining the patterns shown in Table 9.2. The weakness of the USTTA can be attributed in large part to successive administrations' lack of support for public intervention in the tourism sector. Federal policies for tourism in Germany were shown to be recent and not well developed as was also the case in the Netherlands. At the same time, it must be noted that in these cases a lot of government support for tourism, particularly for development, has not been channelled through the NTOs but formed part of other programmes. A more established pattern of government support to tourism has existed in Ireland and New Zealand even if this has not always been strongly expressed in monetary terms. State and local politics account for much of the variation in tourist organizations' budgets at these levels as well.

Finally, Table 9.2 indicates that tourist organizations in general are not very large organizations in terms of their budgets and staff. Indeed, many regional ones in particular have limited funds and only a handful of staff.

Tourist organizations have developed at the different scales shown in Table 9.1 for two interrelated sets of reasons: administrative and functional. In the majority of cases examined, the public sector provides a significant, often a dominant, share of tourist organization funding. The public sector itself is structured hierarchically, with varying forms of national, state/regional and local government. As each of these wants to retain as much control as possible over its own

expenditure, it is not surprising that the resultant tourist organizations almost invariably correspond to existing administrative boundaries and reflect the various responsibilities of different levels of government. By extension, different political systems will exhibit different administrative frameworks which in turn are likely to generate tourist organizations whose importance and functions vary from one scale to another.

Generalizations about the influence of the prevailing political structure can not be carried too far given the limited number of case studies examined. However, in the centralized states, the NTOs – Bord Fáilte, NZ Tourism Department and the Dutch NBT – have had a more dominant role in their countries' networks than the USTTA and the DZT have had in theirs. Conversely, the STOs in the USA and the *Länder* organizations in Germany are generally much stronger than their more weakly developed regional counterparts in Ireland, New Zealand and the Netherlands. Again the special status of the STB reflects the particular case of Scotland.

In Ireland and New Zealand, Bord Fáilte and the Tourism Department respectively encouraged the formation of regional tourist organizations. In the absence of any intermediate tier of government, the RTOs in Ireland did not correspond to other regional structures. In New Zealand an attempt was made to develop regional tourist organizations along the lines of the united councils and later to restructure them to conform with the boundaries of the new regional councils. The restructuring of tourist organizations following centrally induced local government reform in New Zealand and Scotland further testifies to the influence of political structures on tourist organizations. However, in the Netherlands the push for creating the provincial VVVs essentially came from the local organizations upwards rather than being imposed from the top or arising from the initiatives of the relatively weak provincial governments.

Sub-regional tourist organizations may also correspond to some lower-level administrative unit, for example the four *Regierungsbezirke* in Bavaria (Figure 4.4). Elsewhere, the existence of sub-regional organizations may reflect the size and geography of regional units, the scale and diversity of tourism and the strength of local identification. These factors contributed to the development of the island chapters of the Hawaii Visitors Bureau, the reluctance of some New Zealand organizations to restructure into larger regional bodies and, to some extent, the formation of the *streek* VVVs in the Netherlands.

Functional factors have also been a major force leading to the formation of regional, sub-regional and inter-regional organizations. Different functions are seen to be best carried out at particular scales, in some cases at several scales. The push for regional tourist organizations in Ireland and New Zealand came during periods of development. The new regional bodies there were seen to have a key role to play in stimulating and co-ordinating development through the greater contact they had on the ground with local and regional authorities and private sector operators. Provision of infrastructure and planning for tourism were seen to have more than local implications. Similarly in the Netherlands, municipalities came together in *recreatiegemeenschappen* to develop joint recreational projects. In the case of the Maasoevers and Parklands projects, new organizations were created to develop and promote particular products on a larger scale.

Regional organizations also are commonly seen to have a vital role in marketing, often being able to develop and promote stronger images and provide more effective services than smaller, local organizations with their more limited resources. In the Netherlands recognition of the role of regional marketing led to the creation of the provincial or 'promotional' VVVs. Such recognition also underscored the Tourism Department's support for the creation of regional organizations in New Zealand, as evidenced by the technical and financial encouragement given to develop regional marketing plans for the domestic market. However, attempts to develop 'macro-regions' in New Zealand came to nought and STB proposals to promote Scotland as five major regions generated such opposition that the original scheme was subsequently diluted.

Opposition to the creation of larger functional regions can arise for several reasons. Disagreement

may occur over the extent to which larger units bring together like products – those in Ayrshire felt they were not functionally associated with Glasgow even through STB image research had shown they were perceived by potential English visitors to fall within the same region. Likewise, different parts of Otago – Queenstown, Wanaka and Dunedin – see themselves as having different products and serving different markets. Tension may also arise because different functions conflict. Many of the Scottish ATBs are driven by the need to serve their local members. Distribution of local area brochures is seen as one way of achieving this but it is not necessarily the most effective or practical means of promoting the broader region in more distant markets, again another source of conflict in the Scottish case. More generally, reluctance to participate in larger scale activities may stem from a perceived lack of control over funds generated locally, failure to recognize why certain activities are best carried out by a bigger organization or simple parochialism.

Functions

Tourist organizations may undertake a wide variety of different functions (Chapter 1). Some focus on a single function but the majority carry out a range of different activities, the number and mix of these varying from scale to scale and case to case. The multifunctional nature of most tourist organizations results from several factors: the multi-faceted nature of tourism, the interdependence of different functions (marketing, development, research, planning) and the differing interests of different members (big and small operators, the public and private sectors). Monofunctional organizations may reflect a conscious division of responsibility, broader institutional structures, limited resources or particular vested interests.

With monofunctional organizations the most common functions undertaken are visitor servicing and marketing. Visitor servicing, notably through the operation of visitor information centres, is commonly the sole function of many small local tourist organizations, such as many of the Dutch VVVs. Visitor servicing involves delivery of information and assistance at the destination and is appropriately carried out at the local scale, though not necessarily administered at this level, as the operation of Welcome Centers by American STOs and information centres by Irish and New Zealand regional organizations showed. Many small organizations do not have the resources to pursue other activities such as marketing or research even though they might aspire to do so. In other cases there is an explicit recognition that marketing might best be carried out at a larger scale and left to regional bodies, with a clear division of responsibility occurring, as with the Dutch VVVs and some local and regional organizations in New Zealand (eg Auckland and Taranaki).

Local level monofunctional marketing organizations are less common. The Hawaiian destination associations linked to master planned resorts, for example those at Kaanapali, Wailea and Keahou, are very distinctive in this regard. In these cases planning and development have already occurred, membership is tightly defined, resort capacity is substantial, the commercial goals of the associations are paramount and coastal holidays, particularly packaged ones, generate fewer demands for visitor information.

At the other end of the scale, the BTA and DZT are essentially monofunctional marketing organizations which seek to increase international arrivals. Other functions are performed by different agencies or at different scales. Public expenditure on tourist development projects in Germany was shown to be greater than federal support to the DZT but these grants were disbursed through another section of the Ministry of Economic Affairs as part of the regional development programme. In Britain, Section 4 grants were administered by the country tourist boards not the BTA.

When marketing is not the sole function it is, nevertheless, as Figure 9.1 shows, still the most dominant one among national and regional tourist organizations. In this respect the budgets of the NTOs examined appear to be consistent with those elsewhere. Middleton (1988, p.211) cites WTO data which indicate 'that expenditure on marketing accounts for between one half and two thirds of the total budgets of NTOs'.

Strict international comparisons are difficult to make, however, given the different ways in which budgets are presented from country to country. The percentages shown in Figure 9.1 are those directly listed under 'marketing' in each budget; this may or may not include associated personnel and overhead costs. In the case of the DZT such costs are not included in the figure given, but as these are all directly linked to undertaking the marketing function, in effect the entire budget is spent for this purpose and the DZT can be regarded as monofunctional. In the case of the STB, funds for the Section 4 development grants are included in the board's budget whereas in the case of the NZ Tourism Department, only the costs of administering any development grants are. Such differences clearly influence the interpretation of organizations' budgets and contribute to the STB's low ranking in Figure 9.1.

Why is marketing so important for national and regional organizations? There are several interrelated reasons for this. First, the prime goal of most tourist organizations is to promote growth, especially growth in international arrivals as far as the NTOs are concerned. The impetus for this comes from both the public and private sectors, the former seeking increased foreign exchange earnings, more jobs, greater tax revenues; the latter, more revenue and greater profits. Increased expenditure on marketing and promotion is seen as the way to achieve or maintain growth, particularly in the face of increasing competition or depressed market conditions. Spending on an activity which is seen to contribute directly to growth thus has more appeal to politicians controlling the public purse strings and to private sector members than other related functions such as planning and research whose role in increasing arrivals is often perceived to be less direct and essential.

Not all governments share this enthusiasm, as was clearly illustrated with the USTTA, but NTOs and many regional tourist organizations are generally seen to have a leadership and co-ordinating role to play in marketing, particularly in developing new or distant markets. The major reasons for this were outlined in Chapter 1 and substantiated by the examples in the ensuing

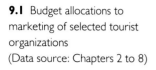

9.1 Budget allocations to marketing of selected tourist organizations
(Data source: Chapters 2 to 8)

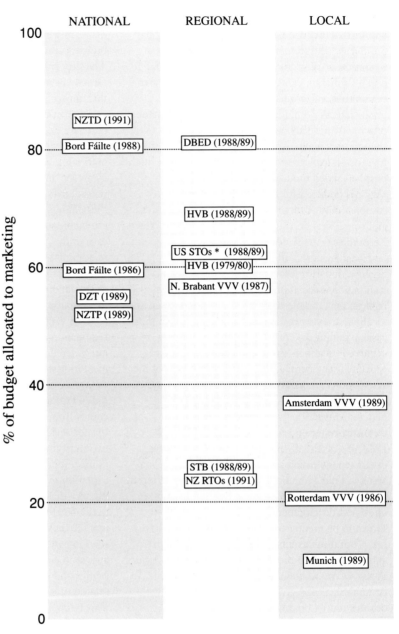

chapters, notably the need for an organization to facilitate and co-ordinate the marketing of an activity characterized by a range of different sectors and a multiplicity of different players and to overcome some of the issues arising from questions of common good and free loaders. National and regional tourist organizations are thus undertaking marketing activities through united action or on behalf of many different players, both members and non-members, who could/would not undertake these activities themselves, for example the maintenance of overseas offices. In this they are demonstrating the underlying rationale of organizations (Table 1.1).

As noted in the preceding section, the relative importance of marketing to national and regional tourist organizations is also a function of their scale. Visitor servicing is a widely recognized and costly function (due to the personnel required) but one which is undertaken at the local level and which thus commonly does not feature in regional budgets and only rarely or as a minimal item in those of NTOs (eg the USTTA's corps of gateway hostesses or departmental subsidies to New Zealand's Visitor Information Network). Many of the larger local organizations will also undertake marketing activities.

While marketing and visitor servicing are almost universal functions at their respective levels, significant differences were found in the extent to which tourist organizations engage in other functions such as development, planning, research, and lobbying.

The involvement of tourist organizations in development has varied considerably from country to country and over time and has taken many different forms. US tourist organizations are characterized by their lack of direct intervention, by the prevailing attitude that the development and operation of tourist facilities and services is best left to the private sector. However, some recent, and still minor, changes were noted in this regard in New York. In the Netherlands development assistance traditionally went on recreational amenities for the Dutch rather than tourist development proper. Changes occurred in the mid-1980s with the Maasoevers and the Parklands projects as well as state grants for other 'spearhead' projects although these were administered by government agencies rather than the VVVs or NBT. A distinctive form of intervention is the role the Gelderland and North Brabant VVVs play as tour operators, putting together packages based on the products of small local operators. In other instances, financial assistance to develop tourism

projects formed part of broader regional development programmes as in Germany (Figure 4.1) and in the cases of the Highlands and Islands Development Board (HIDB) and Shannon Development in Ireland.

Scotland, through both the STB and the HIDB, has had a prominent grant-aiding development programme, with both bodies also taking a more proactive role in the late 1980s to promote and co-ordinate tourist development. Bord Fáilte's intervention in development has varied over time, reflecting more general stages in the growth of tourism in Ireland and broader changes in government policies. During the initial phase of expansion in the 1960s and early 1970s development of tourism plant was encouraged through grants for accommodation, attractions and infrastructure. During the early 1980s general cut-backs in government spending and an increased emphasis on marketing resulted in reductions on capital expenditure for tourism. Later in the decade a product development strategy again became part of the new drive to expand tourism's role in the Irish economy.

New Zealand's Tourism Department stands out with its long and varied involvement in many aspects of development and operations. At its peak this included running hotels, travel agencies and coach tours and managing and developing scenic resort areas. Such functions arose out of broader policies of direct intervention in the economy and the lack of private sector success or willingness and/or capacity to invest in these areas. As facilities were developed, however, and the economy expanded, more effort was directed towards marketing and promotion. Broader policy changes introduced by the fourth Labour government in 1984 saw the department withdraw completely from operational activities, concentrating more of its budget on marketing (Figure 9.1) and leaving a small section to facilitate development rather than undertake it directly.

Planning has not been a conspicuous long-term function of any of the tourist organizations examined, preparation of marketing plans excepted. Earlier chapters have recounted how Bord Fáilte and the STB withdrew from physical planning in the late 1970s or early 1980s after earlier being enthusiastic and how little has resulted from the series of tourism plans prepared in Hawaii. What was to have been a national plan for tourism in New Zealand never eventuated as such and regional tourist organization input into district planning schemes there has been minimal even though the alignment of their boundaries to those of the district (and later regional) councils was in part to facilitate such input. In the Netherlands, the country with the strongest tradition of planning, the first tourism plans (TROPs) were not prepared until the 1980s and then the VVVs did not play a large role in their preparation or implementation.

Several factors appear to contribute to this general neglect of planning. In the Netherlands there has been only belated recognition of tourism as a separate and significant sector of the economy, with earlier effort in this sphere being directed towards recreation. More generally throughout Europe, regional planning reached a peak in the late 1960s and early 1970s then faded as economic conditions tightened. The USA and New Zealand have no tradition of indicative planning. At the regional and local levels where some physical planning may occur, this is usually done by other agencies and tourism, as a relative newcomer, has received little attention from them. With the increased drive towards marketing noted above, physical planning has effectively been pushed into the background, particularly in small under-resourced regional and local tourist organizations where many industry members do not necessarily perceive their interests to be furthered by planning.

Lack of resources and appreciation of its role also appear to explain why research is only a minor function in most organizations and is often missing entirely at the regional and, especially, local level. The largest research sections are to be found in the NTOs. These have more resources, can provide a national overview and have more established links with international markets. Critical issues involve the extent to which NTO research can be sufficiently disaggregated to serve regional and local users and the ways this information is transmitted to them. While the staff of most organizations

would welcome more information and data on a range of topics, research is not a day-to-day priority when funds are limited. Available resources are spent on marketing, running information offices and occasionally development, with little or no funding left to commission research which would help set directions, evaluate the effectiveness of existing activities and so on. Much of the STO research in the USA consisted of economic impact studies undertaken to justify current public sector assistance and/or obtain further funding.

Commissioning studies to increase the profile of tourism and thereby obtain more resources can be seen as a form of lobbying undertaken by tourist organizations. Given their dependence on public sector funding, destination organizations have to be careful that their calls for more support are not seen as being critical of the government. As a consequence, some of the more overt lobbying is undertaken by sector groups or other broadly based organizations. One of the more successful examples of this noted was the adoption of the main findings of the Irish Hotel Federation's report as part of Ireland's Programme for National Recovery. In Germany the Deutsche Fremdenverkehrsverbänd (DFV) is expressly charged with representing the interests of its members to the federal legislature and executive and has commissioned its own studies and others under the aegis of the Deutsche Fremdenverkehrspräsidium to further these aims. At a more localized scale the Waikiki Improvement Association (WIA), a separate organization, but one enjoying the support of both the HVB and the Waikiki Oahu Visitors Association, has been actively lobbying for the redevelopment of Waikiki, sponsoring for example the high-profile Waikiki Tomorrow Conference. Some of the recent upgrading of Waikiki can no doubt be attributed to the WIA's activities. It is likely that lobbying will become an activity which more and more tourist organizations are forced to pursue if they wish to increase funding for their sector by developing a stronger public profile for tourism.

National organizations may also play a role in co-ordinating the diverse activities and policies of federal or central governments, for example through the US Tourism Policy Council. Where there is an NTA (national tourist administration) as well as an NTO (national tourist organization) such co-ordination is often left to the former, in the cases of Germany and the Netherlands, a small section within the Ministry of Economic Affairs. In these cases, however, there appeared to be little co-ordination between marketing support given to the NTOs and the sums spent on developing tourism plant through regional development programmes. At a local level too there often appears to be little input from tourist organizations into urban development projects directly or indirectly associated with tourism.

The number and type of functions an organization may undertake and weight given to each are not constant but change over time. A general trend has been for higher order organizations to trim back their functions and give increased attention to marketing, the restructuring of the Tourism Department in New Zealand being the most dramatic example of this, but similar trends are also found in Ireland and Scotland. The small but growing amount of attention DBEDT in Hawaii has been giving to monitoring social impacts runs counter to this trend, perhaps a reflection of its more mature stage of development. Lower level organizations have shown a tendency to want to add marketing to their functions or increase its importance – the implications of this are outlined later.

Public–private partnerships

Tourist organizations differ in the extent to which they depend on public or private sector funding but in general the public sector is the dominant partner. Figure 9.2 indicates that the majority of the destination organizations examined here rely on the public sector for at least half of their income and in many cases upwards of 80 per cent of their entire budget. The remainder does not always come directly from the private sector but may consist of commissions, publications, advertising, retail sales and other self-generated income. Different practices are used in recording self-generated finance and, in particular, accounting for 'contra' contributions. Figure 9.2 must therefore be

regarded as indicative only. It should be noted also that self-generated finance can generally be raised only once a core organization has been established through public/private funding.

NTOs draw heavily, if not entirely, on central government support, obtaining most other income from self-generated activities. The USTTA and NZ Tourism Department had no private membership while the DZT had a small number of large industry members. The NBT has no private members either but has been successful in attracting industry support for its programmes, thereby progressively reducing central government funding to the point where the public/private input is almost balanced (see also Table 6.4).

The regional tourist organizations also exhibit similar levels of dependence on public sector funding. The survey of STOs (US Travel Data Center, 1988) does not detail STO income in the same way that it treats expenditure but, as was noted in Chapter 2, the STOs, with the exception of the HVB, are either divisions of larger state departments or autonomous cabinet level tourism agencies which are dependent on funding from the state legislature. Even the HVB receives 90 per cent of its revenue from the state. If the LFV Bayern is typical of other *Länder* organizations in Germany then one might tentatively conclude that regional tourist organizations in federal systems are the most dependent on public sector funding, there being stronger levels of government at this level than in the other, more centralized nations. In Ireland the absence of a tier of intermediate government has meant that the RTOs have been heavily dependent on central support – through Bord Fáilte grants – though restructuring in the late 1980s saw attempts to increase local authority, private sector and self-generated funding. The Scottish case again reflects the peculiarities of Scottish Office responsibilities and funding. In New Zealand and perhaps in the Netherlands (if the North Brabant VVV is representative), public funding from regional and !ocal authorities constitutes a smaller but nevertheless still dominant share of these organizations' income. Some variation occurs in New Zealand depending on the functions exercised; regional organizations which

9.2 Public sector support to selected tourist organizations (Data source: Chapters 2 to 8)

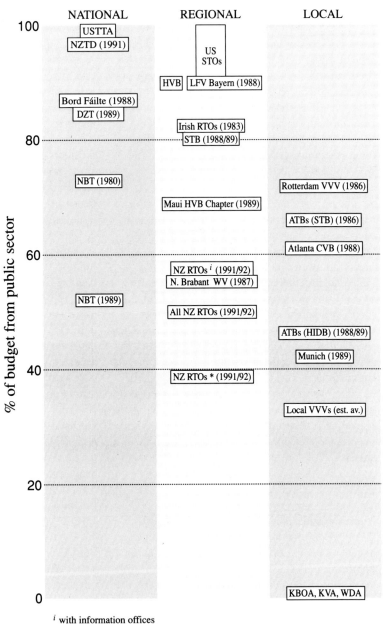

NATIONAL   REGIONAL   LOCAL

100

USTTA
NZTD (1991)

US
STOs

HVB   LFV Bayern (1988)

Bord Fáilte (1988)
DZT (1989)

Irish RTOs (1983)
STB (1988/89)

80

NBT (1980)

Rotterdam VVV (1986)

Maui HVB Chapter (1989)

ATBs (STB) (1986)

Atlanta CVB (1988)

60

NZ RTOs ^{i} (1991/92)
N. Brabant WV (1987)

NBT (1989)

All NZ RTOs (1991/92)

ATBs (HIDB) (1988/89)

Munich (1989)

40

NZ RTOs * (1991/92)

Local VVVs (est. av.)

20

0

KBOA, KVA, WDA

% of budget from public sector

^{i} with information offices
* without information offices

operate information centres tend to derive more income from local councils; those without are often more dependent on regional council funding alone and have lower levels of support.

A much less representative list of local tourist organization budgets has been compiled. None of the examples for which detailed budgets were obtained depended wholly on local municipal funding. At the other end of the spectrum, the Hawaiian resort-based destination associations again stand out: though no budget details were obtained, these appear to be entirely financed by their limited private sector membership. Between these two extremes a wide variety of intermediate situations exist. About one-third of the income from local VVVs in the Netherlands comes from local authorities. As Table 5.1 showed, considerable variation is to be found throughout Scotland in terms of public sector funding at the local level. ATBs in the region supported by the STB derived two-thirds of their support from local authorities and the STB, especially in large cities such as Greater Glasgow, compared with under a half for the northern ATBs funded by the smaller local authorities and the HIDB.

Few generalizations can be made about other local organizations given the small numbers for which sufficient detail was obtained but it should be noted that local organizations often have more direct contact with their members and through the operation of information centres may have greater opportunities for self-generated revenue in such areas as retail sales and reservation commissions. Moreover, there may be a greater need to generate such revenue if municipal resources are limited. As at other scales, local politics can be a decisive factor in the amount of public support accorded to tourism. Such support is often more forthcoming in those areas where tourism is a visibly significant part of the local economy, as in the cases of Queenstown and Rotorua. At a regional and particularly a national scale, larger companies such as airlines and major operators may participate jointly with publicly financed tourist organizations without necessarily being members, as was the case in the Netherlands and Hawaii. In Germany it is only the very large companies who have direct membership of the DZT.

The percentage of the tourist organizations' budget which comes from the public and private sector is only one aspect, though an important and often quantifiable one, of the nature of the partnership between the two sectors. The legal status of the organizations, their management structure and the way they obtain their finance are

significant related factors.

In many cases where revenue is wholly or largely drawn from public funds the tourist organizations are integral parts of government. Although there may be functional links with the private sector (eg joint marketing campaigns) and consultation through advisory boards and the like, the private sector is essentially excluded from management and decision-making except through the broader political process. The United States – the land of free enterprise – stands out in this regard (ie the USTTA and the STOs) but other examples have already been noted (eg Munich and Rotorua). Where tourist organizations are created as boards they are one step removed from government but board appointments are usually the prerogative of the appropriate minister and the state still provides the bulk of the funding (Bord Fáilte, the DZT, the NBT, the STB, New Zealand Tourism Board). Appointments may bring members of leading private enterprises onto the board but representation of smaller operators can be overlooked and political considerations are never far away.

Elsewhere, particularly at a local and regional level, public–private partnerships are promoted much more explicitly. The Stodart Report in Scotland recommended local authorities become involved with the trade through ATBs. The Greater Glasgow Tourist Board stresses the complementarity of public and private sector activities while the Loch Lomond, Stirling and Trossachs Tourist Board emphasizes the need to represent members' interests and encourage local tourist organizations. In the Netherlands, the Rotterdam VVV sees itself as having a bridging role between the public and private sectors while in the case of Parklands a specific Public Private Partnership was formed. Tourism Taranaki puts great emphasis on informing its many small members and receiving input from them (Figure 8.5). This partnership image can of course be overstated, both sectors having a vested interest in increasing funding from the other. At the same time, in many more enlightened areas there appears to be a genuine awareness of the interlocking of the interests and activities of different groups and the mutual benefits to be achieved by working together as partners.

Tourist organizations usually also experience some of the difficulties and frustrations which features of the public and private sectors and a mix of the two can bring. Organizations which depend heavily on public sector funding are frequently limited to short-term horizons, particularly for marketing. Budgets cannot be determined with certainty well in advance as the public sector allocations are made on a year-by-year basis, final amounts often not being known until well into an operating year. Allocations to tourism frequently fluctuate significantly from one year to another as a result of broader political decisions, especially in those places where tourism is not seen as a mainstream government function. STO budgets in the United States, for example, are subject to a fair degree of volatility while regional and local tourist organizations in New Zealand during the late 1980s were subject to much uncertainty due to changing government policies and the restructuring of local government.

Private sector membership is often characterized by high rates of turnover among a large number of small businesses. This can result in a lack of continuity and a considerable amount of staff effort being spent on maintaining members and membership records and generating funds from this source.

Tourist organization executives frequently face the difficulties of trying to satisfy competing and sometimes conflicting interests from both sectors and responding to two different operational environments. Regional and local organizations with a large share of public sector funding frequently have management boards dominated by local politicians, as was noted in the cases of Ireland and Bavaria. This reflects an understandable concern with overseeing the expenditure of public monies. Social functions associated with tourist organizations may also appeal to local politicians. At the same time, such elected officials do not necessarily have any expertise in tourism, and local politics and parochialism frequently come into play. Such a situation can give rise to an absence of objectivity,

delays in decision-making and a lack of professionalism. On the other hand, where private sector membership is dominant, public monies may not always be spent in the interests of the broader community. The long and involved debate over the relationship between DBED and the HVB detailed in Chapter 3 highlighted some of the issues which may arise here.

Recognition of these difficulties has led to a trend towards the creation of more autonomous foundations and corporations which have smaller more functional management boards performing specified tasks under contract, with local and regional government adopting a 'hands-off' approach to day-to-day management. This is seen for example in the Netherlands, where the majority of the provincial VVVs are foundations and where the Rotterdam VVV has recently been restructured in a similar fashion. The tendency for many US cities to contract out their tourist and convention bureaux was noted in Chapter 2. Hawaii has seen an increasingly tighter specification of state appropriations for tourism. In New Zealand, as part of a broader change in government policy the Tourism Department came to be funded to provide specified outcomes bought by government before being further restructured in 1991 into the New Zealand Tourism Board. There have also been general moves towards greater accountability at other levels. Restructuring of the public sector in some places has also brought it closer to the private sector.

Tourist organization networks

Adoption of an interorganizational approach to the study of tourist organizations throughout earlier chapters has emphasized the complexity and significance of networks of tourist organizations to be found in each country. In the preceding sections of this chapter this approach has contributed to the elucidation of key dimensions of tourist organizations – scale, functions and public–private partnerships. Attention in this section is directed to the networks themselves, drawing on concepts introduced in Chapter 1.

Networks bring together in various ways and from different scales a range of tourist organizations, each with its own goals and functions. Basic questions concerning these networks are why do they develop, what form do they take and what types of exchanges occur between the constituent organizations?

As was noted earlier, tourist organizations develop at different scales for functional and administrative reasons. While some overlap in functions does occur, organizations at different scales tend to perform different functions: visitor servicing is essentially a local function, international marketing is carried out by all NTOs though not by them exclusively. These functions exhibit a large degree of mutual interdependence. Concerted promotional campaigns in the markets need to be complemented by delivery of services and development of appropriate products at the destinations and vice versa. Exchanges between different organizations are an expression of this interdependence. Networks of organizations thus foster the pursuit of individual organizations' goals.

As Chapters 2 to 8 have shown, networks of tourist organizations take several different forms. In the Netherlands, the individual VVVs are members of a larger national organization, the ANVV, but intermediate provincial and regional organizations have been created from the grass roots for promotional and administrative purposes. A separate organization, the NBT, was developed to carry out international marketing, with contractual arrangements being made between the NBT and the 'promotional VVVs'. Financial support and representation from government is fed in at different levels but no direct interaction between the commercial operators and the provincial or regional VVVs occurs. Voluntary membership, domain consensus and strong 'bottom up' inputs are characteristics of the Dutch network.

A similar situation exists in Germany. As was shown in Bavaria, organizations tend to be members of other higher level organizations although many were also independently members of the Deutsche Fremdenverkehrsverband (DFV), which was in turn a member of the DZT (Figures

4.2 and 4.3). The DFV, however, is primarily a national lobby group. A major role of the *Länder* and regional organizations is to co-ordinate the marketing efforts of lower level bodies.

The British case is distinguished by the statutory separation of functions among different parts of the network. In particular, the right to overseas marketing was originally limited to the BTA by the Development of Tourism Act 1969. Within Scotland the HIDB has also been able to develop tourism under its broader regional development remit while at lower levels local government reform in 1982 removed regional council responsibility for tourism and limited it to the district councils. The STB and HIDB actively encouraged the formation of the area tourist boards (ATBs) to undertake a visitor servicing role and to foster contact with the trade. The ATBs are voluntary associations but through the grants and other support received from the STB and HIDB are heavily dependent on these bodies.

Similarly in Ireland and New Zealand, Bord Fáilte and the NZTP supported the formation of regional tourist organizations to carry out tasks at this level. Although autonomous, the Irish RTOs depended heavily on Bord Fáilte for funding and were subject to a fair measure of control through their articles of association. Despite the varying degrees of support they have received from the NZTP, regional tourist organizations in New Zealand have always been independent, the official presence of the central department in the regions taking the form of regional offices. The regional organizations are also members of the national Tourist Industry Federation, along with major industry members and sector associations.

The separation of federal, state and local powers in the United States along with the operation of the USTTA and the STOs as wholly government agencies or departments (the HVB excepted) has resulted in the absence of any formal network of destination organizations. While some functional exchanges may occur between the USTTA and the STOs, no membership or financial links exist. Within Hawaii, the strength of local identification with particular islands, coupled with the scale and diversity of tourist activity there, resulted in the emergence of island chapters of the HVB, the HVB and its own complex links with the DBED arising out of the long history of developments detailed in Chapter 3.

Analysis of the networks in Hawaii and elsewhere over time has highlighted their dynamic nature. Tourist organizations evolve and as they do their goals and aspirations change leading to a reassessment of their role in the broader network. In general, as tourist organizations mature and grow they seek to strengthen their position and take on functions which may previously have been the responsibility of higher level bodies. Consequently, there may no longer be a consensus on appropriate roles and interorganizational conflict may arise, the resolution of which may lead to a modification of the network.

The situation in the Netherlands is now characterized by a large measure of domain consensus, a reflection perhaps of the maturity of the Dutch network. Separate and specific roles were assigned to the ANVV and NBT as early as 1968 and general agreement appears to exist in the separation of visitor servicing and marketing up the VVV hierarchy. However, the emergence of the Maasoevers and Parklands foundations which emphasize the development and marketing of localized products does testify to some fluidity, if not conflict, in the system.

On Oahu, consensus exists over the roles of the Waikiki/Oahu Visitors Association (WOVA) and the Waikiki Improvement Association (WIA). WOVA's role is marketing, WIA's responsibility is to redevelop and improve Waikiki – and the two come together in a mutually beneficial street party! The designation of WOVA as the official Oahu Chapter of the HVB marked the last stage in the development of a tier of island organizations in Hawaii. These had emerged because commercial operators on the Neighbour Islands – Maui, Kauai and the Big Island – were not wholly satisfied with the efforts of the HVB and had sought to develop stronger images and niches for their own specific islands. The establishment of island chapters has been followed by continuing attempts to obtain specific allocations from the state legislature through DBEDT.

Marketing conflicts, particularly over the right to promote Scotland overseas, also characterized the STB's struggles with first the BTA, then the HIDB and finally the lower level ATBs. The conflict between the STB and the BTA can also be seen in the context of wider calls for more devolution of power to Scotland. While the STB–BTA struggle was formally resolved by special Act in 1984, the greater resources of the BTA still make it the dominant marketing organization. The STB and HIDB eventually came to work more closely together and the STB–ATB relationship has yet to be worked through completely.

Similarly in Ireland, as the RTOs grew away from their initial visitor servicing and development roles into more ambitious organizations wanting to have a greater say in marketing their own regions abroad, so relations between Bord Fáilte and the regions became strained. Increased integration occurred in the Irish network in the late 1980s as a refocused national programme again emphasized a greater role for the regions in development. A similar parallel in New Zealand has already been noted: the Tourism Department strongly supported the regions during a development phase then largely withdrew to concentrate on international marketing.

The complex debate over which organizations should undertake marketing is, in Benson's (1975) terms, a question of both domain and ideological consensus. NTOs readily leave domestic marketing to the regions and associated visitor servicing to the regions and/or local organizations. The only argument here often is that the NTOs are not doing enough in the domestic market. Conversely, the NTOs make a case for a strong, central co-ordinated marketing effort to make the biggest impact with limited resources in competitive international markets. Multiple campaigns by a host of regional and local organizations are said to confuse the market and lead to duplication of effort. Moreover, central governments' prime reason in funding NTOs is to boost foreign exchange earnings. Regional and local organizations, on the other hand, are less concerned with overall growth and foreign exchange than with increasing visitor numbers and revenue in their own regions and resorts. Such organizations then frequently disagree with national marketing strategies which are rarely seen to give sufficient prominence to specific regions or forms of tourism associated with particular areas. Examples here include 'the Other Holland' campaign in the Netherlands and the concentration versus dispersal debate in New Zealand, whereby emphasis on the American and Japanese markets has favoured growth in the gateways and major resorts but seen little increase in other parts of the country. This lack of ideological consensus in turn generates calls for lower level organizations to embark on their own campaigns. Their ability to do this successfully will depend on a number of factors, especially their size and proximity to international markets. Regional organizations in Germany and the Netherlands are better able to mount campaigns in neighbouring countries, for example in each other, than small regional organizations in New Zealand and Ireland remote from their major markets.

Partial interorganizational conflict according to Litwak and Hylton (1962) is inevitable, it may lead to positive changes in the networks and, in the case of the tourist organizations discussed here, should not obscure the large amount of co-operative work which does occur. A key role for higher level tourist organizations, be they NTOs or some regional organization, has been to facilitate and co-ordinate the activities of lower level organizations and commercial operators, particularly in terms of trade show representation and co-operative advertising campaigns. Lower level organizations feed their publications up the chain for wider distribution than they themselves can achieve; NTOs channel market intelligence and research results downwards to smaller organizations. The programming of familiarization trips, a popular form of promotion with tourist organizations because they are seen to be particularly cost effective, often requires close co-ordination among a variety of organizations at different levels. Product development has also been characterized by a certain amount of inter-level interaction. Development occurs not in head office but out in the regions and resorts where some co-ordination may be needed and from where central

support such as incentives may be sought.

An increasing amount of co-ordinated effort also appears to be occurring on the same level, that is between NTOs, as in the case of the DZT, and especially between regional tourist organizations. Such co-operative efforts are largely driven by perceived scale economies in marketing and market research. In Germany joint marketing activities have been fostered by the DZT, for example the Magic Eight, the Historic Ten and the various thematic routes. Other Bavarian organizations have banded together with those of adjoining regions, for example to promote the Bavarian Alps. In the United States cautious moves towards interregional marketing programmes and organizations are emerging, encouraged by the USTTA. However, international and domestic marketing may generate different demands, the former inducing states to co-operate, the latter to compete with each other. Some STOs belong to several larger inter-regional organizations depending on which particular product they want to promote or specific market they wish to attract.

A common tendency noted throughout the cases examined here has been for many metropolitan organizations to opt out of joint participation with their surrounding regions and to go it alone. Thus in the Netherlands, the VVVs of Amsterdam, Rotterdam and the Hague act as 'promotional' VVVs in their own right, usually independently of the VVVs of North and South Holland. Similarly Munich largely functions apart from the rest of Bavaria as does Bayreuth at the smaller scale of the Fichtelgebirge. In New Zealand, Rotorua and Queenstown essentially promote themselves rather than lead their respective regions. Many US city promotion and convention bureaux have larger budgets than their STOs, as was noted in the cases of Georgia and California. The restructuring of Irish RTOs saw Dublin being separated out from the surrounding Eastern region.

Cities and large resorts may opt out for several interrelated reasons. The sheer size of such cities means that their organizations often have sufficient resources to act alone (Table 9.2) and that they already have a distinctive image to build upon. Local scale in the geographical sense does not equate in these cases with small-scale tourist plant or organizational resources, a factor that was also observed with the Hawaiian resort-based organizations such as the Kaanapali Beach Operators Association. Moreover, metropolitan centres and large resorts may draw on different markets than their hinterlands. Urban tourism, for example, attracts a larger share of business travellers and convention goers. Other cities though recognize the functional interdependence with their surrounding region: Christchurch attempts to increase the length of stay of its visitors by promoting side trips throughout Canterbury. Large cities and resorts also opt out because of the greater delays in decision-making which frequently occur in larger organizations with representatives from a number of local authorities or constituent organizations. Being self-contained means metropolitan organizations can often act more quickly and respond more rapidly to changes in the market. Such opting out may weaken regional organizations but it is not necessarily regretted by the smaller organizations as they may feel less dominated and thus capable of having more of their own input into joint activities.

Throughout the examples examined, existing administrative units and their corresponding organizations have formed the building blocks for larger functional regions even though cases might be made for creating these in terms of homogeneity of products and markets. Even with the Maasoevers Foundation, which was created to develop and promote activities along the Meuse, the constituent bodies were regional VVVs and existing *recreatiegemeenschappen*. Such a structure enables the smaller organizations to retain their identity while acting co-operatively at a larger functional scale.

What becomes critical then are the linkages between the organizations in the network. Clear and effective channels of communication are needed both up and down the hierarchy as well as between organizations at different levels. At the same time care must be taken to ensure that consultation and representation from different organizations does not result in unwieldy, time-consuming procedures. Regional organizations can play a vital role here, providing key links with the

NTOs and co-ordinating the activities of lower level organizations. More formal specification of the functions of different organizations and their relationships with others in the network, for example through performance contracts, may also remove the need for over frequent consultations and delays in decision-making. Given the small size of many tourist organizations, the skill and competence of their staff, particularly in terms of interpersonal relations, cannot be overlooked either.

Achievements and effectiveness

In this seminal study the emphasis has been on examining the structure, functions and interactions of tourist organizations. There has been little scope for carrying out the detailed analysis and auditing needed to evaluate the effectiveness of each. Nevertheless, some general comment on the success, or otherwise, of tourist organizations is called for. What have they achieved? What is a successful tourist organization? These are not easy questions to answer given the lack of research which has to be undertaken and the intangible nature of many tourist organization functions. Nevertheless, some general points can be made.

A successful tourist organization might be considered to be one that is soundly established, well resourced, highly regarded and one that is meeting its goals. On these criteria the balance sheet of the organizations reviewed here is rather mixed. While some of the tourist organizations discussed have a long history, for example the New Zealand Tourism Department, the Hawaii Visitors Bureau and many of the Dutch VVVs, others are comparatively recent, dating from the 1960s or later. Most are not well resourced (Table 9.2, Figure 7.3) and many lead a precarious existence, for example the USTTA, many US STOs and local offices and some regional tourist organizations in New Zealand. Some even disappear periodically. Why should this be?

Tourism in general often appears not to have widespread political support. The comparative recency and weakness of national policies on tourism was noted in most of the cases examined with significant variations in support at the local and regional levels also occurring. As public grants were the major source of funding for many tourist organizations, lack of political support and recognition are major constraints. At the same time, many tourist organizations are struggling to maintain membership and increase private sector contributions. Factors accounting for this may include the fragmentation of the tourism sector and difficulties occasioned by the opportunities for freeloading.

Nevertheless it could be argued that if tourist organizations were doing an essential job well then they should readily attract resources and recognition. How then can their effectiveness be measured? The clear answer is, not easily. This point is well illustrated by a review of the annual reports of the New Zealand Tourist and Publicity Department. While acknowledging that in a period of high growth 'many claimants should emerge for the accolades', the NZTP in its annual report for 1985 claimed that 'the interest so generated [by its marketing activities] is a key underpinning of tourism growth' and the following year reported 'The record arrivals represented a triumph for market diversification'. For 1989, when the annual rate of increase had dropped to 1.4 per cent (Figure 8.1), the annual report noted 'overall the year reflected the intensely competitive international market for tourism'. In other words, in times of growth tourist organizations say they are doing a good job, in harder times relative or absolute decreases in visitor arrivals are attributed to exogenous factors such as exchange rates, changing market conditions, world events and so on. While there is no doubt a great deal of truth in both relationships, the effect of tourist organizations *vis-à-vis* other factors cannot be readily measured. Herein lies much of the difficulty in judging the effectiveness of tourist organizations be it the USTTA's activities, those of the NZTP or of lower level organizations.

Likewise, a range of exogenous factors also comes into play with domestic tourism. In each of the countries studied, domestic tourism was shown to be stable, declining or increasing only very

slowly. This trend might be in part attributed to the NTOs' exclusive or almost complete concentration on increasing international arrivals and to the sub-national organizations' lack of success in competing with the highly industrialized packaging of outbound tourism. At the same time, other more general factors undoubtedly have had a major impact, notably general levels of economic development and improved communications. The more detailed analysis of the US situation which the STO data allowed also did not reveal any conclusive patterns to be established. Hunt (1990) reported some association between aggressiveness of STO activity and increased market share but the findings were very tentative. Likewise, little systematic correlation between STO expenditure and other variables was found (Table 2.5).

Additional difficulties arise here because each tourist organization starts from a different base of attractions, market accessibility, private sector activity and so on. The 'I Love New York' campaign has been widely credited as being very successful, as witnessed by the other states' emulation of this campaign, but California continues to attract the largest amounts of domestic travel expenditure with very little state-level marketing. Small, secondary destinations might frequently have to work harder to achieve an increase in arrivals and any evaluation of their tourist organizations needs to take this into account.

Moreover, many tourist organizations have a range of functions, each of which may contribute in varying degrees to meeting the organizations' goals. While the interdependence of functions is generally recognized, for example development and research or visitor servicing and marketing, few if any attempts at measuring the relative contribution of each appear to have been made. Evaluation techniques in this field appear to work best when a more specific problem is examined, for example a particular marketing campaign. Measuring one function against another or trying to evaluate the overall effectiveness of an organization is much more difficult. In the Netherlands, for example, a dense well-organized network of visitor information centres, the VVVs, has been put in place but the precise contribution these make to developing tourism relative to the marketing and operational activities of the provincial VVVs and the NBT, let alone private sector activities, is extremely difficult to assess.

Other difficulties arise out of the range of goals which tourist organizations may pursue. Growth in absolute numbers of visitors, overnights or expenditure is the most common goal of tourist organizations but other questions such as the regional distribution of demand or the social and environmental impacts of tourist development may also come into play, particularly at the regional and local levels. Judging the effectiveness of tourist organizations should therefore also take account of these factors, the perception of which may vary from region to region and one scale to another. Variations in the perceived effectiveness of the HVB and DBEDT, for example, might occur from one island to another as well as among different groups within society depending on the importance they attach to economic, social or environmental matters. Measurement of organizations' performance on other than growth criteria may be even more complicated than linking their activities to visitor numbers.

Despite all these qualifications tourist organizations do have an important role to play and, in many cases examined here, they appear to be fulfilling that role reasonably well. There can be little doubt that scale economies and efficiencies are achieved by joining forces and pooling resources, whether this be in co-ordinating trade fair representation, maintaining overseas offices, advertising, distributing information, carrying out research, lobbying and so on. Through the leadership and common resources they provide, tourist organizations can be a useful, perhaps even essential, means of achieving united action. At the same time, it must be recognized that they are not the only way. Much tourism research in the Netherlands and Germany, for instance, is carried out by consulting firms (the NRIT and the Studienkreis für Tourismus) and many information centres in Hawaii are in effect commercial sales outlets or ticket offices. Elsewhere, however, particularly in areas with small-scale tourist operations, many of these activities would just not

happen without the leadership or resources of some tourist organization.

No single organization would appear to be capable of carrying out all the different roles which tourist organizations might fill in any given country. Rather, a network of organizations with different functions at different scales is needed. What is important here is that some domain consensus is established to avoid unnecessary duplication of effort and that well established means of exchange exist to enable effective interorganizational interaction to occur. There is no single best type of organization nor interorganizational network, rather each country must evolve a system which best reflects local, regional and national conditions. There would appear to be merit in giving tourist organizations more operational flexibility, freeing them up from day-to-day management by public sector officials while retaining or increasing accountability. This trend, already noted in some recent moves towards corporatization, presents a number of challenges, particularly given the methodological difficulties outlined above. As a consequence, much more research on tourist organizations remains to be done.

Avenues for future research

Conclusions drawn in the preceding section must be viewed in terms of the examples on which they are based. The case studies were consciously chosen from developed Western economies, selected so as to represent a range of political structures, from the federal systems of the USA and Germany to the centralized states of Ireland and New Zealand. While certain general characteristics have been attributed to tourist organizations in federal as opposed to centralized states, it is conceivable that a different set of federal examples, for instance Canada or Switzerland, or consideration of other centralized nations such as France, might have resulted in different interpretations and conclusions. One obvious way of extending this research and testing the validity of the findings presented here is simply to increase the number and range of examples used, both from developed and developing countries. The organizational changes consequent upon recent and more general upheavals in Eastern Europe constitute a more specific research problem.

Others may choose to highlight different issues and relationships or base their research upon some other conceptual framework. However, in the early phases of research in a field which has so far attracted little attention, the comparative approach offers much potential for rapid advances in knowledge. In this, explicit recognition of the influence of broader environmental factors has been shown to be important, both in presenting and understanding the individual case studies and in enabling generalizations to be made from them. Likewise, adopting a temporal perspective has also yielded important insights into tourist organizations. The different examples have highlighted the dynamic nature of tourist organization networks and shown how organizations and their relationships with other organizations change over time, particularly in response to changing external factors. A static examination at only one point in time would reveal only a partial picture of roles and relationships. Interorganizational analysis, it is also argued, provides a very valuable approach to research on tourist organizations. No tourist organization exists in isolation and the examination of the interaction between organizations can help increase our understanding not only of the wider network but also of its constituent parts. In these regards, Figure 1.1 has proved to be a robust and useful model which might be applied elsewhere.

While Figure 1.1 emphasizes a holistic approach to the study of tourist organizations clearly there is also scope for much more detailed and specific research on some of the issues raised here and others which have not been explored. In particular, there is a growing need for more evaluative research, especially in the face of growing calls for increasing accountability for expenditure of public monies. A particularly useful programme of accountability research emphasizing marketing was commissioned by the United States Department of Commerce (Wynegar, 1989; Davidson and Wiethaupt, 1989; Burke and Lindblom, 1989;

Burke and Gitelson, 1990; Siegel and Ziff-Levine, 1990; Perdue and Pitegoff, 1990; Fleming and Toepper, 1990). Other recent related research deals with the effectiveness of destination marketing strategies (Woodside, 1990), travel trade shows (Pizam, 1990) and press briefs (Gladwell and Wolff, 1989). These are all key areas in which tourist organizations are involved. This research shows that while measuring the effectiveness of these activities, and thus of the organizations which undertake them, is no easy matter, it is possible. Some of the organizations examined already have established research programmes in some of these areas (eg STB, 1984c, 1987) but much remains to be done.

Other non-marketing functions have attracted less attention. How effective have the various development programmes of the different organizations been? What effects have tourist organizations had on influencing the way tourism develops and the types of impacts it has? Little monitoring appears to be carried out by the organizations themselves; most barely have the resources to vet grant applications let alone follow projects up in terms of jobs created or revenue generated. The limited success tourist organizations have had with implementing tourism plans warrants further investigation. Their technical ability to prepare plans does not appear to be in doubt, the will or wherewithal to implement them does. Certain tourist organizations appear to have a significant and sometimes successful lobbying function but what they actually achieve and how they go about it requires more research. Here basic research techniques need to be established, or adapted from other areas, before these aspects of tourist organizations can be widely studied.

Tourist organizations might also be viewed from other perspectives than that adopted in this book. In concentrating on the organizations and their role in a broader network, comparatively little attention has been given here to the perceptions of other groups: members, non-members, tourists and host communities. Surveys of members and potential members for example, might shed further light on the roles and effectiveness of organizations as well as on more specific questions associated with funding and membership. Much more work also needs to be done to assess the role of tourist organizations *vis-à-vis* commercial operators. Just what share of all marketing activities do national, regional and local tourist organizations have? Other types of tourist organizations might also be examined in greater detail than has been possible in this book which has concentrated on destination organizations. The role and structure of some sector and allied organizations have been discussed briefly in some chapters, notably those on Ireland and Germany, but more work could usefully be undertaken on such organizations.

Tourist organizations then offer many challenges, not only to tourism researchers but also to those interested more generally in the study of organizations. Indeed, future research might also explore in detail the differences and similarities between tourist organizations and those that have developed in other sectors. Research in this field, as this book has attempted to demonstrate, can make both theoretical and more applied contributions, leading to a better understanding of tourism, and ultimately more effective tourist organizations. For this to happen, however, a more explicit recognition of the role and significance of tourist organizations is needed. If this book has contributed towards this then its aims will have been achieved.

References

Adams T H (1984) One hundred years later: does Scotland exist? *Scottish Geographical Magazine* 100(2): 123–34.

Agel P (1987) West Germany. National Report No. 139, *International Tourism Quarterly* 49–60.

Ahmed Z M and Krohn F B (1990) Reversing the United States' declining competitiveness in the marketing of international tourism: a perspective on future policy. *Journal of Travel Research* 29(2): 23–9.

Airey D (1983) European government approaches to tourism. *Tourism Management* 4(4): 234–44.

Airey D (1984) Tourism administration in the USA. *Tourism Management* 5(4): 269–79.

An Foras Forbartha (1973) *Brittas Bay: a planning and conservation study*. Dublin, An Foras Forbartha.

Anon (1989) Tourism and the tourist industry: latest statistics. *Employment Gazette*, August: 433–42.

Armstrong R W (ed) (1983) *Atlas of Hawaii*. Honolulu, University of Hawaii Press. 2nd edn.

Ashworth G J and Bergsma J R (1987) New policies for tourism: opportunities or problems. *Tijdschrift voor Economische en Sociale Geographie* 78(2): 151–5.

Ashworth G and Goodall B (1988) Tourist images: marketing considerations. In Goodall B and Ashworth G (eds) *Marketing in the Tourism Industry: the promotion of destination regions*. Beckenham, Croom Helm.

Assael H (1968) The political role of trade associations in distributive conflict resolution. *Journal of Marketing* 32(2): 21–8.

Bayerische Staatsregierung (1978) *Fremdenverkehrsforderungsprogramm 1978*. Munich, Bayerisches Staatsregierung.

Bayerische Staatsregierung (1989) *Fremdenverkehrsprogramm*. Munich, Bayerisches Staatsregierung.

Beaman J and Meis S (1987) Managing the research function for effective policy formulation and decision making. In Ritchie J B and Goeldner C R (eds) *Travel Tourism and Hospitality Research: a handbook for managers and researchers*. New York, Wiley.

Becker C (1987) Domestic tourism in FRG: trends and problems. *Annals of Tourism Research* 14(4): 516–30.

Beckman M J (1988) *Tinbergen Lectures on Organization Theory*. Berlin, Springer-Verlag. 2nd edn.

Bennett A D (1984) The application of alternative theories in political geography: the case of political participation. In Taylor P and House J (eds) *Political Geography: recent advances and future directions*. Croom Helm, London, and Barnes and Noble, New York.

Benson J K (1975) The interorganizational network as political economy. *Administrative Science Quarterly* 20(2): 229–49.

Blacksell M (1987) West Germany. In Clout H D (ed) *Regional Development in Western Europe*. London, David Fulton Publishers.

Blanton R and Jackson T H (1979) Organization and structure. In Council of State Governments, *Tourism: state structure, organization and support*. Washington DC, US Govt Printing Office.

Bodlender J A and Davies E J G (1985) *A Profile of Government Financial Grant Aid to Tourism*. WTO/Horwath and Horwath International.

Bollard A and Buckle R (eds) (1987) *Economic Liberalisation in New Zealand*. Wellington, Allen and Unwin, Port Nicholson Press.

Boonman A (1986) *De TROPometer: een TROP evaluatie*. Eindexamenscripte (unpublished). Breda, Nederlands Wetenschappelijk Instituut voor Toerisme en Recreatie.

Bord Fáilte (nd) *Tourism and the Business Expansion Scheme*. Dublin, Bord Fáilte.

Bord Fáilte (1973) *Tourism Plan 1973–1976*. Dublin, Bord Fáilte.

Bord Fáilte (1978) *Tourism Plan 1978–82*. Dublin, Bord Fáilte.

Bord Fáilte (1987) *Report and Accounts, 1986*. Dublin, Bord Fáilte.

Bord Fáilte (1988) *The Regional Tourism Organizations*. Dublin, Bord Fáilte.

Bord Fáilte (1989) *Tourism Facts 1988*. Dublin, Bord Fáilte.

Bowes S (1988) The role of the tourist board. In Goodall B and Ashworth G (eds) *Marketing in the Tourism Industry: the promotion of destination regions*. Beckenham, Croom Helm.

Britton S G (1982) The political economy of tourism in the Third World. *Annals of Tourism Research* 9(3): 331–58.

Broos LFHC and Ziegler FWM (1984) Integrated tourism and recreation planning for the 80s: the experience in the Netherlands. In *Planning for Leisure and Tourism: the next 10 years*. London, Planning and Transport Research and Computation.

Brunt B (1988) *The Republic of Ireland*. London, Paul Chapman Publishing.

Bryans P and Cronin T P (1984) *Organization Theory*. New York, Facts on File Publications.

Burfitt A (1988) Marketing Australia overseas: a corporate perspective. *International Journal of Hospitality Management* 7(4): 321–32.

Burkart A J and Medlik S (1974) *Tourism: past, present and future*. London, Heinemann.

Burke J F and Gitelson R (1990) Conversion studies: assumptions, accuracy and abuse. *Journal of Travel Research* 28(3): 46–51.

Burke J F and Lindblom L A (1989) Strategies for evaluating direct response tourism marketing. *Journal of Travel Research* 28(2): 33–7.

Callanan B (1984) The work of Shannon Free Airport Development Company. *Administration* 32: 342–50.

CERT (1988) *Manpower Survey of the Irish Hotel and Catering Industry, update 1988*. Dublin, CERT.

CHL Consultants (1987) *Scope of the Tourism Industry in Ireland*. Dublin, CERT.

Collins C O (1979) Site and situation strategy in tourism planning: a Mexican case study. *Annals of Tourism Research* 6(3): 351–66.

Committee on Public Expenditure (1984) *Review of Shannon Free Airport Development Company Ltd*. Dublin, Stationery Office.

Cook S D (1987) Research in state and provincial travel offices. In Ritchie J B and Goeldner C R (eds) *Travel Tourism and Hospitality Research: a handbook for managers and researchers*. New York, Wiley.

Cooper C (1987) The changing administration of tourism in Britain. *Area* 19(3): 249–53.

Cork/Kerry Regional Tourism Organisation Ltd (1964) *Memorandum and Articles of Association of Cork/Kerry Regional Tourism Organisation Ltd*. Cork

Cornelissen J A T (1986) Dutch tourism; a big industry in a small country. *Tourism Management* 7(4), 294–7.

Coughlan G and Kearsley G (1991) Selling southern landscapes: the role of local and regional government in New Zealand's tourism development. In Kearsley G and Fitzharris B (eds) *Southern Landscapes*. Dept of Geography, University of Otago, Dunedin.

Council of State Governments (1979) *Tourism: state structure, organization and support*. Washington DC, US Government Printing Office.

Davidson T L and Wiethaupt W B (1989) Accountability marketing research: an increasingly vital tool for travel marketers. *Journal of Travel Research* 27(4): 42–5.

Davidson-Peterson Associates Inc (1990) *The Economic Impact of Expenditures by Tourists on Georgia, 1989*. York, Maine, Davidson-Peterson Associates Inc.

Dawson S (1986) *Analysing Organisations*. Basingstoke, Macmillan Education.

DBED (1987) *The State of Hawaii Data Book 1987*. Honolulu, Department of Business and Economic Development.

DBED (1988) *Strategic Marketing Plan: tourism*. Honolulu, Dept of Business and Economic Development.

DBED (1989) *State Tourism Office 1988 Annual Report*. Honolulu, Dept of Business and Economic Development.

Deloitte, Haskins and Sells (1989) *The Community Journal on Tourism*. Honolulu, Dept of Business and Economic Development.

Deutscher Bundestag (1975) *Tourismus in der*

Bundesrepublik Deutschland-Grundlagen und Ziele. Druchsache 7/3840. Bonn, Deutscher Bundestag.

Deutscher Bundestag (1985) *Vierzehnter Rahmenplan der Gemeinschaftsaufgabe Verbesserung der regionalen Wirtschaftsstruktur.* Drucksache 10/3562, Bonn, Deutscher Bundestag.

Deutsches Fremdenverkehrspräsidium (1988) *Tourismus Bericht 1988.* Deutsches Fremdenverkehrspräsidium.

DFV (nd) *Die Mitgliedsverbände und-Stadte des Deutschen Fremdenverkehrsverbandes E.V.* Bonn, DFV.

DFV (1986a) *Grundsatzfragen der Fremdenverkehrspolitik in der Bundesrepublik: Stellungnahme des Deutschen Fremdenverkehrsverbändes.* Bonn, Deutscher Fremdenverkersverband.

DFV (1986b) *Tourismus und Verkehr: Verkehrspolitische Stellungnahme des Deutschen Fremdenverkehrsverbändes.* Bonn, Deutscher Fremdenverkehrsverband.

DFV (1986c) *Naturschutz und Fremdenverkehr.* Bonn, Deutscher Fremdenverkehrsverband.

DFV (1987a) *Geschäftsbericht 1987.* Bonn, Deutscher Fremdenverkehrsverband.

DFV (1987b) *Marketing Empfehlungen für den deutschen Fremdenverkehr: Ergebnisse und Schlussfolgerungen aus der Grundlagenuntersuchung 'Urlaub in Deutschland'.* Bonn, Deutscher Fremdenverkehrsverband.

Doering T R (1979) Geographical aspects of state travel marketing in the USA. *Annals of Tourism Research* 6(3): 307–317.

Dollimore E S (1971) *Thomas Edward Donne (1859–1945): a biographical essay.* Wellington, Tourist and Publicity Department, mimeo.

Doube P (1985) How California went from $0 to $5 million for tourism and the results. In *The Battle for Market Share, 16th Proceedings of the Travel and Tourism Research Association.* Salt Lake City: 269–72.

DPED (1984) *State Tourism Functional Plan.* Honolulu, Dept of Planning and Economic Development.

DPED (1986) *The Hawaii State Plan Revised.* Honolulu, Dept of Planning and Economic Development.

Drake M (1985) Life in an established destination – Los Angeles. In *The Battle for Market Share, 16th Proceedings of the Travel and Tourism Research Association.* Salt Lake City: 141–4.

DRV (1989) *Wirkschaftsfaktor Tourismus, eine Grundlagenstudie der Reisebranche.* Frankfurt, Deutscher Reisebüro-Verband.

Duffield B S and Long J (1981) Tourism in the Highlands and Islands of Scotland. *Annals of Tourism Research* 8(3): 403–31.

Duffield B S and Long J (1984) The role of tourism in the economy of Scotland. *Tourism Management* 5(4): 258–68.

Dundler F (1988) *Urlaubsreissen, 1954–1987. 34 Jahre Erfassung des touristischen Verhaltens der Deutschen durch soziologische Stichprobenuntersuchungen.* Starnberg, Studienkreis für Tourismus.

Dunkerley D (1972) *The Study of Organisations.* London, Routledge, and Boston, Mass. Kegan Paul.

DZT (1985) *Deutsche Zentrale für Tourismus e.V. Jahresbericht 1985.* Frankfurt, Deutsche Zentrale für Tourismus.

DZT (1989) *Deutsche Zentrale für Tourismus e.V. Jahresbericht 1988/89.* Frankfurt, Deutsche Zentrale für Tourismus.

Easton B H and Thomson N J (1982) *An Introduction to the New Zealand Economy.* St Lucia, University of Queensland Press.

Edgell D (1984) US governmental policy on international tourism. *Tourism Management* 5(1): 67–70.

Edgell D L (1985) *International Trade in Tourism: a manual for managers and executives.* Washington DC, US Dept of Commerce.

Elazar D J (1966) *American Federalism: the view from the states.* New York, Thomas Y Crowell.

Elliott J (1987) Government management of tourism – a Thai case study. *Tourism Management* 8(3): 223–32.

ETB (1981) *Planning for Tourism in England.* London, English Tourist Board.

Etzioni A (1964) *Modern Organisations.* Englewood Cliffs, Prentice-Hall.

Ewing R C (1989) Industrial museums in Scotland: development and prospects. *Scottish Geographical Magazine* 105(3): 178–81.

Farrell B H (1982) *Hawaii, the legend that sells.* Honolulu, University Press of Hawaii.

Feldman E J (1978) Comparative public policy: field or method? *Comparative Politics* 10: 287–305.

Feldmann O (1988) The German tourism industry is based on a two-fold approach. In *ITB Katalog.* Berlin: 65–7.

Fielding G J and Johnston D C (forthcoming) Restructuring land transport in New Zealand. *Transport Reviews.*

Flachmann C (1989) Inlandsreiseverkehr 1988: Ergebnis der Beherbergungs-statistik. *Wirtschaft und Statistik* 4, 220–4.

Fleming W R and Toepper L (1990) Economic impact studies: relating the positive and negative impacts to tourism development. *Journal of Travel Research* 29(1): 35–42.

Ford L R (1979) Urban preservation and the geography of the city in the USA. *Progress in Human Geography* 3(2): 211–38.

Forer P C and Pearce D G (1984) Spatial patterns of package tourism in New Zealand. *New Zealand Geographer* 40(1): 34–42.

Frank T C (1985) Established vs. emerging destinations. In

The Battle for Market Share, Proceedings of 16th Travel and Tourism Research Association. Salt Lake City: 139–40.

FVV München-Oberbayern (1988) *Oberbayern Geschäftsbericht 1988.* Munich, Fremdenverkehrsverband München-Oberbayern.

GBT (1989) *Gelderland Activiteitenplan 1989.* Arnhem, Gelders Bureau voor Toerisme.

GGTBCB (1988) *Annual Report and Accounts 1987/88.* Glasgow, Greater Glasgow Tourist Board and Convention Bureau.

Gillmor D A (1985) *Economic Activities in the Republic of Ireland: a geographical perspective.* Dublin, Gill and Macmillan.

Gladwell N J and Wolff R M (1989) Assessment of the effectiveness of press kits as a promotion tool. *Journal of Travel Research* 27(4): 49–51.

Godau A (1991) Tourism policy in the new Germany. *Tourism Management* 12(2): 145–9.

Governor's Ocean Resources Tourism Development Task Force (1988) *Interim Report.* Honolulu, Governor's Ocean Resources Tourism Development Task Force.

Groenendijk (1988) *Kerncijfers Toerisme Amsterdam.* Amsterdam, VVV Amsterdam.

Gunn C A (1988) *Tourism Planning.* New York, Taylor and Francis, 2nd edn.

Hage J (1978) Toward a synthesis of the dialectic between historical-specific and sociological-general models of the environment. In Karpik L (ed) *Organization and Environment: theory, issues and reality.* London, Sage.

Hall C M (1991) *Introduction to Tourism in Australia: impacts, planning and development.* Melbourne, Longman Chesire.

Hall P (1970) *Theory and Practice of Regional Planning.* London, Pemberton Books.

Hall R H, Clark J P, Giordano P C, Johnson P V, and Roekel M (1977) Patterns of interorganizational relationships. *Administrative Science Quarterly* 22(3): 457–72.

Hayman D A (1983) Development of a tourism plan for New Zealand. In *Proceedings from the First Tourism Planning Workshop: planning for tourism development.* San Francisco, Pacific Area Travel Association: 20–5.

Hayward B M (1989) Development of tourism and recreation policy in New Zealand. In Welch R (ed.) *Geography in Action, Proc. 15th New Zealand Geography Conference.* Dunedin, N.Z. Geographical Society.

Heeley J (1981) Planning for tourism in Britain: an historical perspective. *Town Planning Review* 52(1): 61–79.

Heeley J (1985) Tourism: A Highland stramash. *Fraser of Allander Quarterly Economic Commentary* 10(4): 57–9.

Heeley J (1986a) Big company involvement in Scottish tourism. *Fraser of Allander Quarterly Economic Commentary* 11(2): 75–9.

Heeley J (1986b) An overview of the structure of tourism administration in Scotland. In Houston L (ed) *Strategy and Opportunities for Tourism Development*, Planning Exchange Occasional Paper No. 22, Glasgow.

Heeley J (1986c) Tourism in England: a strategic planning response? In Houston L (ed) *Strategy and Opportunities for Tourism Development*, Planning Exchange Occasional Paper No. 22, Glasgow.

Heeley J (1989) Role of national tourist organizations in the United Kingdom. In Witt S F and Moutinho L (eds) *Tourism Marketing and Management Handbook*, Hemel Hempstead, Prentice-Hall.

Heeley J and McVey M (1985) Overseas tourism to Scotland: patterns, problems and prospects. *Fraser of Allander Quarterly Economic Commentary* 10(3): 57–63.

Henshall B D (1982) *Tourism and New Zealand – a strategic analysis.* Working Paper NTA/81/8, Auckland, Dept of Management Studies, University of Auckland.

Heydebrand W V (ed) 1973 *Comparative Organizations: the results of empirical research.* Englewood Cliffs, Prentice-Hall.

Hicks H G and Gullet C R (1975) *Organizations: theory and behaviour.* New York, McGraw Hill.

HIDB (1984) *Annual Report*, 1984. Inverness, Highlands and Islands Development Board.

HIDB (1988) *Tourism Development in the HIDB Area: an outline strategy.* Inverness, Highlands and Islands Development Board.

HIDB (1989) *Annual Report, 1988.* Inverness, Highlands and Islands Development Board.

Hills T L and Lundgren J (1977) The impact of tourism in the Caribbean: a methodological study. *Annals of Tourism Research* 4(5): 248–67.

Hodgson P (1983) Research into the complex nature of the holiday choice process. In *Proceedings of the Seminar on the Importance of Research in the Tourist Industry*, Helsinki, 8–11 June 1983. Amsterdam, ESOMAR: 17–35.

Hughes H L (1989) Resorts: a fragmented product in need of coalescence. *International Journal of Hospitality Management* 8(1): 15–17.

Hunt J D (1990) State tourism offices and their impact on tourist expenditures. *Journal of Travel Research* 28(3): 10–13.

HVB (1967) *An Evaluation of Hawaii Visitors Bureau Programs: Report to the Fourth State Legislature, State of Hawaii.* Honolulu, Hawaii Visitors Bureau.

HVB (1989a) *Westbound Visitors to Hawaii, 1988.* Waikiki, Hawaii Visitors Bureau.

HVB (1989b) *Visitor Plant Inventory 1989.* Waikiki, Hawaii Visitors Bureau.

ITIC – Bord Fáilte (1990) *Promoting Irish Tourism 1991–93.* Dublin, Irish Tourist Industry Confederation and Bord Fáilte.

ITIC (1989) *Doubling Irish Tourism: a market-led strategy.* Dublin, Irish Tourist Industry Confederation.

Jefferson A and Lickorish L (1988) *Marketing Tourism: a practical guide.* Harlow, Longman.

Jeffries D (1973) The role of marketing in official tourism organizations. In *Tourism and Marketing.* Berne, Association Internationale d'Experts Scientifiques du Tourisme.

Jeffries D (1989) Selling Britain – a case for privatisation? *Travel and Tourism Analyst* 1: 69–81.

Jenkins R L (1978) Family vacation decision-making. *Journal of Travel Research* 26(4): 2–7.

Johnson J H (1987) Republic of Ireland. In Clout H D (ed) *Regional Development in Western Europe.* London, David Fulton Publishers.

Johnston R J (1988) The political organization of US space. In Knox P L et al, *The United States: a contemporary human geography.* Harlow, Longman, and New York, Wiley.

Kenneth Leventhal & Coy (1987) *Special Report: State of Hawaii Tourist and Lodging Industry.* Los Angeles, Kenneth Leventhal & Coy.

Kloss G (1976) *West Germany: an introduction.* Basingstoke, Macmillan.

Knox P L, Bartels E H, Boyland J R, Holcomb B and Johnston R J (1988) *The United States: a contemporary human geography.* Harlow, Longman, and New York, Wiley.

Kotler P (1967) *Marketing Management.* Englewood Cliffs, NJ, Prentice-Hall.

Lavery P (1987) *Travel and Tourism.* Huntingdon, Elm Publications.

Law C M (1985) *Urban Tourism in the United States.* Working Paper No. 4, Department of Geography, University of Salford, Salford.

Lee G P (1987) Tourism as a factor in development cooperation. *Tourism Management* 8(1): 2–19.

Legislative Auditor (1987) *Management Audit of the Hawaii Visitors Bureau and the State's Tourism Program.* Report No. 87–14, Honolulu, Legislative Auditor of the State of Hawaii.

Legislative Auditor (1989) *Management of Financial Audit of the State Tourism Office, Department of Business and Economic Development.* Report No. 89–2, Honolulu, Legislative Auditor of the State of Hawaii.

Levine S and White P E (1961) Exchange as a conceptual framework for the study of interorganizational relations. *Administrative Science Quarterly* 5: 583–601.

LFV Bayern (1987a) *Der Landesfremdenverkehrsverband Bayern e.V. : Geschicte-Organisation-Aufgaben.* Munich, Landesfremdenverkehrsverband Bayern.

LFV Bayern (1987b) *Landeswerbeplan Bayern 1987.* Munich, Landesfremdenverkehrsverband Bayern.

Lickorish L J (1988) UK tourism development: a 10-year review. *Tourism Management* 9(4): 270–8.

Litterer J A (1973) *The Analysis of Organisations.* New York, Wiley.

Litwak E and Hylton L F (1962) Interorganizational analysis: a hypothesis on coordinating agencies. *Administrative Science Quarterly* 6(4): 395–420.

Liu J C (1983) *Advertizing Expenses of Airlines and Hotels Promoting Hawaii as a Destination.* Honolulu, Report prepared for the Hawaii Visitors Bureau (mimeo).

Liu J C and Var T (1986) Resident attitudes toward tourism impacts in Hawaii. *Annals of Tourism Research* 13(2): 193–214.

Lloyd P (1964) *The Economic Development of the Tourist Industry in New Zealand.* Wellington, Institute of Economic Research.

LLSTTB (1988) *Annual Report for the period ending 31 October 1988.* Stirling: Loch Lomond, Stirling and Trossach Tourist Board.

Lundgren J O J (1982) The tourist frontier of Nouveau Quebec: functions and regional linkages. *Tourist Review* 37(2): 10–16.

Lynch B and McQueen E (1987) Geography in public policy: the changing role of the state. In Holland P G and W B Johnston (eds) *Southern Approaches: geography in New Zealand.* Christchurch, NZ Geog Soc.

Lythe C and Majmudar M (1982) *The Renaissance of the Scottish Economy?* London, Allen and Unwin.

McDermott Millar (1988) *The Implications of Tourism Growth in New Zealand.* Wellington: New Zealand Tourist and Publicity Department.

McEniff J (1987) Republic of Ireland. *International Tourism Report* 4: 5–26.

McKay D (1990) The constitutional structure of the USA. In *Regional Surveys of the World: The USA and Canada, 1990.* London, Europa Publications.

McTaggart W D (1980) Tourism and tradition in Bali. *World Development* 8: 457–66.

McVey M (1986) The strategic role of local authorities in tourism: the Welsh experience. In Houston L (ed) *Strategy and Opportunities for Tourism Development.* Glasgow, Planning Exchange Occasional Paper No. 22.

McVey M and Heeley J (1984) Tourism and public policy in Scotland. *Fraser of Allander Quarterly Economic Commentary* 10(1): 63–70.

Martins M R (1986) *An Organisational Approach to Regional Planning.* Aldershot, Gower.

Masser I (1981) *Comparative Planning Studies: a critical review.* TRP 33, Department of Town and Regional Planning, University of Sheffield, Sheffield.

Mathieson A R (1985) Social impacts of tourism: a state of the art. In *Issues in Tourism Research in the South Pacific,* Les Cahiers du Tourisme, B44, Centre des Hautes Etudes

Touristiques, Aix-en-Provence: 15–19.

Michigan Travel Bureau (1989) *Travel Promotion Under the Yes Michigan Program, 1982–1988*. Lansing, Michigan Travel Bureau.

Middleton V (1986) England and Wales, National Report No. 112, *International Tourism Reports* 2: 5–26.

Middleton VTC (1988) *Marketing in Travel and Tourism*. Oxford, Heinemann Professional Publishing.

Mill R C and Morrison A M (1985) *The Tourism System: an introductory text*. Englewood Cliffs, NJ, Prentice-Hall International.

Mings R C (1980) A review of public support for international tourism in New Zealand. *New Zealand Geographer* 36(1): 20–29.

Miossec J M (1976) *Eléments pour une Théorie de l'Espace Touristique*, Les Cahiers du Tourisme, C-36, Centre des Hautes Etudes Touristiques, Aix-en-Provence.

Moran F (1979) *The Role of Government in the Development of the New Zealand Tourist Industry 1901–1979*. Unpublished MA thesis, University of Canterbury, Christchurch, NZ.

Morrison A M (1987) Selling the USA: part 2: Tourism promotion by the states. *Travel and Tourism Analyst* April: 3–18.

Murphy M J (1979) Legislative participation and support. In Council of State Governments, *Tourism: state structure, organization and support*. Washington DC, US Govt Printing Office.

Murphy P E (1985) *Tourism: a community approach*. New York and London, Methuen.

Murray-North (1991a) *Options for Regional Tourism*. Report prepared for the N.Z. Tourism Department, Auckland.

Murray-North (1991b) *Future Directions for Regional Tourism in Canterbury*. Christchurch, Canterbury Regional Council.

National Economic and Social Council (1978) *Tourism Policy*. Dublin, Stationery Office.

NBT (1985) *Strategic Plan 1985–1989: summary*. Leidschendam, Nederlands Bureau voor Toerisme.

NBT (1988a) *Toerisme, Trends en Toekomst*. Leidschendam, Nederlands Bureau voor Toerisme.

NBT (1988b) *A Summary of the 1987 Annual Report and Tourism Statistics*. Leidschendam, Netherlands Board of Tourism.

NDC (1969) *Report of the Targets Committee to the National Development Conference*. Wellington, Government Printer.

New Jersey Division of Travel and Tourism (1988) *New Jersey Tourism Profile*. Trenton, New Jersey Division of Travel and Tourism.

New York State Dept of Economic Development (1988a) *Tourism Master Plan*. Albany, NY State Dept of Economic Development.

New York State Dept of Economic Development (1988b) *Tourism Master Plan: 1989 Evaluation and Review, 1990 Annual Strategy*. Albany, NY State Dept of Economic Development.

NRIT (1989) *Trendrapport Toerisme 1988*. Breda, Nederlands Research Instituut voor Recreatie en Toerisme.

NRIT (1991) *Trendrapport Toerisme 1990*. Breda, Nederlands Research Instituut voor Recreatie en Toerisme.

NZTD (1990) *Brief to the Minister of Tourism, November 1990*. Wellington, New Zealand Tourism Department.

NZ Tourism Council and Tourist and Publicity Dept (1984) *New Zealand Tourism: issues and policies*. Wellington, NZ Tourism Council and Tourist and Publicity Department.

NZTP (1989a) *The Economic Review of Tourism in New Zealand 1987/88*. Wellington, New Zealand Tourist and Publicity Dept.

NZTP (1989b) *Tourism 2000 New Zealand Grow For It: Conference Proceedings*. Wellington, New Zealand Tourist and Publicity Department.

NZTP (1989c) *Report of Taskforce 2000*. Wellington, New Zealand Tourist and Publicity Department.

NZTP (1989d) *Brief to the Minister of Tourism, Vol. II: Current issues facing New Zealand tourism*. Wellington, New Zealand Tourist and Publicity Department.

NZTP (1989e) *New Zealand International Visitors Survey 1988/89*. Wellington, New Zealand Tourist and Publicity Department.

NZTP (1989f) *New Zealand Domestic Travel Study 1988/89*. Wellington, New Zealand Tourist and Publicity Department.

O'Hagan J, Scott Y and Waldron P (1986) *The Tourism Industry and the Tourism Policies of the Twelve Member States of the Community: summary of main findings*. Brussels, Commission of the European Communities.

O'Neill T P (1979) Preface to Council of State Government's report. In Council of State governments, *Tourism: state structure, organization and support*. Washington, DC, US Govt Printing Office.

O'Toole L (1983) Interorganizational co-operation and the implementation of labour market training policies: Sweden and the Federal Republic of Germany. *Organization Studies* 4(2): 129–50.

OECD (1987) *Tourism Policy and International Tourism in OECD Member Countries*. Paris, Organisation for Economic Cooperation and Development.

OECD (1989) *Tourism Policy and International Tourism in OECD Member Countries*. Paris, Organisation for Economic Cooperation and Development.

Ohio Office of Travel and Tourism (1986) *Tourism in Ohio: a prime economic motive*. Columbus, Ohio Office of Travel and Tourism.

Ohio Office of Travel and Tourism (1988) *1987/1988 Tourism Program Economic Development Results*. Columbus, Ohio Office of Travel and Tourism.

Oireachtus Eireann (1984) *Third Report of the Joint Committee on Small Businesses, Tourism, Catering and Leisure*. Dublin, Stationery Office.

Ollendorff M J (1988) Regional cooperative marketing programs in tourism. *Business American*, 15 February: 6–7.

Paddison R (1983) *The Fragmented State: the political geography of power*. Oxford, Blackwell.

Pearce D G (1980) Tourist development at Mount Cook since 1884. *New Zealand Geographer* 36(2): 79–84.

Pearce D G (1981) L'espace touristique de la grande ville: éléments de synthèse et application à Christchurch (Nouvelle Zélande). *L'Espace Géographique* 10(3): 207–13.

Pearce D G (1983) The development and impact of large-scale tourism projects: Languedoc-Roussillon (France) and Cancun (Mexico) compared. In Kissling C C, Thrift N J, Taylor M J and Adrian C (eds) *Papers 7th Australian/NZ Regional Science Assn*, Canberra: 59–71.

Pearce D G (1987a) *Tourism Today: a geographical analysis*. Harlow, Longman, and New York, Wiley.

Pearce D G (1987b) Motel location and choice in Christchurch. *New Zealand Geographer* 43(1): 10–17.

Pearce D G (1988) Tourism and regional development in the European Community. *Tourism Management* 9(1): 13–22.

Pearce D G (1989) *Tourist Development*. Harlow, Longman, and New York, Wiley. 2nd edn.

Pearce D G (1990a) Tourist travel patterns in the South Pacific: analysis and implications. In Kissling C C (ed) *Destination South Pacific: perspectives on island tourism*, Aix-en-Provence, Centre des Hautes Etudes Touristiques.

Pearce D G (1990b) Tourism, the regions and restructuring in New Zealand. *Journal of Tourism Studies* 1(2): 33–42.

Pearce D G (1991) *Comparative Studies in Tourism Research*. Paper presented at the meeting of the International Academy for the Study of Tourism, Calgary (mimeo).

Pearce D G and Booth K L (1987) New Zealand's national parks: use and users. *New Zealand Geographer* 43(2): 66–72.

Pearce D G and Cant R G (1981) *The Development and Impact of Tourism in Queenstown*. NZ Man and Biosphere Report No. 7. Christchurch, NZ National Commission for UNESCO/Department of Geography, University of Canterbury.

Pearce D G and Richez G (1987) Antipodean contrasts: national parks in New Zealand and Europe. *New Zealand Geographer* 43(2): 53–9.

Perdue R R and Pitegoff B E (1990) Methods of accountability research for destination marketing. *Journal of Travel Research* 28(4): 45–9.

Perrow C (1961) The analysis of goals in complex organizations. *American Sociological Review* 26: 854–66.

Pizam A (1990) Evaluating the effectiveness of travel trade shows and other tourism-sales promotion techniques. *Journal of Travel Research* 29(1): 3–8.

Presthus R (1962) *The Organisational Society*. New York, Knopf.

Price Waterhouse (1987) *Improving the Performance of Irish Tourism*. Dublin, Stationery Office.

Provinciale VVV Noord-Brabant (1988) *Jaarverslag, 1987*. Vught, Provinciale VVV Noord-Brabant.

Raelin J A (1982) A policy output model of interorganizational relations. *Organization Studies* 3(3): 243–67.

Randall J N (1987) Scotland. In Damesick P and Woods P (eds) *Regional Problems, Problem Regions and Public Policy in the United Kingdom*. Oxford, Clarendon Press.

Richter L K (1985) Fragmented politics of US tourism. *Tourism Management* 6(3): 162–73.

Ritchie J B and Goeldner C R (eds) (1987) *Travel, Tourism and Hospitality Research: a handbook for managers and researchers*. New York, Wiley.

Ronkainen I A and Farano R J (1987) United States' travel and tourism policy. *Journal of Travel Research* 24(4): 2–8.

Roth P and Wenzel G (1983) *Der Auslandertourismus in der Bundesrepublik Deutschland Die Entwicklung von 1950–1981*. Starnberg, Studienkreis für Tourismus.

Schaffer B (1979) Regional development and institutions of favour: aspects of the Irish case. In Seers D, Schaffer B and Kiljunen M L (eds) *Underdeveloped Europe: studies in core-periphery relations*. Hassocks, Harvester Press.

Schmidt S M and Kochan T A (1977) Interorganizational relationships: patterns and motivations. *Administrative Science Quarterly* 22(2): 220–7.

Schnell P (1975) Tourism as a means of improving the regional economic infrastructure. In *Tourism as a Factor in National and Regional Development*. Occasional Paper 4, Dept of Geography, Trent University, Peterborough.

Schnell P (1988) The Federal Republic of Germany: a growing national deficit. In Williams A M and Shaw G (eds) *Tourism and Economic Development: Western European Experiences*. London, Belhaven Press.

Scott W R (1964) The theory of organizations. In Farig E (ed) *Handbook of Modern Sociology*. New York, Rand McNally.

Scott W R (1981) *Organizations: rational, natural and open systems*. Englewood Cliffs, NJ, Prentice-Hall.

Seely R (1987) USTTA's cooperative marketing program stimulates new business. *Business America*. 16 February: 11–12.

Sewel J (1987) Reorganised Scottish local government: a review. *Scottish Geographical Magazine* 103(1): 5–11.

Shaw G, Greenwood J and Williams A M (1988) The United Kingdom: market responses and public policy. In Williams A M and Shaw G (eds) *Tourism and Economic*

Development: Western European Experiences. London, Belhaven Press.

Shaw G, Williams A, Greenwood J and Hennessy S (1987) *Public Policy and Tourism in England: a review of national and local trends*. Cornish Tourism Project Discussion Paper 3, Dept of Geography, University of Exeter, Exeter.

Shih D (1981) The birth of a state travel research unit: the Pennsylvania experience. In *Innovation and Creativity in Travel Research and Marketing, 12th Proceedings of the Travel and Tourism Research Association*. Salt Lake City: 363–9.

Siegel W and Ziff-Levine W (1990) Evaluating tourism advertizing campaigns: conversion vs advertizing tracking studies. *Journal of Travel Research* 28(3): 51–5.

Smith S L J (1983) Identification of functional tourism in North America. *Journal of Travel Research* 22(4): 13–21.

Smith S L J (1989) *Tourism Analysis: a handbook*. Harlow, Longman, and New York, Wiley.

Smyth R (1986) Public policy for tourism in Northern Ireland. *Tourism Management* 7(2): 120–6.

Stationery Office (1987) *Programme for National Recovery*, Dublin, Stationery Office.

Statistisches Bundesamt (1988) *Tourismus in Zahlen, 1988*. Wiesbaden, Statistisches Bundesamt.

STB (1977) *Annual Report, 1976–1977*. Edinburgh, Scottish Tourist Board.

STB (1980) *Annual Report, 1979–80*. Edinburgh, Scottish Tourist Board.

STB (1982) *Annual Report, 1981–82*. Edinburgh, Scottish Tourist Board.

STB (1983) *Annual Report, 1982–83*. Edinburgh, Scottish Tourist Board.

STB (1984a) *Tourism and the Economy of Scotland*. Research and Planning Report Synopses, C.53. Edinburgh, Scottish Tourist Board.

STB (1984b) *Annual Report, 1983–84* Edinburgh, Scottish Tourist Board.

STB (1984c) *The Effectiveness of Area Tourist Board Promotional Campaigns*. Research and Planning Report Synopses, C.60. Edinburgh, Scottish Tourist Board.

STB (1986a) *Business Plan*. Edinburgh, Scottish Tourist Board.

STB (1986b) *Annual Report 1985–86*. Edinburgh, Scottish Tourist Board.

STB (1987) *Tourist Information Centre Visitor Survey, 1987*. Research and Planning Report Synopses, C.78. Edinburgh, Scottish Tourist Board.

STB (1988a) *Overseas Visitors Survey – 1988*. Research and Planning Report Synopses, C.83. Edinburgh, Scottish Tourist Board.

STB (1988b) *The Supply of Hotels in Scotland: 1988*. Research and Planning Report Synopses, C.81. Edinburgh, Scottish Tourist Board.

STB (1989a) *National Survey of Tourism in Scotland: 1988*. Research and Planning Report Synopses D2.37. Edinburgh, Scottish Tourist Board.

STB (1989b) *Overseas Visitors to Scotland 1988*, Market Research Results Fact Sheet D.2.40. Edinburgh, Scottish Tourist Board.

STB (1989c) *Annual Report, 1988–89*. Edinburgh, Scottish Tourist Board.

Stephens G R (1974) State centralization and the erosion of local autonomy. *Journal of Politics* 36: 34–76.

Stewart T (1985) The birth of regional tourism. *The Kerryman/Corkman*, 25 January: 18.

Stodart A (1981) *Report of Committee of Inquiry into Local Government in Scotland*. Edinburgh, HMSO.

Stöhr W P and Taylor D R F (eds) (1981) *Development from Above or Below? The dialectics of regional planning in developing countries*. Chichester, Wiley.

Stokes Kennedy Crowley et al (1986) *Tourism Working for Ireland: a plan for growth*. Dublin, Stokes Kennedy Crowley, Peat Marwick, Davy Kelleher McCarthy.

TAC (1978) *Report of the Tourism Advisory Council to the Minister of Tourism*. Wellington, Government Printer.

Taylor G D (1987) Research in national tourist organizations. In Ritchie J B and Goeldner C R (eds) *Travel, Tourism and Hospitality Research: a handbook for managers and researchers*. New York, Wiley.

Taylor M and Thrift N (1983) Business organization, segmentation and location. *Regional Studies* 17(6): 445–65.

Taylor P J (1984) Introduction: geographical scale and political geography. In Taylor P and House J (eds) *Political Geography: recent advances and future directions*. London and Sydney, Croom Helm.

Tennessee Department of Tourist Development (1989) *Marketing Plan 1989–90*. Nashville, Tennessee Department of Tourist Development.

Tietz B (1980) *Handbuch der Tourismus-Wirtschaft*. Munich, Verlag Moderne Industrie.

Tourism Auckland (1990) *Tourism Auckland Business Plan 1990–1991*. Auckland, Tourism Auckland.

Tourism Taranaki (1991) *Annual Action Plan 1991–92*. New Plymouth, Tourism Taranaki.

Tourist and Publicity Department (1964) *The Pattern of Tourist Organization in New Zealand*. Wellington, NZ Tourist and Publicity Department.

Tourist and Publicity Department (1976) *75 Years of Tourism*. Wellington, NZ Tourist and Publicity Department.

Tourist and Publicity Department (1983) *Annual Report*. Wellington, NZ Tourist and Publicity Department.

Tourist and Publicity Department (1984) *Brief Prepared for the Minister of Tourism*. Wellington, NZ Tourist and Publicity Department.

Town and Country Planning Directorate (1984) *Tourism Reconnaissance Conclusions.* Wellington, Ministry of Works and Development.

TSMG (1990) *Destination New Zealand: a growth strategy for New Zealand Tourism.* Auckland, Tourism Strategic Marketing Group.

Usdiken B (1983) Interorganizational linkages among similar organizations in Turkey. *Organization Studies* 4(2): 151–64.

US Travel Data Center (1988) *Survey of State Travel Offices 1988–89.* Washington DC, US Travel Data Center.

US Travel Data Center (1989a) *Impact of Travel on State Economies 1987.* Washington DC, US Travel Data Center.

US Travel Data Center (1989b) *The 1988–89 Economic Review of Travel in America.* Washington DC, US Travel Data Center.

US Travel Data Center (1989c) *The Economic Impact of Travel on Tennessee Counties.* Nashville, Tennessee Department of Tourist Development.

US Travel Service (1978) *City Government, Tourism and Economic Development.* Washington, US Travel Service.

USTTA (1982) *1st Program Report of the United States Travel and Tourism Administration.* Washington DC, US Department of Commerce.

USTTA (1986) *5th Program Report of the United States Travel and Tourism Administration.* Washington DC, US Department of Commerce.

USTTA (1987a) *6th Program Report of the United States Travel and Tourism Administration.* Washington DC, US Department of Commerce.

USTTA (1987b) *Developing a US Regional Approach for Promoting Travel from Foreign Markets.* Washington DC, US Travel and Tourism Administration.

van Doren C S and Gustke L D (1982) Spatial analysis of the US lodging industry, 1963–1977. *Annals of Tourism Research* 9(4): 543–63.

van Raaij W F and Francken D A (1984) Vacation decisions, activities, and satisfactions. *Annals of Tourism Research* 11(1): 101–12.

VVV Amsterdam (1988) *Amsterdam Toeristisch Marketingplan 1989.* Amsterdam, VVV Amsterdam.

VVV Rotterdam (1987) *Adviesnota m.b.t. Het Toeristisch/Recreatief Beleid in Rotterdam.* Rotterdam, VVV Rotterdam.

Wahab S, Crampon L J and Rothfield L M (1976) *Tourism Marketing.* London, Tourism International Press.

Walsh J A (1987) *Regional Development Strategies in Ireland and Europe,* mimeo.

Warren R L (1967) The interorganizational field as a focus for investigation. *Administrative Science Quarterly* 12(3): 396–419.

Warriner C K (1984) *Organizations and their Environments: essays in the sociology of organizations.* Greenwich, Connecticut, JAI Press Inc.

Waters S (1990) *Travel Industry World Yearbook, the Big Picture – 1990.* New York, Child and Waters.

WBOA (1988) *1988 Annual Report and 1989 Marketing Strategy.* Honolulu, Waikiki Beach Operators Association.

WIA (1989) *Annual Report 1988–1989.* Waikiki, Waikiki Improvement Association.

WIA (1990) *Final Report, Waikiki Tomorrow, a conference for the future.* Waikiki, Waikiki Improvement Association.

Wild M T (1981) *West Germany: a geography of its people.* London, Longman.

Wilde F (1990) *Announcement of New Tourism Structures.* Wellington, mimeo.

Wolff I (1983) Organisationen, Verbände und Institutionen des deutschen und internationalen Fremdenverkehrs. In Haedrich G, Kaspar C, Kleinert H and Klem K (eds) *Tourismus-Management, Tourismus-Marketing und Fremdenverkehrsplanung.* Berlin, de Gruyter.

Woodside A G (1990) Measuring advertizing effectiveness in destination marketing strategies. *Journal of Travel Research* 29(2): 3–8.

Wright R G (1977) *The Nature of Organizations.* Encino, Dickenson Publishing Coy.

WTO (1979) *Role and Structure of National Tourism Administrations.* Madrid, World Tourism Organisation.

WTO (1980) *Physical Planning and Area Development for Tourism in the Six WTO Regions, 1980.* Madrid, World Tourism Organisation.

Wynegar D (1984) USTTA Research: new tools for international tourism marketing. *Travel Research: the catalyst for worldwide tourism marketing.* Salt Lake City, Proceedings of 15th Annual Travel and Tourism Research Association Annual Conference: 183–200.

Wynegar D (1989) US Department of Commerce Task Force on Accountability Research. *Journal of Travel Research* 27(4): 41–2.

Yuill D, Allen K and Hull C (1980) *Regional Policy in the European Community.* London, Croom Helm.

Author Index

Subject and Place Index